LAYING IT ON THE LINE

LAYING IT ON THE LINE

DRIVING A HARD BARGAIN IN
CHALLENGING TIMES

BUZZ
HARGROVE

HarperCollins*Publishers*Ltd

HarperCollins Publishers Ltd
2 Bloor Street East, 20th Floor
Toronto, Ontario, Canada
M4W 1A8

www.harpercollins.ca

Hargrove, Buzz, 1944–
Laying it on the line : driving a hard bargain in challenging times / Buzz Hargrove.

ISBN 978-1-55468-445-8

1. Automobile industry and trade—Canada. 2. Manufacturing
industries—Canada. 3. Industrial relations—Canada—History—21st
century. 4. Industrial relations—Canada—History—20th century.
5. Hargrove, Buzz, 1944–. 6. CAW-Canada—History. 7. Collective labor
agreements—Automobile industry—Canada—History. 8. Collective labor
agreements—Canada—History. I. Title.

HD6528.A8H38 2009   331.0971'090511   C2009-903110-8

Printed in Canada
TRA 9 8 7 6 5 4 3 2 1

To my family—my wonderful wife, Denise; our children,
Ena and Albert Small—and to the CAW leadership, membership
and retirees who allowed me the honour of over 40 years of social,
economic and political activism on behalf of working people and
the underprivileged in our society.

Work is of two kinds: first, altering the position of
matter at or near the earth's surface relative to other such matter;
second, telling other people to do so. The first kind is unpleasant
and ill-paid; the second is pleasant and highly paid.
Bertrand Russell

Few men of action have been able to
make a graceful exit at the appropriate time.
Malcolm Muggeridge

CONTENTS

Saturday, September 6, 2008

I was big news that day.

CBC Television carried video of a small portion of my speech, the part where I had to pause and get my emotions under control before continuing. My almost tearful expression had nothing to do with stepping down as national president of the Canadian Auto Workers union. I had been trying to explain the love and support I enjoyed from my wife, Denise, and how much it meant to me. So there was this rough, tough union leader blinking back tears in front of a thousand union brothers and sisters and much of the TV-viewing audience in Canada.

The tears had nothing to do with my departure from the CAW. I love Denise and I also love the union and the workers it represents. But I was leaving my position as the president of the CAW with no regrets. It was time for me to go—six months earlier than I planned. One of my first actions after assuming the presidency of the CAW had been to introduce a resolution calling for mandatory retirement from the office for presidents who turned 65, which was still several months away for me.

I've always believed unions should, and must, remain flexible to changing realities, and responsive to the concerns of union members. The members deal with the everyday challenges of labour in ways that union leaders, not to mention corporate executives, do not. The best way to avoid the risk of union leaders losing touch with day-to-day challenges is to prevent them from becoming too entrenched in their jobs. When they do, they lose sight of the needs of the members, and the members lose faith in the ability of their leaders to understand their concerns, and to fight for their rights.

I had been prepared to leave the CAW in March 2009, when I turned 65 years old. I had not been prepared, however, for the aggressive actions and open hostility shown by some within my union who wanted to fill my role before my scheduled departure date. That's why I stepped down early.

For almost 40 years I had sat across the table and exchanged tough words with snarling corporate presidents and angry government officials without flinching. It was my job, and theirs, to express feelings and disagreements directly, whether during bargaining for a new contract or while telling a prime minister in which direction we thought he should take the country. There was nothing personal about it. If we disagreed—and we usually did—we disagreed. I respected their opinion and they, I believed, respected mine. But when Hemi Mitic, a guy I had appointed to be my executive assistant 16 years earlier, leaned across a restaurant table and said, "What are you hanging around for? Why don't you get the hell out?" I figured it was time to go.

You can lead a union as long as you stand firm and tall. But the moment you stumble and fall, you'll be surprised at how many people you thought were your friends begin putting their boots against your back.

I had no worries about dealing with Hemi and the two or three other CAW staff who wanted my job. I might even have enjoyed watching the battle while I prepared to take retirement on the day everyone expected me to leave. But I knew an extended dispute over my position would be divisive to the union. It would create open wounds that take a long time to heal, divert the CAW from critical decisions, create concern among the workers who relied on the union to defend their rights, and persuade politicians and corporate executives that we were weak and conflicted.

I had long ago decided that the first serious challenge to my leadership by an executive member would be enough impetus for me to step down, whatever my age. The most valuable quality a successful trade union can have is solidarity between its rank and file and the leader they choose to make decisions. I would not have the CAW divided over who felt entitled to be the next president; this was a decision to be made according to the union's constitution, and I strongly believed whoever was chosen should be the candidate supported by the administration caucus, which should choose my successor with a minimum of wrangling and find a way to make the decision unanimous.

A few days after my lunch with Hemi, at a meeting of the national executive board, I announced I would be leaving my position as soon as the board was able to schedule and organize a special constitutional convention to elect a new president. Some members of the board were surprised by my announcement. Others weren't.

"I love my job," I told the board. "I love my union. I love the people in this room. I love the debates we have, the discussions and the dialogue, and I probably have had an argument with everybody in this room at some time or other. But at the end of the day, I always felt we were all respectful of each other. I know enough about politics and the labour movement, both here and around the world, that if you let a conflict go on for eight or ten months, boy, you'll wind up with ruptures that will take years to heal, if you're able to heal them at all."

I asked for the transfer of power to a new president to be completed as soon as possible. With many of our members locked into summer vacation times, and a limited number of facilities available in which to hold the event, it was delayed until September 6.

So there I was, making my final speech as CAW president in the Metro Toronto Convention Centre to about 1,000 delegates, staff, retirees, visitors, and media. I expressed my thanks, offered my best wishes for the union's future, had that emotional moment when mentioning Denise, and turned the proceedings over to Ken Lewenza, my replacement. After Ken's acceptance speech and the end of the meeting, I walked into a crowd of well-wishers who shook my hand, slapped me on the back and said all the things they wanted me to hear.

It felt good, no doubt about it. But eventually the cheering ends, the crowds go home, the nice words no longer ring in your ears, and you're left with your own thoughts.

My thoughts, when I sat alone in our home that evening, bounced back and forth between the past and the future. I thought about all the battles won and lost over the previous 16 years, and the amazing people I had encountered. The memories usually brought a smile to my face, even if the incidents were not amusing when they occurred. I thought about the future as well, but with fewer warm feelings. I worried about my union, and the men and women who depended on it for their security; about the industry that employed so many of us and its ability to deal with frightening realities in a changing world; and about my country, whose prosperity was so closely linked to the automotive industry and the many other goods and services industries whose workers were represented by the CAW.

Within a week, Lehman Brothers collapsed, stock markets around the world melted down, and my early departure from the union became insignificant. Nothing has been the same since. The collapse of a Wall Street investment bank would normally make a good story for the business section of a newspaper but, as we all know by now, it marked the first rock in an avalanche of disastrous events that continues rumbling as I write now, several months later. Bad economic news always hits working people the hardest, but in this case the biggest impact was being felt by the North American automotive industry, and it was giving rise to comments and predictions I never expected to hear.

"Let 'em go broke," some otherwise intelligent Canadians said and wrote, meaning General Motors, Ford and Chrysler. These people didn't care, or hadn't thought, about the human beings behind the companies. Whatever you may think of North American automakers and the people they employ, how could you possibly advocate throwing hundreds of thousands of Canadians out of work and assume that the damage—economical, social, political—wouldn't be felt by the rest of the country?

Much of this attitude grew out of animosity toward the companies and the CAW members who work for them, animosity built up over the years by misapprehension, bias and a basic lack of knowledge. For sure, the Big Three automakers have made errors, as has every major corporation—or have we forgotten about Nortel already? Their primary problems were rooted not in they way they dealt with the market but in the way the politicians dealt with offshore competition. And despite what many believed and spouted in newspaper reports and editorials, wages and benefits paid to CAW members in Canada or UAW members in the United States did not bring down the car companies. Anybody who believes that garbage doesn't know the facts.

The CAW has become much more than an auto worker's union. Only one in four CAW members works in the auto assembly and parts sectors, but its leadership remains as committed as ever to protecting workers' rights in that industry. Whether the union is representing health care providers, food service workers, airline clerks, hardrock miners or workers in any other industry, the same principles apply. Helping people understand these principles and implementing them into contracts and agreements remains as challenging a struggle as it was when I obtained my first union card more than 40 years ago.

That's what *Laying It on the Line* is about—the lessons I learned in leading one of the largest unions in Canada, and the fears I have for the future, not just for the automotive industry but also for Canada's overall prosperity. Many of the stories I tell here were whirling around in my head while I stood on the stage that Saturday accepting cheers from the crowd and thinking back over nearly four decades as a union activist—40 years of being called a hero and a bum, of experiencing terrific successes and crushing failures, of encountering enormous support and surprising betrayal. Others occurred while I watched with sadness and alarm as predictions of the end of our automotive manufacturing industry flew back and forth between those who understood the true situation and cared and those who neither knew nor cared.

My experiences have provided me with a unique outlook not just on unionization and the concerns of working Canadians, but on business generally. All those years of dealing with top executives of some of the largest, most aggressive corporations in the world helped me understand both the strengths and weaknesses of business corporations, especially as they apply to working people. It's easy enough to grasp the effects of business decisions and activities on executives, shareholders, clients and customers, but it takes another view, behind the scenes, as it were, to evaluate fully decisions made in the boardroom and their impact on wage-earning employees. And I'm talking about a hell of a lot more than deciding whether to risk a strike.

My tenure at the CAW began with a sharp focus on the automotive industry. I was there when we broke from the American-controlled UAW and risked total collapse by insisting that, among other things, the U.S. government could not make laws that affected Canadian auto workers. And I left on the brink of a worldwide economic collapse triggered not by the so-called greed of unionized workers that much of the right-wing press delights in condemning but by the gluttony of investment bankers, stock traders, hedge fund operators and insatiable CEOs who claimed severance packages of hundreds of millions of dollars as a reward for doing little more of substance than handing pink slips to tens of thousands of employees.

Business can do better. I know it can. Some of the most intelligent, hardest-working and even compassionate people I met and worked with over 40 years wore starched white collars, not blue ones. And while business and unions will naturally disagree over certain issues, and must be true to their respective constituents (the union's members and the company's shareholders, respectively), we need to find effective and constructive ways of managing those differences. This is especially true in this era of global economic turmoil.

I believe that business needs to acknowledge that many of the market-driven and profit-motivated practices that have dominated its activities since 1980 no longer apply. But unions also need to adapt to the reality of the 21st-century world, not by abandoning their principles but by finding new and more effective ways of applying them.

This book is no academic, blue-sky treatise; I'm still a grease-to-the-elbows kind of guy. Theories are fine, but no theory ever mounted an axle on a Chrysler or strung a communications line across the prairie. The events, opportunities and challenges I talk about are real. From some of them came a reward and from others came nothing but experience, which is the most effective way of learning a lesson, in my book.

It doesn't do much good to complain about a situation without putting your neck on the line by proposing solutions, so I've attempted to do just that. Of course, I've been putting my neck on the line for a lot of years now. Sometimes I consider myself lucky that my head is still attached to it. But it is, and the risk has been worth it.

Most of the time . . .

ONE

Born in the Bush and Raised on an Assembly Line

The chief difference between corporations and unions is that the first are all about profit and the second are all about people. This is the basis of the adversarial attitude between the two sides. It also explains why each side needs the other. Corporations cannot achieve their profit goals without the talents and efforts of their employees, and unions cannot expect to earn suitable income for their members unless corporations reach their goals.

I enjoy the company of most people. I gravitate toward people and most seem to like me, as well. Indeed, my attitude toward people may be the most influential factor in my long career. As a high school dropout, I sure can't credit education. And as one of 10 children growing up in Holmesville, New Brunswick, in the 1940s and 1950s, I can't say that I was fired with ambition to become an executive of any kind, in any organization. I rose out of poverty and hopelessness because I needed to, and I saw unions as a means of other people doing the same thing.

There was little pride in the poverty of my childhood. All 12 of us were crowded into a small frame house. It had no central heating, no running water and no electricity until I was almost a teenager. My father worked as a carpenter in the summer and cut trees for pulp and paper in the winter. My mother did everything she could to hold the family together and keep us clothed and fed. We grew and raised most of the food we ate—carrots, potatoes, turnips and berries from the garden; eggs from the chickens we kept (and, for a special Sunday treat, perhaps one of the chickens); milk from a couple of cows; and pork that was salted in barrels in the basement from a few pigs. Our water came from a brook, the heat came from tossing pieces of wood into an iron stove, and much of our clothing was hand-me-downs.

Dad worked for a company owned by Hugh John Flemming, a former premier of New Brunswick. Even working as hard and steadily as he did, his wages weren't sufficient to support my mother and 10 children. In the spring my mother worked on local potato farms, cutting seed potatoes into pieces, walking through the tilled fields with a burlap bag of "eyes" on her back and planting them in the ground, bent from the waist for hours on end. When the potato harvest was ready, she would gather us kids and off we would go to bring in the crop, all of us on our hands and knees, filling empty barrels with potatoes. We were paid 15 cents a barrel.

My father, who showed about as much affection to his family as he did to the animals we kept, died at age 53 of a heart attack while working deep in the bush in the middle of winter. He never had a kind word or gesture for my mother or any of his children, and about the only time he related to me and my brothers and sisters was in the summer when he loaded us in the car and drove along the roads, sending us to look for discarded pop and beer bottles to be cashed in for the refund, maybe two cents a bottle. Later in the year we drove along the roads next to the potato farms, where he sent us to pick up the bruised and discarded potatoes. The ones that weren't rotten we dropped in bags and took home for supper.

A tough life? You bet. But it's the kind of life that teaches you lessons you never forget. The ones I learned—which proved far more valuable to me than any lessons picked up during my 10 years of formal education—stayed with me throughout my career as a union leader. Many were handed down from my mother, including the importance of being honest and open with people, and the need to always stand up for your rights. She also advised me never to be angry with anyone or about anything for more than five minutes. Boy, has that lesson proved valuable!

Her most important lesson might have been the example she set for us. Despite our father' coldness and verbal abuse, and despite the hard, unending work to provide for her children, she maintained a warm, outgoing personality. Maybe her cheerfulness was the result of her French and Irish heritage. Or maybe it was because she insisted on looking at people as individuals, trying to understand what makes them tick, seeing them as human beings and accepting all their talents ands flaws. That's another good lesson I learned from her.

By the time my father died, he and my mother had separated. My father had taken us kids with him to live in Hartland, New Brunswick. Mom managed to get a job in the hospital in Woodstock, New Brunswick, where she helped organize the workers into a local of the Canadian Union of Public Employees.

I'm not sure who gave up on my education first, me or the school, but I left at age 16, ready to go to work. I had been living with the family of a friend, Cyril Clark, in Hartland. This took some pressure off my mother, but changing schools proved to be a problem for me. I was basically shy, and felt like the poor kid from the sticks who couldn't fit in. I soon gave up trying, choosing to hang out in poolrooms rather than attend school. A few weeks after the start of grade 10, I said the hell with it, and Cyril and I headed down the road to Toronto, where I worked for a dollar an hour in a warehouse. Over the next few years I was back and forth between New Brunswick and the rest of Canada, wherever I found employment—working a jackhammer and driving a truck for Alberta Government Telephones (AGT) in Calgary, cutting timber on a pipeline project in northern Alberta, and joining a survey crew in Saskatchewan.

On a trip back east with my sister Mildred and her children in 1964, we stopped to visit my brother Carl in Windsor, Ontario. Carl worked in one of the city's automobile plants, and he kept urging me to submit a job application there. I had no intention of working in a car plant, but Carl was persuasive, and I filled out an application before continuing on to New Brunswick. I had barely arrived on the east coast when Carl called to say my application had been accepted, and Chrysler had a job for me in their maintenance department. For a while I was torn between returning to the open fields of Saskatchewan or heading to the factory floor in Windsor. Almost on a whim I chose Windsor. In many ways, my timing couldn't have been better.

It was the spring of 1964, and the auto companies were coming off a few bad years. The automotive industry still represented the single biggest manufacturing activity in Canada, but it was full of inefficiencies caused by the smallness of our market. The major auto companies were owned and operated by American firms that would gladly have produced all the cars and trucks they could sell in this country out of their own factories in the United States. To prevent this, the Canadian government had slapped heavy duties on imported vehicles, forcing manufacturers to build cars in Canada.

But it didn't make sense for U.S. manufacturers to create an all-Canadian car from the ground up. And like it or not, Canadians, exposed as they were to U.S. advertising in the media and to the cars driven by American tourists, usually wanted to buy the same cars Americans were buying. They were content to have minor changes made to some American models and have them labelled "Canadian," even though the differences were superficial.

This strategy proved effective everywhere except on the assembly line. One factory would be assigned to assemble several different car models simultaneously, creating a production nightmare. Chrysler could build Dodges in a single dedicated plant in the U.S., but in Canada the company turned out Dodges, Plymouths, DeSotos and Chryslers on the same production line.

The costs were enormous. Each assembly line worker might have to choose between several different parts to bolt on each car, depending on the model and nameplate. Parts stacked all along the production line produced inefficiencies and accidents. And most of the parts were manufactured in the U.S., which meant they were hauled hundreds of kilometres to the Canadian plants, requiring the plants to maintain massive parts inventories or risk shutdowns. For years, Canada ran a large trade deficit with the U.S. when it came to cars, car parts, trucks and buses. Nobody was happy with the arrangement until someone came up with a solution. The major problem was the import tariffs. They had to go. But the answer wasn't free trade; it was "managed trade," more commonly known as the Canada–U.S. Auto Pact.

At the same time I was driving out of New Brunswick headed for Windsor, with mixed emotions about my decision to become an auto worker, Canada and the U.S. were drawing plans for the Auto Pact.

Over the 35 years of its existence, the Auto Pact changed the face of auto manufacturing across North America, generating lower vehicle prices for buyers, tens of thousands of jobs for workers, billions of dollars in taxes for government programs and profits for manufacturers. What's not to like about a deal like that? Yet the lesson has still to be learned.

The basic principle of the Auto Pact was that for every car sold in Canada, one car had to be built in Canada *at equal dollar value* and with at least 60 percent Canadian content in parts and labour. As simple as that.

Introduced in January 1965, the Auto Pact completely changed the industry on both sides of the border. Now each plant would produce a single brand or model, eliminating massive warehousing, production line confusion and unnecessary costs. It didn't matter where each vehicle was sold as long as the manufacturers maintained the balance between production and sales in Canada. In 1964, the year I began working at Chrysler in Windsor, barely seven of every 100 cars built in Canada were shipped to the U.S. Four years later, 60 out of every 100 Canadian-made cars crossed the border. In 2008 the number of cars and trucks made in Canada and shipped to the U.S. had risen to 85 out of 100.

It's difficult to overstate the impact of the Auto Pact on Canada. About 75,000 Canadians worked in the auto industry when the pact was signed in 1964. By 2001, the year the World Trade Organization declared the pact illegal, almost a half-million Canadians made their living from automotive manufacturing and related industries, and the industry represented 12 percent of the country's manufacturing GDP. Nothing supports the argument in favour of managed trade better than those figures.

The U.S. benefited from the Auto Pact as well. Auto manufacturers grew wealthy from greater efficiencies and wider markets, and their wealth spread across the country. Workers, dealers, service industries and the general public all shared in the bounty to one extent or another.

The automakers' success didn't always trickle down to the workers on the line. In many cases, new efficiencies in the factories inspired managers and supervisors to demand more from the workers. Some of the demands were well beyond the workers' capacity. I had seen this situation in the various non-union jobs I had held before arriving at Chrysler. In shops without unions, workers had no more rights than the machinery they operated. They were told what to do, how much they would be paid, when to work overtime, and never to question supervisors. The power of the corporate employer was unchallengeable without a union.

As a unionized worker at Chrysler, I learned to appreciate the union's role and admire most of its leaders for their dedication. I voiced my support for the union often enough on the job that I was elected shop steward. For the first time in my life I was responsible to someone besides myself, and almost overnight I changed from a hell-raising young guy spending his off-hours in beer halls and at the racetrack to a union advocate discussing left-wing politics and strategy. I began relating better to people, and while I remained something of a hothead for several years, I began to understand the motives of the people around me, who believed in the union and relied on it for their security and fairness, and the people above me, who kept demanding more sacrifice from employees in their search for higher profits and bigger dividends. I didn't agree with the guys on the employer side, and I didn't like all of them as people, but I began seeing them as individuals and understanding what drove them, what pleased them and what infuriated them.

Later, as chairperson of the shop stewards in my union local and as a staff member of the UAW, I broadened my vision. I saw things in a political light, and recognized that the kind of struggles we faced on the shop floor and in the offices and warehouses at Chrysler existed elsewhere. I joined the New Democratic Party, attracted to their socialist principles, such as countries owning their own natural resources instead of having them owned and controlled by international corporations.

Between the goals of the NDP and the influence of the unions, I recognized it was possible to change the way people lived and how they were treated by their employers and by society. In 1964, when I first began working at the Chrysler plant, your working life and your personal life were considered two separate worlds, and one was rarely allowed to influence the other, unless it was the working world controlling the personal world. Back then, the lives of workers and their families were dictated by the schedules of the employers and their factories. During my first year at Chrysler, everyone had to work four hours on Christmas Eve. Christmas itself was a day off but you were expected back on the job the next day, without fail.

A lot of my inspiration in those days came from the example set by Walter Reuther, the American labour leader, a remarkable man who worked for social justice, workers' rights and peace. Other labour leaders influenced me as well, but none more than the UAW's Reuther, maybe because he was so passionate and articulate about the union. He believed that people, working collectively, can improve their lives, the lives of their children and the lives of others, and he dedicated his life to achieving that goal, something I have never forgotten.

I also became a ferocious reader of history and biographies, especially those dealing with union activities and strategies. I learned different methods of applying pressure to create change on behalf of workers, such as sit-down strikes, plant occupations, slowdowns, deadline bargaining and other tactics. Each situation had to be examined before a decision was made on the response, and the decision had to be based on the best way of getting the most benefits for union members with the least amount of sacrifice.

The idea that a union has several ways to reach its goals, and that effective leaders choose from among these alternatives, made a major impact on me, and I applied it during my years as CAW president. In 1996, for example, General Motors refused to agree to the bargaining pattern we had set with Chrysler earlier that year. The first reaction from most union members was to launch a complete walkout, striking all of the company's Canadian operations. The trouble was that this would create some problems we didn't need. Striking the GM parts plants in Canada would shut down the American assembly plants that relied on those parts for U.S.-built cars, just as striking the assembly plants in Canada would cause problems for U.S. parts plants. GM was making some investment decisions that potentially involved Canada, and I didn't want to give anyone in Detroit a reason for favouring some other location on the basis that the CAW was being unreasonable. Besides, I had a suspicion that Jack Smith, the CEO of GM, didn't fully grasp the position being taken by the people we were bargaining with on this side of the border. If Jack knew the whole story, I suspected, things would be different.

So in place of a full strike we launched staged strikes, in which different areas go on strike one after another (in this case the assembly plants, then the parts plants and finally all operations), building step by step to a full walkout. We were doing more than striking. We were sending a message to the company, to CAW members and to the public generally that we didn't want a strike, and that we didn't want to be more disruptive than we had to be. We simply wanted GM to continue a 50-year policy of agreeing to pattern settlements. After 17 days Smith called me. I knew him from his days running the Canadian operations, and we got along well. "Maybe I should have called you myself," he said when I painted the whole picture for him, and we quickly reached an agreement.

This idea of exploring every avenue that's open before calling a general strike is something I stressed all through my years as CAW president. Unions don't exist just to authorize strikes against the employers. A strike should be considered the last weapon in their arsenal, one they use only when absolutely necessary. Strikes are costly to both sides, and the price is paid in dollars and in public image. Workers walking off the job reflect and create conflict between workers and the employer, and there's nothing like a strike with a large corporation such as one of the auto companies to generate lots of headlines and hand-wringing.

* * *

Throughout all my years on the shop floor at Chrysler and in offices as a union leader, I recognized that many workers worried about their job security, their pensions and their children's futures, and that families everywhere were facing the same kind of poverty I had encountered as a child. I knew the pain and hopelessness that constant deprivation can create, and I believed it shouldn't happen in a wealthy country like Canada. But it happens more often than we care to admit.

I don't believe in handouts alone as a means of eliminating poverty, and I have never met anyone in dire economic need who wanted a handout. The last thing that many poverty-stricken people possess is their pride, and as long as they can hold onto it they prefer to help themselves by working for a fair wage or salary. Business people who fixate on the bottom line alone seem to have difficulty recognizing this fact. In a free enterprise society we will accomplish little in solving the problem of poverty until that perception is changed.

It was the union that proved to me that change is possible. Unions provide their members with more than a voice and fair wages. They provide security and pride, an idea in the mind of every member that he or she is not alone, and that their individual identities and ambitions will be respected. Maybe you have to watch your mother work 12 hours a day just to keep a roof over your head and meals on the table, rarely having any hope of better days, to appreciate those ideals. People have to break down their stereotypes, positive or negative, of corporations and labour unions, and recognize that they are made up of people not much different from themselves.

Whenever I encounter a story in the media about union activities—and the stories are usually negative—I want the readers or listeners or viewers to see beyond the picketers and understand them not just as protesting workers but as individuals with real concerns and needs. Of course, this means seeing the people on the other side of the bargaining table as individuals as well, something I always tried to do. Employers were my adversaries when we were in the middle of bargaining, but I never lost respect for them as individuals, which helped me understand them. Most of all, I rarely grew angry with someone who happened to disagree with me, even if the differences between us were substantial. I would never want a world where everybody agreed with Buzz Hargrove: boy, would that be a boring place! I love debating ideas and goals, trying to impress the other side with my point of view and remaining open to their attempts to impress me.

This outlook has led to some surprising friendships over the years—surprising to those who don't know me, and who don't understand the principle of collective bargaining. Magna International Chairman Frank Stronach, for example, has been anti-union for much of his career, building a multibillion-dollar empire while defying almost every effort by unions to certify his plants. Obviously I wasn't happy with this strategy, but I kept the communications between us open, and I began to understand why Frank acted the way he did. Much of his attitude was based on his own beginnings. He was born in the middle of the

Great Depression and grew up in Austria during the Second World War, arriving in Canada in 1954 as a 22-year-old tool and die maker. He built his company from scratch, relying on nobody, and you have to admire him for that. Unfortunately, he became convinced that all of us could rely on ourselves alone to succeed as he had, and that's simply not true. One person cannot go up against a giant multinational corporation alone and expect to be treated with respect. That's the job of unions, but Frank refused to accept that idea.

The employees in Frank's companies needed unions, but on at least two occasions Frank needed the unions too. In the early 1990s, Magna International got itself in to a financial pickle. The company had too much debt. Then the recession of 1990 struck. Frank needed an injection of cash but was over his borrowing limit with the banks, which were reluctant to lend another dime. Without money, Magna risked falling into bankruptcy. Incredibly, Frank turned to the same group of people he had scorned for years—our union, the CAW.

It began with an invitation to have lunch with him. With no idea what he had in mind I agreed to go along, bringing my assistant, Hemi Mitic, with me. It had been almost five years since Canadian auto workers had broken away from the United Auto Workers to become the CAW, and at some point in his search for investment funds Frank had learned that the UAW's strike fund totalled about $500 million. With no strikes looming on the horizon, he figured he could tap the union strike fund, deliver a better return to the union than the banks could offer, and climb out of his financial hole.

I don't know whether Frank confused us with the UAW or believed we had a strike fund as large as theirs or thought we could access the American union's treasury with the stroke of a pen. Whatever it was, he believed we could supply him with ready cash. "Here's the deal," he said over lunch. "If you will loan me the money I need to keep Magna afloat, or buy enough of my Magna shares to provide the cash I need, you'll have my assurance that we will encourage our employees to join the CAW. It's a good deal. It'll benefit you and us."

Unionizing Magna workers would add to our bargaining power enormously, and bring benefits to Magna employees that they could not enjoy outside the union. I wasn't that interested in buying the Magna shares, but I couldn't reject his suggestion out of hand either. "Just how much money do you need from this deal?" I asked.

"How much do you have in your strike fund?" he asked.

"About $22 million," I replied.

Frank turned pale. "That's all?" he said.

I don't know how much Frank needed, or how much he thought the CAW had in its strike account, but he told me our entire strike fund wasn't going to put much a dent in his company's debt.

His quick reversal from an anti-union capitalist to the working man's friend was impressive, and proved that many business principles go out the window when enough money is involved. I took no joy in Frank's situation, or in his turning to me and the CAW to bail out him and his company. Like it or not, Magna International filled an enormous role in the industry, and the financial collapse of his company would cause a large ripple everywhere. In addition, Magna was the only major Canadian player in the auto parts business; if it filed for bankruptcy, an American conglomerate would almost certainly pick up the pieces.

"Let me speak to Bob Rae," I suggested. Premier of Ontario at the time, Rae was then still on speaking terms with me (and I was still a member of the NDP). Rae's government did not provide any direct emergency aid, but his officials did play a role in facilitating restructuring talks with Magna's lenders and customers. In the end, Stronach negotiated a complete overhaul of Magna's debt, including new terms with the banks and other lenders, better payment arrangements with Ford and GM (two of Magna's key customers) and continuing provincial and federal support for investments in new technology. The whole experience changed Frank's attitude toward debt. Today Magna runs with minimal corporate debt, and this caution has helped the company survive the current downturn in the industry better than most of its peers.

I like Frank Stronach. Many people consider him dogmatic, but that's just one side of the man. Here's another side.

In August 2005, during a telephone conversation, Magna executive Dennis Mills and I discussed the enormous impact Hurricane Katrina had made on New Orleans. I was stunned to learn how desperate the residents of New Orleans and of the nearby Gulf Coast were, and I began calling business leaders to ask if they would join our union in creating a committee to offer assistance. One of the first people I contacted was Frank Stronach, and he responded immediately. "Leave it with me," Frank said. "I'll contact some people and get back to you." Well, he didn't. Four or five days later I saw him on television news beamed from New Orleans. He'd taken the situation in hand on his own and created a village to house homeless people. There he was in the middle of things, creating a community of new homes that became known as Canadaville. Frank always was impatient with committees. When I sparked the idea for him, he took charge on his own. That's the nature of the guy, and I admire him for that.

Frank is a practical business man, and when his company was in trouble he took steps to correct things without letting his personal feelings get in the way. One of these steps was offering to throw his years of anti-unionism out the window and work with me or anyone else who could help save his company—and, from my point of view, save the jobs of his workers. Later he and I found a new way to collaborate, which brought a lot of criticism down on my shoulders, but I'll deal with that later.

The idea that anyone who holds power in business is automatically opposed to working people is wrong. I don't agree with the perception that all wealthy business people concentrate only on making themselves richer and neglect everything else. Many, perhaps, but not all.

Frank's daughter, Belinda, became the target of all kinds of abuse when she entered politics. The point is, she didn't have to get into the game. She enjoyed all the power, influence and money anyone could want as president of her father's company. She chose to enter politics out of other concerns, including support for abortion rights, gun control and same-sex marriage. Anyone familiar with federal election campaigns knows that knocking on doors, attending debates and rallies, and putting yourself in the spotlight ready to take criticism from all sides is not a day at the beach. It's exhausting and often humiliating, and I admired Belinda's determination to contribute something to society rather than relax in the executive suite. The pressures on her, along with health issues, drove her out of politics. Too bad. She is a bright, hard-working woman.

Gerry Schwartz, founder and CEO of Onex Corporation, is another self-made man with enormous influence. Like Frank Stronach, Gerry Schwartz represents the Other Side to working people, who are often surprised, shocked and even disappointed when I say positive things about him.

Throughout my life in the CAW I never gave a damn about who owned the company employing our members. I cared only about the rights of the CAW members under our collective agreement. What was the company's commitment to our members and how well were they living up to it? I'd ask. Ultimately, that's all that mattered.

So it's easy for me to get along with Gerry Schwartz and his wife, Heather Reisman. He is tough as nails when it comes to negotiations, but he is as good as his word when the deal is done. We like each other, and if this surprises people on either side of the political spectrum, it proves that we are all prone to stereotypes where labour and management are concerned.

My relationship with Gerry and Heather goes well beyond words expressed over lunch, by the way. In June 2008, around the time I announced my decision to step down earlier than expected, they helped organize a fundraiser in my honour to support Eva's Initiative, a Toronto-based inner-city project for youth. The event generated almost $3 million to fund programs designed to keep disadvantaged kids off the street and in school. Who can fault that kind of activity, or the people who get it done?

Robert Milton, who steered Air Canada through its near-bankruptcy in 2003, is a very different guy from both Stronach and Schwartz. Unlike them, Milton worked his way up the ladder of an existing company; where Stronach and Schwartz created their business worlds, Milton assumed control of a corporation built by someone else. He is a cool, calculating manager and probably one of the most capable airline executives in the world. If you doubt it, just ask him. He is very knowledgeable about aircraft, and can tell you which plane can carry the most passengers to a given destination at the least cost. This technical bent, which some see as arrogance, may hinder his ability to reach out to people. I know that no one calls Robert Milton "Rob" or "Bob" or "Bobby." He insists on "Robert," and maybe that's a measure of his personality.

In my dealings with him, Milton has shown little appreciation for many of Canada's social programs, including universal health care. I had my share of run-ins with Milton and with Air Canada, but he and I managed to do a deal when the chips were down, and both of us lived up to our promises.

Robert Milton, however, is Winnie the Pooh compared with Darren Entwistle, CEO of Telus. I found him to be the most arrogant and aggressive executive I dealt with in my years at the CAW. He used his powerful voice, with its slightly upper-class English accent, to intimidate anyone who disagreed with his goals or management style, a style he himself described as "FIFO": Fit In or Fuck Off. While I always tried to find a positive aspect in everyone I dealt with, Entwistle was a real challenge.

So was Lee Iacocca, who seemed to be more interested in creating an impression than on getting down to business. Iacocca knew a lot about the automotive business, to be sure, but he knew at least as much about theatrics. If he had taken a different turn in his early life he might have had a career as an actor. He showed it during Chrysler's many financial crises. Iacocca and his team, like other top executives in Detroit, would show up on our doorstep demanding concessions from the workers, and when we didn't give in he would blame the UAW or the CAW for all of Chrysler's problems.

During one crisis Iacocca called our bargaining committee to a meeting at Chrysler and began his doomsday scenario. "Guys," he said to us in his I'm-just-one-of-you-working-men style, "this is what I need. We've got to cut your hourly wages by a buck-fifteen an hour," which just happened to be our COLA (cost of living allowance). "And if we don't get it," he said, raising his voice, "all the factories will go dark!" That was the cue for somebody on his staff to flick the light switch, and suddenly the room was black. Sitting there in the dark I almost laughed out loud at Iacocca's attempt to dramatize the situation. Whatever theatrics he used to make his point, he was not going to change our attitude about concessions. We stood our ground, which led to a five-week strike during the fall of 1982. After saying he would never agree to our union's demands, arguing it would bankrupt the company, in the end he realized we wouldn't bend. That's when he reached into his "big barrel of cash"—that's his phrase, not mine—and found the money needed to settle the strike. Within six months of our members going back to work, Chrysler recorded its most profitable quarter in history.

Much of Chrysler's success, in Canada at least, came not from Lee Iacocca's dramatics and substantial ego but from the personality and abilities of Yves Landry. President and CEO of Chrysler Canada from 1990 to 1998, Landry proved that while union and management take adversarial positions during bargaining sessions, this does not mean they're at each other's throats all the time. Here's something for those people who view trade unionists as snarling blue-collar bullies: when Yves Landry died suddenly in March, 1998, CAW shop stewards from Chrysler formed an honour guard at his funeral. They were as saddened as anyone by his death because he had earned their respect and their friendship. How? By being a Canadian nationalist and a guy who understood and appreciated the concerns of workers.

In bargaining with us, Landry would fight hard over wages, benefits, charges of featherbedding and the usual union-management conflicts, but he fought just as hard with Chrysler's U.S. bosses to get products manufactured in Canadian plants, providing income and security for our members. Landry would walk through the plant, introduce himself to the workers, shake their hands, ask how they were doing and listen to their suggestions. Beyond the plants he worked like hell for the industry and for Canadian workers generally. He lectured governments and educators about the need for our educational system to adapt to new realities, acting as a link between industry, education, government and unions. He wanted to improve our global competitiveness and make this a better country. Many Canadians believe that less strife between management and unions would benefit everyone, and in many cases they are correct. Yves Landry knew this, and he promoted it by leaving his ivory tower executive suite and getting down on the factory floor to mingle with everybody in the company, not just the white-collar crowd.

If more top executives saw union–management relationships his way, everyone would be better off. Landry was the exception.

There was nothing arrogant about Yves Landry, but lately we've encountered incredible arrogance at the federal political level with Jim Flaherty, Stephen Harper's federal finance minister. How and why a federal minister from a riding in which the country's largest and most successful auto complex is located could suggest, as Flaherty did, that Ontario is a lousy place to do business is beyond me. I can usually find something pleasant to say about almost anyone, but my encounters with Jim Flaherty have left me at a loss.

I first became acquainted with Flaherty when he was part of Mike Harris's government in Ontario. I found him stubborn and short-sighted then, and he has proven just as incompetent since. There's a long and growing list of economic and financial issues that Flaherty and his government have seriously mishandled since the Harper government squeaked into office in January 2006. Think of the tax cuts, weighted so heavily in favour of corporations, that Flaherty implemented in his first national budget. He claimed Ottawa's coffers were overflowing, and he wanted to downsize government's role in the economy. Lo and behold, recession soon hit, and those tax cuts laid the groundwork for a return to massive government deficits. When the Canadian dollar soared to unsustainable heights in 2007, fuelled by speculative pressure in commodity prices and foreign takeovers of Canadian resource companies, not only did Flaherty fail to use his influence to bring the loonie back to earth; he actually *endorsed* the dollar's value at near-parity with the U.S. dollar—a level that could only spell bankruptcy for Canadian manufacturers and others who must sell into global markets. His mishandling of the income trust controversy was erratic and damaging; his sudden reversal of direction caught personal investors unaware and contributed to unnecessary losses.

More recent was the incredible error in judgment in his economic and fiscal update of November, 2008. It was already clear Canada was plunging deep into recession. Yet Flaherty put on rose-coloured glasses and pretended everything was fine. He even claimed—fantastically—that his government would eke out small surpluses in the troubled years ahead. Worst of all, he used the opportunity of that statement to launch a partisan and divisive attack on the opposition parties (attempting to eliminate public funding for parties) and unions (trying to ban strikes in the federal civil service) that Canadians rightly rejected. Flaherty's misstep plunged his government, and the whole country, into an unprecedented period of political turmoil (sparking the creation the opposition coalition and the subsequent unprecedented proroguing of the House of Commons). It's incredible to me that after all these blunders, he still holds his position as Finance Minister. Where's the accountability in that?

I criticized Flaherty many times in the media, an action I don't like taking, believe it or not. I would much rather say good things about politicians and CEOs, as I have about Paul Martin and Yves Landry, than criticize them. I've told Flaherty this and I've told his boss, Stephen Harper, the same thing. "Nothing would give me more pleasure," I said to Harper in 2007, "than to leave a meeting with you and announce to the press that the CAW fully supported you and your party over your plans, for example, to end unfair trade with Asia."

Harper told me that this was not going to happen. No surprise there. My point was that I will give credit where credit is due, an attitude that got me in trouble with the NDP, who believe you should never say anything positive about the Other Side no matter how they respond to demands.

* * *

Of all the people I encountered in my years with the CAW, no one's story was more tragic than that of Bud Jimmerfield. When I first met him, Bud was a big man with a heart to match. Weighing maybe 240 pounds, he worked as a tool and die maker for an Ontario auto manufacturer and was president of CAW Local 89 in Amherstberg, Ontario. For over 30 years Bud was exposed to mists from oily fluids used to cool the machinery, along with asbestos and silica dust from the manufacturing process. "My clothes were saturated with the fluids 90 percent of the time," Bud told me. "You could taste the oil, the air was a cloud of oil mist." People working under these conditions, according to a study conducted by Harvard University back in the 1980s, were *12 times* more likely than the national average to contract cancer of the esophagus, the disease that took Bud's life, as well as laryngeal, rectal and pancreatic cancers.

Bud died in January 1998 at age 49. When I saw him in his last days he weighed perhaps 90 pounds. It didn't stop him, however, from travelling from plant to plant, visiting health and safety committees to alert them of the dangers of working in the kind of environment that he had laboured in for so long. He left behind his wife and eight children. Despite his doctors' testimony that the fluids had caused his cancer, and the decision by his employer not to contest the case, for several years the Workplace Safety and Insurance Board (WSIB) refused to allow his claim for benefits before caving in to pressure from the CAW. The International Agency for Research on Cancer (IARC) recognizes 24 substances directly linked to lung cancer in humans, and 23 of them have been found in mortality studies on Canadian blue-collar workers.

I think of Bud and others like him whenever I hear anyone suggest that our union members "have it easy." Bud Jimmerfield never had it easy. Not when he was putting in 40-hour weeks in the plant, and certainly not during the two years of suffering he endured while cancer ravaged his body. In honour of Bud, I supported the creation of the annual Bud Jimmerfield Award to be given to a CAW member who demonstrates outstanding effort on behalf of workplace health and safety issues.

* * *

Political disasters like Jim Flaherty and workplace tragedies like Bud Jimmerfield are balanced in my memory by people who demonstrate the best side of human nature. One of these is Phil Fontaine, national chief of the Assembly of First Nations. Phil has outstanding leadership qualities, as good as any leader of any political party, community group or labour organization in Canada, and better than most. He's bright, thoughtful and concise in what he says, is not prone to flying off the handle when something upsets him, and is a powerful presence in any setting.

Like most First Nations people, Phil experienced extreme poverty as a child. He had the love and support of his family for a time, but this was taken away thanks to the Canadian government's policy of removing aboriginal children from their families and depositing them in residential schools. During 10 years spent at the Fort Alexander Indian Residential School, Phil learned first-hand about racial prejudice, physical and sexual abuse, and the powerlessness of poverty. Despite all of this, Phil grew determined, not angry. His experience and attitude remind me of the most impressive human being I have been privileged to meet: Nelson Mandela.

Generations from now, people will still speak of Nelson Mandela with great admiration. History, I hope, will record the efforts by Canadian trade unionists to free him from his long prison term. While he was still imprisoned, the CAW created Free Mandela! committees at local unions across the country, collecting contributions from union members and funnelling the money to South Africa through the South Africa Congress of Trade Unions (SACTU) and later the Coalition of South African Trade Unions (COSATU).

Nelson Mandela's story is so well known that it is almost a cliché, but I don't believe you can fully appreciate the man until you have met and talked with him, one on one, as I was privileged to do. I found him thoughtful, bright, kind and committed, a man who will be more celebrated in history than Gandhi who, for all of his achievements, did not spend 27 years in prison. Both men demonstrated that change can be brought about through peaceful means, especially among the most needy and downtrodden of society. They also proved that courage and determination alone cannot succeed without effective leadership.

These are just a few of the people I encountered during my years as CAW president. You'll meet many of them and others on the following pages. They are all different in their own way—some inspiring, some exasperating, but all of them individuals with unique personalities and unique needs. Just like, in some ways, every member of the CAW.

TWO

Let's Hear It for the Middle Class!

Once upon a time, long, long ago, groups of Canadians were treated with great respect by people who knew the role they played in providing prosperity and security for millions of their members and families. These groups were called "unions."

Sounds like a fairy tale, doesn't it? It's true. As a young man, my membership in the United Auto Workers of Canada, as it was called at the time, marked me as someone to be envied, as most trade unionists were. We represented the solid, hard-working core of Canada's industrial power. We mined the ore, made the steel, forged the parts, built the tires, assembled the cars, drove the trucks and trains, and performed many other essential and difficult tasks. We did it with the security of a hard-bargained contract, the support of other unions and the respect of the public generally. Unions were as essential to Canada's productivity and economic success as the corporations that employed them and the consumers who bought the goods they made.

Many things have changed. Many things have not.

One of the changes, and it's a good one, involves the number of women who make up union membership in Canada today. Back in 1977 only 12 percent of female workers in Canada were unionized; today it's well over 30 percent and climbing. In fact, there are now more women than men in trade unions today. The days when all workers, especially female workers, were exploited by bosses and corporations are long past.

Other changes are less positive and very disturbing, like the attitude toward employment by governments in Canada, the United States and elsewhere. In the years following the Second World War, lawmakers saw full employment as a prime economic goal. Anyone who wanted a job and was qualified to fill the position, everyone agreed, should have the opportunity to work. Full employment would allow every Canadian to make a contribution to our national prosperity, and would avoid the many economic costs and social problems associated with unemployment. For three decades after the war, this emphasis on full employment—while never fully achieved—contributed to a climate of prosperity and optimism among working people. Things changed. Sometime in the 1980s the idea of making jobs available for every qualified Canadian who was capable of putting in a day's work was abandoned in favour of massive deregulation, privatization and globalization.

The result of this change in goals has been a reduction in the expectations of working people. In my early years of employment, workers like me truly believed that our children would be better off than we were, and their children would be better off still. I don't hear that kind of talk anymore. I don't believe that most working people buy it, and that's sad. When ordinary people stop dreaming of better times for themselves and their families, something leaves them, and leaves society generally. A generation ago workers shared in the fruits of their labour, an idea that made perfect sense to almost everyone regardless of their political leanings. Sadly, almost no one proposes this concept anymore. Labour's share of Canada's gross domestic product has dropped to less than 50 percent since the late 1970s, meaning workers receive less than half of the economic pie they produce.

And let's get something straight. This isn't the result of some benign development in world economics. It's the direct outcome of a conscious strategy against organized labour, an approach that's never been more clearly illustrated than by the actions of the Mike Harris Conservatives when they gained power in Ontario. The very first piece of legislation introduced by the Harris government had nothing to do with education, health care, transportation or any other government responsibility. No, Harris and his cabinet thugs, some of whom graduated to Stephen Harper's federal cabinet a few years later, took aim at organized labour with an omnibus bill that repealed the province's anti-scab law, eliminated union certification procedures and made it easier for existing unions to be decertified. The impact of this legislation extended well beyond Ontario and set the stage for a broadly based anti-union attitude by governments throughout Canada that remains alive today.

Actions like these are behind the decline in union membership among Canada's workers. Less than 30 percent of the paid labour force in Canada was unionized in 2008, down from 40 percent two decades ago; in the private sector the figure was below 20 percent. That's shocking to me, but not as shocking as the figures on union membership in other countries. In the U.S., for example, union penetration in the private sector workforce is barely 8 percent.

Historically, a direct link can be plotted between the extent of trade union membership in a country and the standard of living enjoyed by its citizens—the higher the penetration of effective trade unions in the workforce, the higher the standard of living. On average, union members in Canada earn $4.59 more per hour than non-union members doing the same job. And here's an eye-opener: The union advantage is strongest among lower-wage work, such as security guards and trades helpers, and among women. Women union members average 36 percent more in hourly wages than women who are not in a union. So, true to their roots, unions provide more assistance to those who need it most—in this case, women workers who for generations before unions were expected to accept less pay for the same work as men.

Trade unions produce a prosperous middle class, and it's the middle class that defines and nurtures democracy and many of the freedoms we value so highly. Expand the definition to include middle-class families and the benefits of union membership really strike home. About 80 percent of union members in Canada have a workplace pension plan, three times the percentage of non-union members, and 76 percent enjoy dental benefits versus 43 percent of non-union members. These and other aspects of union life help families feel secure and cared-for, especially children, and the positive ripple effect flows through all of society.

The middle class in a free democracy defines the country's values and standards. In the absence of a vibrant middle class, a country can fall under autocratic rule with widespread injustices to the majority of its citizens, and the best way to generate a solid middle class is with effective trade unions.

For proof, you don't have to look further than to developing countries in Central and South America, Asia and Africa that lack a large-scale trade union influence. In every case you'll discover a small, obscenely wealthy level of society and a lower, desperately poor level. What you won't find is a large, active, and secure middle class, because they lack the power of a trade union to lift workers out of poverty. A similar situation may be growing much closer to home. While other factors may play a role, concern has been expressed lately about the decline in size and wealth of the American middle class, a decline that has occurred in clear parallel with the drop in trade union membership.

Anti-union people fail to recognize this connection between unions and a solid middle class, and other benefits that unions provide. They also tend to overlook a similar linkage between trade unions and a nation's productivity and work quality. On average, nations with large union representation score higher on both counts than countries with little or no union activity. This surprises people who assume unions are a barrier to productivity, quality and profits. In reality, the opposite is true.

The GM automotive plant in Oshawa has been unionized since 1937. In 1989, Toyota built an entirely new assembly plant about 200 kilometres down the road in Cambridge, Ontario. The new Toyota facility boasted the newest, most efficient technology available, importing every cutting-edge Japanese system to be had, a showplace of know-how as modern as today's date. Yet the unionized Oshawa plant consistently exceeds the non-union Toyota plant in overall quality and productivity.*

* * *

While organized labour has been getting a kick in the ass from most governments, business leaders are being warmly kissed in the same place by many of the same people. Over the past several years,

---

* *The Harbour Report, North America, 2008:* "GM's Oshawa #1 and #2 plants finished second and third (as most productive assembly plants in North America) behind CAMI Automotive, which produces Chevrolet Equinox, Pontiac Torrent and Suzuki XL-7 in Ingersoll, Ontario. Also J. D. Power & Associates, Initial Vehicle Quality Awards, September 2008: "J.D. Power and Associates is pleased to present GM's Oshawa Assembly Plant with a Founder's Award. During the past seven years, the General Motors Oshawa Plant has received four Gold and two Silver Awards for plant quality in North America in the annual J.D. Power and Associates Initial Quality Study. This is far more awards than any other plant has received over this period."

business profits represented the largest portion of GDP in Canada's history, thanks to booming profits and steep reductions in both the corporate tax rate and the federal capital tax. These cuts, we were told, would encourage capital investment in Canada and create new jobs, new prosperity and new hope for the future.

Well, they didn't. Measured against GDP, business investment in Canada has been stagnant since 1999. In fact, if you strip away the Alberta oil sands development and related projects, the share of GDP dedicated to new business capital spending has dropped significantly lower in the past decade.

So add it up: business gets lower taxes and earns higher profits while reducing investments in new projects. Workers get stagnant incomes, government restrictions on organizing and lower future expectations. You can call this anything you want. What you cannot call it is "fair."

* * *

The union movement in North America grew out of manufacturing, and until recently in Canada manufacturing represented a prime source of employment and security for working people. "Union-made" became a symbol of quality on the products we and our parents bought through the last half of the twentieth century. People looked for the union label not just because it represented fair wage and working conditions but also because it meant good value. Thanks to NAFTA and globalization, our manufacturing base has eroded and continues to shrink, and the quality of many manufactured goods we buy is suspect.

As I write this, less than half of CAW members are involved in manufacturing. The rest work in a wide range of transportation, resource and service industries. The work of service industry employ-ees is essential, and the men and women of the CAW who work in ser-vice industries ranging from airlines and hospitality to health care and gaming are proud union members, and their number keeps increasing. Unionism in the service sector continues to grow because wages and benefits represent a large portion of the cost of doing business. This encourages employers to squeeze every available penny from their staff where possible, and only a strong union can ensure that every employee is treated justly.

Many Canadians shrug off the decline in this country's manufac-turing activities, suggesting that employment in one sector is just as important as in another. As vital as service industries are, whether it's nursing us back to health or repairing our plumbing, they can never fill the same role in our national economy as high-value manufactur-ing. Productivity is much higher in manufacturing; the typical CAW member in a vehicle assembly plant produces $300,000 worth of value-added per worker per year. That's one reason manufacturing incomes are 20 percent higher on average than those in the rest of the economy. What's more, most manufacturing output is exported, so money flows into the country to pay for needed imports. And let's not forget that more than half of all business R & D spending in Canada comes out of the manufacturing sector, despite the fact that it represents less than 15 percent of our total GDP, an investment that spills over into the rest of our economy, lifting incomes in other sectors. Those are just a few good reasons why the jobs of many service-sector workers depend, directly or indirectly, on a healthy manufacturing sector.

When a unionized worker builds an automobile, truck, aircraft or other complex item to be sold here or elsewhere, the product they create represents an asset that did not exist before, and it can be exported to generate income for the country in ways that most services cannot. If it remains in Canada, the newly manufactured product will create opportunities for service people to operate and maintain it over many years to come. So those who shrug at our vanishing manufacturing base, especially the automotive industry that provides so much employment for so many Canadians, are simply wrong. They are wrong to suggest that manufacturing doesn't matter, they are wrong to say that unions are responsible for the loss of manufacturing jobs, and God knows they are wrong about promoting the so-called benefits of globalization.

The wealth of Canada, as much as any country's and more than most, is based on our ability to produce goods and sell them around the world. We should never forget this, and we must do all we can to preserve Canadian manufacturing. The decline of appreciation for manufacturing in Canada has paralleled the decline in regard for unions generally. Part of the blame lies with the media, which frequently place unions in a bad light by using terms such as "union bosses" to describe labour leaders. When did you ever hear CEOs called "corporate bosses" by the press? Treatment of unions—especially my union, the CAW—by some people in the media has been outrageous and I will deal with it in a later chapter.

Supporting this negative picture of unions disregards all union activities beyond those related to the concerns of their members, a situation that ignores many aspects of unions. Union supporters look past their own concerns to those of others, especially people who suffer poverty, discrimination and exploitation, in Canada and elsewhere. More than most Canadians, CAW members support the idea of making a commitment to assist those in need, and members have done this for years without the expectation of reward or recognition. Good thing, too. If CAW members produced peace in the Middle East, cured the common cold and eliminated problems of global warming, the *National Post* and other newspapers might give us a grudging mention somewhere between ads for hemorrhoids and the weather forecast.

Okay, I'm exaggerating. But not much. Too many people in the media keep promoting old stereotypes of unions and their members. Whisper "wildcat strike" and a platoon of reporters and cameras will tear across town. Mention community service or the generosity of union members when disaster strikes, and their eyes glaze over.

Need an example? Here's one.

The day after Christmas 2004, a devastating tsunami struck Southeast Asia. More than 200,000 people died and millions were made homeless. I asked CAW local unions and councils to dig into their pockets for cash to assist these victims. Within days we raised more than $1 million, which ultimately grew to the $2.1 million that we turned over to the Canadian Red Cross for tsunami relief. No other private organization came close to matching this amount. I saw press coverage for people who raised $30,000 or $40,000 but nothing about a union that gave more than $2 million.

I was so impressed with the generosity of our members that I called a press conference to announce it. One TV camera and two print reporters showed up. They listened and left. Nobody in the press covered the story. Nobody beyond the CAW and the Canadian Red Cross knew about it until now.

Our members didn't toss their money in the hat just to see their union be praised on the evening news. They did it from a sense of solidarity and the desire to support those in need. But when the local Lions Club or sewing circle can be congratulated for raising a few hundred bucks for a good cause, it is disheartening to see our union ignored time after time when it demonstrates generosity and concern.

And our social unionism goes beyond just writing a cheque and then feeling smug about it. In August 2008, I flew to Yellowknife to join

CAW members who were spending a week or more doing important work that our own federal government failed to do. These members were among the most highly skilled workers in our union—pipefitters, electricians and carpenters—and they travelled north and worked without pay to bring drinkable water to First Nations people at the Little Salmon/Carmacks community. These 30 or so CAW members gave up as much as $2,000 a week to drill wells and bring clean water into homes, working with First Nations leaders.

For more than three years, the residents of Little Salmon/Carmacks had been under a "boil water advisory" by the federal government. Instead of dealing with the root of the problem—water polluted by distant industries—local officials simply issued orders for First Nations people to solve it by boiling every litre of water they consumed. Meanwhile, politicians and bureaucrats in Ottawa leapt into action. They announced they would study the situation. They studied the damn thing for three years while First Nations families grew sick or trucked water in from kilometres away. That's when CAW leaders and I, supported by skilled tradespeople, said, "To hell with studies, we need action." And we took it.

The federal government's treatment of the Little Salmon/Carmacks people has been disgraceful. Basic rights of every Canadian, including access to drinkable water, must not be left to the private sector. Have we forgotten the people who died when the water treatment facility in Walkerton, Ontario, was privatized? At the CAW, we created a partnership with Little Salmon/Carmacks as a challenge for all levels of government to stop using "studies" as an excuse for doing nothing. I have no doubt that the avoidance of government action to assist these natives was the result of prejudice. Do you believe those in Ottawa would have twiddled their thumbs for three years if it were a non-native community in Ontario or Quebec with polluted water? Not a chance. The problem at Little

Salmon/Carmacks was dismissed because they were First Nations people, who habitually suffer from social, political and economic inequality.

Want proof? Here it is: as I write this, 100 First Nations communities in Canada are under the same boil-water advisory. Most are waiting for government studies to be completed. Have you ever drawn a glass of drinking water from a government study? Nothing is being accomplished by the federal government.

When they finish their work, CAW volunteers will have created 57 wells delivering drinkable water to the Little Salmon/Carmacks residents. That leaves about 99 more communities to go. I join with former AFN National Chief Phil Fontaine in demanding our federal government move immediately to fix the water problem facing First Nations communities. We wouldn't put up with it in our own communities. Why should we expect anyone else to accept it?

You don't have to venture as far north as Yukon to discover ways of helping people, and CAW members don't. Two of our most successful assistance programs have focused on the needs of families in Toronto's inner city. Governments and private corporations always seem to drop the ball on basic poverty issues, either by throwing money around and claiming they've done something good, or blaming the victims for their own desperate situations. It really does take socially active organizations such as unions, the CAW in particular, to get to the heart of the problem and solve it.

Consider the Pathways to Education program, or P2E, that CAW has supported since its inception. A few years ago, 56 percent of the students living in Toronto's Regent Park social housing development dropped out of high school. Regent Park residents were primarily people of colour, which led right-wing observers to attach racial labels to the problem. In reality, the problem had nothing to do with skin colour and everything to do with lousy planning.

The city had built no high schools within an easy walk of Regent Park. Students had to take public transportation, and spending even a couple of bucks a week per child for streetcar and bus tickets put a strain on these low income families. Why not help these kids get to school and see what happens? Along the way, why not add tutoring and mentoring support, and the attraction of a $1,000 contribution toward post-secondary education for every year of high school completed by a Regent Park student?

It sounded like a great idea to us, and the CAW has been supporting P2E, along with various other groups and individuals, since 2001. The program, which offers academic, social and financial support to students, has cut absenteeism by two-thirds, increased the academic success rate by an equal proportion, and assisted almost 1,000 Regent Park kids to acquire an education and break the cycle of poverty. And how about this: P2E is also responsible for a substantial decrease in drug use and crime in Regent Park.

Maybe it's because of my own rough childhood that I feel a personal obligation to kids in need, but I'm also an enthusiastic supporter of Eva's Initiative, another effort to reach out to youngsters and show them a bright alternative instead of a dark future. Eva's Initiative provides a residence and emotional support for up to a full year to homeless kids or those with severe family problems—long enough for them to shake off their difficulties, stay in school and get themselves resettled. At my suggestion, the CAW national executive board decided to contribute to the program, and we worked closely with various business leaders to raise significant funds each year through golf tournaments, fundraising dinners and other events, all in support of Eva's Initiative.

It's important for Canadians to know about these activities because they balance the skewed image that too many people have of unions. True, unions represent the best opportunity to workers to receive fair treatment and earn fair wages. But they also serve to promote various principles that everyone in a civilized society can and should support.

One of these is the concept of democratic unionism, in which every rank-and-file member understands the organization's goals and activities and has an opportunity to oppose, support and contribute to them, depending on their values and circumstances. All trade unions pay lip service to this idea, but I believe the CAW's emphasis on the principle was at the root of its success.

Another key principle deals with social unionism—the idea that the labour movement's moral credibility rests on its claim to speak for all working people, not just its dues-paying members. Our volunteer work on behalf of the First Nations people in Little Salmon/Carmacks is a perfect example but, as I indicated, it's not the only one. And we don't restrict our efforts to Canada.

More than 20 years ago, the union created a CAW Social Justice Fund to divert money from employers through collective bargaining that might otherwise have gone into our members' pay packets, using it to help those in need around the world. About $3 million a year has been generated to assist people in Africa, Latin America and Eastern Europe whose health and quality of life are suffering due either to the impact or the neglect of governments and private enterprise.

In 2008, the CAW's efforts to build awareness of the dangers of asbestos in countries around the world were recognized with the Tribute of Unity Award from the Asbestos Disease Awareness Organization, headquartered in California. The CAW also represented the largest contributor to the land mine removal initiative of the Chrétien government, under the leadership of its foreign affairs minister, Lloyd Axworthy. Contributions from CAW members helped remove land mines in Mozambique, where each year hundreds of people, many of them children, lose their limbs and their lives to these horrific weapons.

Millions of dollars from CAW members have been spent there to clear the land and build a factory to produce prosthetic limbs for victims of land mines.

Back in Canada, the CAW is a major contributor of funds and volunteers to support women's shelters and food banks. And guess which Canadian city boasted the most successful United Way campaign year after year? It's Windsor, Ontario, where CAW members consistently outstrip the national average in individual donations, despite the hard times that have fallen on that city in recent years.

I don't know of any organization in Canada that works harder to keep its members attuned to serious developments in the social, cultural, political and economic arenas than the CAW. That's not empty boasting; it's solid fact. No other union in the world, for example, brings its elected and local leaders together as often as the CAW does. Three times a year they gather to hear and debate not only reports on union matters but enlightening presentations by guest speakers on topics such as mental health, poverty, health care, homelessness and other concerns extending beyond the factory and office walls where members are employed. Many of these speakers are internationally recognized experts on their topics brought to this country at the CAW's expense to inform union members about critical points of view. This is not a union that looks constantly inward. It's an organization that is in tune with serious issues concerning all Canadians, challenging its members to think hard and long about these matters.

The CAW is also concerned with employment safety, producing and distributing brochures in several languages around the world to alert workers about the dangers of many industrial chemicals, and showing the steps to take when handling them. In many cases, workers alerted by these communications wind up knowing more about the chemicals used at their worksite than their bosses.

I never received one word of criticism from CAW members regarding our investment of time and money in projects such as these. Assisting others is part of the union culture. In fact, we are as unified over our social obligations as we are about our collective bargaining.

Finally, unions must put their faith in the value of collective action as a means improving the status of workers. When aiming to eradicate poverty and suffering, only solidarity among workers, and among citizens generally, will produce the results we all agree are worth fighting for. As CAW national president, I recognized that we would never win every fight that we took up on behalf of workers against poverty and suffering, but if we didn't fight we would never win a thing.

I suppose, if someone wanted to sum up the philosophy of Buzz Hargrove in one sentence, that would be as good as any.

THREE

The Art of Bargaining

Many Canadians believe that, because the union tries to speak with one voice, its members are like some robotic army that marches in whatever direction its leaders point. Boy, have they got that one wrong.

When CAW members face a common challenge that goes to the root of their cause, they become unified as much as any member of a Rotary Club or chamber of commerce would under the same circumstances. But the idea that a union is composed of people who either can't or won't think for themselves; or that their union leaders are treated like infallible gods whose word cannot be challenged; or that whenever Buzz Hargrove raised his hand everybody else in the room did too—well, it's laughable.

Anyone who wants to see democracy in action, stripped to its basic freedoms, should participate in a CAW membership or leadership meeting. Collective bargaining in the CAW begins and ends with the members. They call the shots and they approve or reject the results. When deciding on a bargaining position with an employer, for example, every member of that union local has a right to insert a demand. Whether the demand is as broad as a substantial wage increase or as trivial as the colour of the shop floor washroom, it's put on the table.

Contrary to the thinking of many non-union people, the bargaining process does not always involve wages or direct benefits. It often involves basic fairness, such as scheduling policies and mandatory overtime. Other issues vital to workers, and difficult if not impossible to handle without the backing of a strong effective union, include health and safety issues, job training, seniority rights and job postings. Each of these and more can be inserted in the union's initial contract demands, according to the democratic vote of the members. The CAW's approach to collective bargaining is a rare and notable example of participatory democracy. Canadians believe they live in a democracy and they are correct, to a degree. Compared with the process of collective bargaining, however, our democracy leaves Canadians virtually powerless. In the CAW and other unions with similar policies, rank-and-file members truly "own" the bargaining process. The majority select the terms to be negotiated in a new contract and they must approve—ratify—any proposal agreed to by the bargaining committee. This ownership, more than any other aspect, forces the union leadership to acknowledge and remain true to the members' values and expectations. Can anyone make the same claim about our elected governments? I don't think so.

Every worker who submits a contractual demand naturally feels that his or her idea is valid. Obviously that's not always the case, and while all tabled demands are incorporated in the union's proposal, it's up to the bargaining committee to recognize the practical limits. When the committee returns to the meeting and says, "The employer has met our demands for items A, B, D, F and G but refuses items C and E so we dropped them," they expect a response from the people who submitted those demands. Sometimes it's disappointment, sometimes it's anger—not always, but frequently enough for the committee to be concerned when they make the announcement. It's not that the members are unreasonable. It's just that they're passionate about the issues and their role in the process.

Passion was the first quality I looked for in selecting staff members and executives for duties within the union. Many members saw the union not just as a source of strength and support for workers, but as a career choice, and that was fine. But I knew that the most effective and successful people at all levels in the CAW included those who were sincerely dedicated to achieving the union's goals and meeting the challenge of improving the lives of workers and their families.

You need passion and a deep belief in the union's objectives, not just to keep fighting for workers' rights, but also to stand up to attacks from within your own union. This is where the emotional quality of unionism could turn around and bite you on the ass. I don't know any industry or corporation where the employees feel comfortable telling their boss from time to time that he or she is a dumb SOB. You can't get away with doing that in a company, because the target of your venom is responsible for the income you earn, not to mention any chance you might have of getting a promotion or a raise.

Some union people, however, direct that kind of language and worse at their leadership from time to time, because they're passionate about things and because the roles have been reversed: the target is no longer the source of income but the *recipient* of income, paid via dues by every union member. So you have to love what you're doing as a union executive or staff member because you'll hear a lot of rough language during bargaining debates, ratification meetings and policy discussions. On some occasions after I won a hard-fought battle by getting barely 51 percent of the votes, I left the meeting with the air still blue from all the curses tossed at me. I'd take a break, calm myself down and, at my next meeting a few minutes later, I might make a speech asking for contributions to help the homeless or provide accommodation for battered women from some of the same people who had called me an SOB in the previous session.

Rank-and-file union members drive the system, especially when it comes down to sitting across the table from the employer and negotiating a contract.

Three guidelines framed the CAW bargaining strategy while I was national president. The first was the importance of members owning the process through democratic means, as I described earlier. The second was the requirement that bargaining committees must take responsibility for every agreement they successfully negotiate; there must be no room for excuses. Finally, we insisted that no agreement could represent a backward step for the union, even in tough times. This has been a challenge to follow in the past, and it's clearly a challenge now, but the principle remains: no concession in wages, pensions and core benefits.

Every time I was involved in a collective bargaining session, I assumed both the union and I were being put to the test. And we were. Once a collective agreement expired, all the gains we had made in previous negotiations expired with it. Nobody could assume anything would be extended from an expired contract. Sure, there were precedents from the old contract, but I assumed that we had to be ready to fight for the renewal of every clause. Yet I never started a session with a chip on my shoulder. I always figured you could get more of what you want with a smile than a snarl, knowing that the other side would use every tool available to them. As would we. Sometimes a new approach works and sometimes it turns around and bites you on the ass.

Back in the late 1990s, for example, the Canadian dollar's value against the American greenback had slipped below 70 cents. We used to meet for a casual, relaxed dinner with the CEOs of the car companies about twice a year and discuss whatever issue came up. At one of these sessions with the GM team, we talked about new investment in Canada and I pointed out the much lower Canadian dollar's value to CEO Rick Wagoner. GM should expand its investment in Canada with new plants and facilities, I suggested, because it would cost the company 30 percent less than the same move would cost in the U.S. I wanted more production volume on this side of the border because it would generate more Canadian jobs and more security, and the best way of doing this would be to convince Wagoner to put his money here instead of in Michigan or Missouri or some other place.

"Buzz," Wagoner replied, "we never make investment decisions based on currency value, because currency values can change." And that was that.

A few years later, when we gathered to start negotiating a new contract with GM, the company submitted a presentation opposing the CAW's new wage goals, and the key argument was the fact that the Canadian dollar had rebounded over the years to almost 95 cents American. "The higher exchange rate," GM noted, "makes labour costs in Canada much too high compared with those in our U.S. plants," giving them the basis for arguing against our demands.

"But, Rick," I said across the table to Wagoner, "we never make negotiating decisions based on currency value, because currency values can change." I'm not sure Wagoner got the joke but it didn't matter, because within a few weeks the Canadian dollar began to slide back to about 80 cents.

No matter how well the CAW bargaining committee and the employer representatives got along, the sessions themselves were intense. Some lasted just a few hours. Most extended across several days or weeks. The longer the bargaining went on, the more emotional things could get. That's understandable. In complex contract negotiations such as those conducted with GM, Ford and Chrysler, the sessions became a seemingly endless string of demands and rejections, proposals and counter-proposals, compromises and trade-offs. Stress levels rose. Words were exchanged. Patience was lost.

While wages and benefits were always at the core of bargaining, the agreements we produced were more than economic documents. I always saw them as charters for dignity and respect in the workplace. They dealt with health and safety issues, with family and lifestyle concerns, and with human rights and community support.

CAW members understand these values and principles, and they support them with few, if any, reservations, although things can get complex once the process begins. A union leader can misread the attitude and intent of the members. When this happens, more than words can fly back and forth, and I have the scars to prove it. Some are old. Some are still fresh. Here's how I acquired the oldest one.

In 1978, shortly after the UAW's Canadian director, Bob White, asked me to be his assistant, he sent me back to Windsor to help settle an extended strike at Hiram Walker, the distiller of Canadian Club whisky. The union at Hiram Walker had recently broken away from the American distillers union, set up their own Canadian union, and chose to join what was then the United Auto Workers of Canada.

Hiram Walker maintained two plants at the time. In addition to the Windsor plant, it operated a small plant in Kelowna, B.C., employing 120 people. Both locations were on strike. Years earlier, employees at the Windsor plant had bargained a contract that guaranteed a minimum number of employees. Under the terms of the agreement, the company's workforce could not be fewer than this agreed-upon number. Changes in technology and the whisky market, however, made it impossible for the company to live up to the agreement and it wanted to eliminate the minimum workforce clause. The two sides were dead-locked over this issue.

Playing the role of honest broker, I talked to management, who made a strong case for their position. "The only way we could continue to guarantee the minimum workforce for another three years," they told me, "would be to close the Kelowna plant." Throwing more than 100 people out of work, especially in a small community like Kelowna, was something we couldn't allow to happen.

I suggested an alternative. "Instead of insisting on the minimum number of employees," I said to Bob White, "why not aim for a guar-anteed annual income over the term of the agreement?" This alterna-tive had been accepted in principle by management; all we had to do now was sell it to the Windsor workers. Bob agreed, and off I went to a meeting of the Windsor local, but not before sending a staff member, Al Johnson, to Kelowna. Al was to schedule a meeting in Kelowna at a time following my meeting in Windsor. If Windsor rejected my guaranteed income idea, as I suspected they would, Al would inform the Kelowna employees and ask for a vote on the same deal.

What I really wanted was the chance to talk directly to the local members, explain this was a no-win situation, and plant the seeds that could lead to eventual acceptance of a lower guaranteed income for everybody, leaving nobody unemployed. If Kelowna bought into the agreement to save their jobs, which seemed likely, it would pressure the Windsor local union leadership to settle as well.

By the time I walked into the meeting, the Windsor employees had heard about my proposal and they didn't like it at all. They liked me even less. As I walked toward the podium, some members spit on me, and others flicked lighted cigarettes at me. I hear things can get rough in corporate boardrooms, but I'll bet no CEO was ever greeted this way by shareholders!

I began speaking, but I couldn't hear my own voice over all the boos being directed at me. Finally Dick Tighe, the local president, grabbed the microphone and in his thick drawl he barked, "Now folks, we're going to be respectful here. Brother Hargrove has a different point of view and we're gonna hear him out." This was enough to cut maybe half the booing, but at least I didn't have to dodge more cigarette butts. When I finished, the members voted 96 percent against my proposal, which was enough to ensure me another rough ride as I left the union hall.

Things were set in motion. I passed the results on to Al Johnson, who informed the Kelowna workers that, in effect, Windsor had voted against their jobs. Kelowna, naturally, voted in favour of the proposal. This carried enough weight to send the Windsor local's bargaining committee back to management where an apples-and-oranges settlement took place. Management's proposals were apples; the union's were oranges. Both sides moved their ideas around, but in the end there were the same number of apples and oranges on the table. The arrangement looked different enough for the bargaining committee to recommend and the members to support it, however, and within days the strike ended.

With the local union bargaining committee recommending acceptance, the members ratified the agreement by a 94 percent vote. This reinforced my belief that regardless of what head office leadership recommended, the membership would always follow their local leadership recommendation, and that's the way it should be. Still, for several years after, so I've been told, a few of the Windsor workers continued to snarl whenever anybody mentioned my name.

I've had more serious things than saliva and cigarettes hurled at me. Another time when Bob White was heading the union, I accompanied him to a meeting of workers at the McDonnell Douglas aircraft plant in Malton, just outside Toronto. We had settled what we thought was a pretty good contract on behalf of the workers. The next day the employer shut the plant early so the union members could vote on the deal, and the workers walked across the road to a crowded hall in the International Centre to hear the details. As soon as Bob and I stepped from our car to enter the meeting one of the workers approached Bob and said, "I hear you're a pretty good speaker."

Bob said he wasn't bad.

"Well, you better be damn good today," the McDonnell Douglas worker warned, "because you're gonna need every good word you've got."

Bob and I looked at each other. What the hell was going on here? Then we walked into the hall. Jesus, you'd think a wrestling match was going on and Bob and I were the villains. People started booing and jeering us, and some members of the Marxist-Leninist party were walking up and down the aisles waving signs saying "Better Red than White"! We finally made it to the podium, and all the time we were trying to make the case for the contract, men marched up and down the aisle carrying protest signs or grabbed the microphone to call Bob and the union leadership every name they could think of, urging the members to turn down the deal.

They lost. The deal passed with barely more than 50 percent of the vote.

A few years later, Boeing Corporation, having spent hundreds of millions of dollars to acquire the De Havilland aircraft plant in Toronto, decided they could not make money building the smaller aircraft that De Havilland had produced for many years, and decided to sell the plant. If they couldn't find a buyer, they would close it. Our union persuaded Ontario Premier Bob Rae to partially fund the purchase of De Havilland from Boeing. We wanted those jobs saved, and Rae struck a deal with Laurent Beaudoin at Bombardier to purchase De Havilland.

As part of the sale, our union agreed to extend our collective bargaining agreement for a year in exchange for the company making improvements in benefits for our retirees. When the contract came up for renewal, the bargaining was difficult. After several tough sessions, Bombardier still had done nothing to address our demands, so we authorized a strike. Within a couple of days we were back at the bargaining table making progress until we encountered a problem involving employees of a Japanese supplier who had done lousy work.

The company's primary product was the Dash 8 passenger aircraft. The plane was assembled in Canada, but primary components came from elsewhere. Short Brothers built the fuselage in Belfast, Ireland, and a Japanese subcontractor built the wings.

Around the time we were trying to settle the strike, Bombardier noted that the Japanese supplier's work on the wings was not up to standard, and insisted that the firm send technicians to Canada to make the necessary repairs. The idea of 30 or 40 Japanese workers on the floor of the plant, even for a couple of weeks, did not sit well with CAW members. They wanted to do the work themselves and get paid for it. Bombardier President Bob Brown saw things differently. The company had already paid for the wings. They weren't acceptable to Bombardier, and the supplier agreed to correct them without extra cost. If CAW workers fixed the wings they would expect to be paid for their efforts, which didn't make sense to Brown. "Why should I pay twice for the same work?" he asked.

He had a point, but the local leaders wouldn't budge. If there was work to be done in the plant, the leaders insisted, it would be done by CAW members earning CAW wages.

I called Bob Brown and asked for a meeting, which took place at the Prince Hotel in Toronto. National Secretary Treasurer Jim O'Neil and his assistant, Peter Kennedy, came along with me.

Brown laid things out for us. "If we can't get the Japanese supplier to make good on those wings," he said, "we're getting out of the business. The Ontario government has more money in this deal than Bombardier has. We'll write off our investment and you guys and Bob Rae can have the plant and do what the hell you want with it. But we're not going to pay twice for the same damn work."

Had Bombardier shipped the wings back to Japan to have them repaired there, Brown said, we wouldn't have cause to complain, and he was right. I believed he was serious about pulling out. If he did, we would lose a few hundred permanent jobs for the sake of getting temporary work for a handful of employees. I said as much to Merv Gray, the chair of the bargaining committee, who called a meeting of the members to discuss the proposal, and I agreed to attend.

Once again I walked into a hornet's nest. To call the members unhappy is like saying it gets chilly in Whitehorse in January. Before I could speak a word into the microphone, one guy stood up and yelled, "Hang him! Hang the sonofabitch!"

I assumed he was being a little dramatic and kept talking, hoping I could escape the meeting without wearing a rope around my neck. I managed to avoid being lynched and later I persuaded Merv Gray to speak to Bob Brown directly, something he hadn't done until then. Merv travelled to Montreal for a meeting with Brown, and he returned convinced that Brown was serious. The temporary presence of Japanese workers on the floor of the plant to correct work they should have done right in the first place was not important enough to lose the whole factory, Merv explained to his members. They finally understood and things got settled quickly.

Successful unions are driven by the demands of their members, not by the personal goals or ambitions of union leaders. Leaders need vision, of course. They need to know how to acquire power and how (and when) to apply it. But that power is granted by the workers, and woe betide any leader who ignores the fact. In this sense, I submit, the CAW is more democratic than any federal or provincial government system in Canada. Prime ministers of the day may hear about dissatisfaction among citizens on the editorial pages of newspapers and in reports from their MPs, but they are rarely the target of lighted cigarettes or threats of hanging, no matter how far they might have strayed from the path of their principles.

The media rarely picked up on the threats and insults I received, but they sure had fun with a strike of CAW support staff in 2000. As their employer, we negotiated contracts with the 100 or so secretaries and other office staff, most of whom earned well above the industry average for their work.

The support staff's problem with the proposed contract in 2000 was based on pensions. We had long maintained two separate pension benefits for CAW employees in the auto plants: one for assembly line workers, and one for skilled workers like pipefitters and electricians. A parallel agreement was in place for our own CAW staff; secretaries received a pension similar to that of the assembly line workers, and national representatives (who worked in the field with our local unions) had a pension equal to that of skilled workers in the plant. It's not a two-tier system; it's an income replacement program. Skilled tradespeople earn substantially more than those on the assembly line as a result of their training and education, so they deserve a higher income level when they retire, too. Everyone had been satisfied with this set-up for years, but in 2000 the support staff chief negotiator, Nancy Kearnan, decided that her members should be classified the same as skilled workers in the plant when it came to pensions.

This didn't make any sense to us and, when things came to an impasse, the support staff went on strike. Well, why not? That's what unions have a right to do when contract negotiations break down, and much was made in the media of our offices being picketed. Much was made as well about my daughters Laura and Jaime, who were support staff employees at the time, picketing their old man. Unlike other employers, however, as part of the settlement the CAW made payments to the strikers to cover most of their lost wages while off the job. Still, the media and anti-unionists everywhere had a good laugh over a union office being picketed. Eventually the strike was settled and we all went happily back to work, but for a month or so I went through yet another test of being a union leader.

Leadership is never about trying to make everybody happy. It's about studying and debating issues with the people involved in the process. Then you make the decision and move on. You don't look back and you don't falter in your commitment. You must be prepared to be challenged and, in some circumstances, attacked. The most important thing is to listen to the local leadership and their members. If you fail to listen or avoid responding to their concerns, they'll turn on you.

I was the target of attacks dozens of times during my time as CAW president, sometimes by employers and governments, sometimes by other unions, and sometimes by CAW members. Did I enjoy it? Not a bit. I'm no masochist. Everybody loves to be loved, and I'm no different. I respect their right to protest my decision, yet I can think of only a couple of times when, after all the shouting had died down, I realized I might have done things differently.

One of those times involved Telus. It was 2005, and we were in the midst of bargaining with GM after settling with Ford and Chrysler when I received a call from Bruce Bell, president of the Telecommunications Workers Union. TWU bargainers had been trying to reach a deal with Telus for several months without success. There didn't seem to be an end to the dispute. While I was aware of the work stoppage, and the fact that the CAW had made a $4 million interest-free loan to the TWU to provide their members with strike pay, I had been concentrating on dealing with the auto companies, so I wasn't entirely on top of developments.

Bruce wanted me to intervene, perhaps by pulling the federal labour ministry into the picture. "If you can get the minister or somebody to put this thing to compulsory arbitration," Bruce said, "we can finally get it settled." I agreed to help and, after calls to Prime Minister Paul Martin and Joe Fontana, the federal labour minister at the time, Telus said they would return to the bargaining table.

When I turned my attention to the situation, I was amazed at what a mess it was. There were more demands on the table from both sides than there had been in the negotiations from all three auto companies combined. Compared with Telus negotiations, the Ford, GM, and Chrysler deals were picnics. The complex state of affairs evolved out of the history of Telus, and it contributed to mistrust between the parties.

Telus had been assembled from three different firms, so three different contracts and three different pension plans were involved. Seeking to make more profit, the corporation wanted benefits pulled back, especially from former employees of the two publicly owned telephone companies in the original merger. The employees, who had been enjoying the benefits for years, said the hell with that. They were angry with the employer and just as angry with many of their fellow Telus employees.

About 7,000 British Columbia workers remained on the picket lines, while over half the 9,000 Alberta workers had crossed the lines and returned to work in response to urgings from Telus management. This meant the company was recruiting scabs from its own union. On top of that, the union had recently won the right by a decision of the Canada Industrial Relations Board (CIRB) to represent Ontario- and Quebec-based Telus workers. These people from Ontario and Quebec had no union loyalty, no bargaining experience and no familiarity with union culture, yet there they were, sitting at the table with everyone else. Joining them were representatives of union members who had honoured the picket lines, and representatives of other union members who had crossed it. It was a hell of a mess.

Some of the union people resented my being asked to help out. The TWU had no affiliation with the CAW or any other union, and there were suggestions that some kind of quid pro quo was involved, which was untrue. I was there strictly as a union brother at the request of Bruce Bell and the rest of his members who wanted to settle the thing and hold the union together. Despite this, I became the target of some uncomplimentary remarks from others seated around the table. At one point things became so tense that I said, "Hey, I don't have to be here. I've spent weeks bargaining with GM, Ford, and Chrysler. I'm tired and ready to relax on a beach somewhere for a week or two. If you don't want me here, I'm gone." Bruce and the entire bargaining committee asked me to stay, and I did, which brought me face to face with Telus CEO Darren Entwistle.

Entwistle is a good dresser, I'll say that for him. He strutted into the room and made it clear that he didn't appreciate my involvement in the situation. This didn't impress me, but his grasp of the situation did. Entwistle was more knowledgeable about collective bargaining agreements than any CEO I ever encountered. He knew every paragraph and every sentence of the agreements right down to each comma and semicolon. He also knew he held the upper hand. The TWU had long ago used up its strike fund and had borrowed substantially to replenish it, including those few million dollars from the CAW.

I often break the ice in situations like this one by injecting a little humour, so when after the introductions I said to Entwistle, "One of my first jobs was with Alberta Government Telephone, now part of Telus. Hell, if I hadn't been laid off in 1963 and not gone into the union business, I might've had your fucking job and we'd be sitting on opposite sides of this table!"

Nothing. Not even a hint of a smile. All right. Down to work.

It was November 2005, and Entwistle informed us that if we didn't reach a settlement right away he would suspend talks for at least two months. The coming Christmas season represented a major sales period for Telus, and he didn't need these talks diverting his people from selling as many telephone contracts as they could. A few words were exchanged and we took a break.

I needed the break to consult with the bargaining team. Everything that happens in the bargaining procedure is a matter of power. The employer has the power to hold back on demands, and the union has the power to call a strike. With half the Alberta employees crossing the picket lines and a hard-nosed CEO prepared to ignore us for at least two months, the union had very little power in the situation. My philosophy has always been to obtain the most benefits with the least sacrifice from union members, and always to have an exit strategy should the deal go sour. I suggested the group seek a quick end to the conflict. "The government's not going to help, you're out of money to cover strike pay, and there's not much chance of getting more money from other unions," I said. "Hundreds of union members are crossing your picket line in Alberta and others are preparing to cross the line in British Columbia if talks fail. If you keep this up, you're liable to destroy the union."

It seemed like a reasonable position to me. But to some members of the bargaining committee it sounded like high treason. "I'm not going back into the office to work with those scabs who crossed our picket line!" somebody shouted. Lila Hackett, who had been one of the more strident members of the group, snarled, "I don't give a goddamn if we destroy the union as long as we destroy the company in the process!"

I had never encountered bitterness like this before. Hackett and many of her supporters were prepared to burn down the house to get rid of the mice. They directed their anger at me even though I had volunteered to offer advice and had no power to make any decision. Like it or not, however, I was in the middle of the situation and couldn't simply walk away, although the idea appealed to me. A lot.

"Whatever happens," I advised the TWU workers at one point, "after this gets settled you should affiliate with another, larger union. It doesn't matter if it's the CAW or not. You need the research facilities, resources and expertise to draw from, to help you set your strategy, lobby the government and conduct your bargaining."

You'd have thought I was asking them to join the Conservative Party. They wanted none of it. Nobody was going to tell these people what to do or even offer advice on how to do it. I suspected at least some of the TWU bargaining committee members were more interested in carving out their own fiefdoms than in finding a better way to meet the demands of their members. I soon gave up trying to convince them of the idea, and we resumed our long series of meetings.

Sometimes the negotiations felt like being lost in the Tower of Babel on a dark and stormy night. Everybody seemed to be talking about something else, all at the same time. Amazingly, we began to make progress, although it was slow and painful. Some days stretched beyond six or seven hours of constant wrangling, but after three weeks we had a deal worth submitting to the workers at a ratification meeting. I was barred from attending, but I heard the session went on for several hours with lots of shouted threats and raised fists. The first vote was barely defeated. Bell managed to get a second vote, which passed with 64 percent approval, and the strike ended.

But the animosity didn't. Some union leaders attacked Bell's leadership and managed to have him expelled as president of the union. As I write this, a new president is running things and the situation remains in turmoil. Meanwhile, the five-year agreement expires in 2010, they don't appear to be making any preparations, and hard-nosed Darren Entwistle is likely to be still calling the shots.

The whole exercise was a disappointment for me. As after all failures, however, I walked away with a lesson learned. My lesson from Telus: Never go into an employer-employee dispute without a clear mandate about who is in charge. I needed to say to Darren Entwistle, "When I speak, I have 100 percent support from the unionized employees." I couldn't say that. Entwistle was aware of this and knew that everything I proposed was from a position of weakness.

I also didn't fully appreciate how deeply the views of the more agitated TWU members went, and how totally opposed they were to any compromise with Telus management. Understanding the views and values of members is essential for any union leader. Go into a bargaining session without fully understanding the overall mood of the workers and you're setting yourself up for failure.

I learned this in 2004 when negotiating a contract with CN Rail. Given the nature of the railroad business, CAW members were scattered across the country, making it impossible to gather them in one place. To assist in the bargaining process, my staff and I had to rely on the national bargaining committee to guide us. The bargaining committee was elected by members from all regions of the country, and when the committee announced they had reached a deal with CN, I supported their recommendation to seek ratification. Everybody appeared happy. The bargaining committee was happy to get the new agreement that resolved a lot of tough issues, CN was happy to avoid a strike, and I was happy that things had run so smoothly that I hadn't had to participate to any great extent. This was a relief to me because a few weeks earlier I had torn my knee ligaments and was still recovering from the operation to repair them. Sitting for long days in a crowded meeting room arguing over contract details was the last thing I wanted to do.

The only people who weren't happy with the deal were the workers themselves. Their objections had nothing to do with the contract and everything to do with the way CN management had been treating CAW members. This wasn't about money. It was about respect. I soon began hearing about this in e-mails, letters and telephone calls sent from across the country. "We're not looking for more money," they were all telling me in so many words. "We're looking for a change in attitude from CN, and a way we can sit down and solve our disputes."

The 18-member CAW bargaining committee had underestimated the anger and frustration of CN workers during the negotiations. A union bargaining committee must be totally confident that an agreement will be ratified before accepting the deal, and understanding the attitude of the members is essential. In fact, accurate reading of the members' mood has been one of the strengths of the CAW. Whenever we shook hands at the end of bargaining—and management knew this—the deal was as good as ratified, because we knew the concerns of our members and we did our best to get a favourable outcome. If management suspects that a union bargaining committee has a so-so reputation for getting deals ratified, they'll hold something back. When management is sure a deal recommended by the bargaining committee will be accepted by the workers, they'll hasten the process by putting everything they can on the table.

Over the period of the previous contract, CN managers believed the union had no power, and they exploited this belief by suspending workers for minor infractions that should never have justified removing them from their job. When bargaining was completed, the CAW committee shook hands with CN management and assumed that ratification from the members would be a formality. Like hell it would. CN workers wanted to address the poor management policies as much as if not more than their income, and refused to support the new agreement. Based on the extreme frustration and anger of our members, I had to approve a strike despite the bargaining committee's success. CAW's policy was that once we shook hands with management on a deal it was our responsibility and obligation to ensure it was ratified. With the exception of CN and a couple of other cases, the CAW never authorized a strike once the elected committee signs on to a tentative agreement. This was an exception, and it brought a lot of abuse down on our heads.

Crippling a national railroad is a serious matter. I didn't need to be told that. But developing and maintaining a good employer-employee relationship is also serious. In fact, it's essential. By striking, the CAW members demonstrated they had power that many CN managers refused to acknowledge, and it took a nationwide strike to get the message across. Happy employees are an asset to every corporation, and since the strike every attempt has been made by our union and CN management to deal with the attitude issue. The effort has led to a much better relationship at most CN locations across Canada.

Some people outside the union movement find it strange that the Canadian Auto Workers union represents railway workers. Even more confusing for them, the CAW also represents airline workers, fishery workers, health care workers, hospitality and gaming workers, mining and smelting workers, and retail and wholesale workers. What do all of these people have to do with the automotive industry? Very little, but they have everything to do with worker concerns.

Of all the things I managed to accomplish during my years as CAW president, none gave me more pride than widening the list of industries whose unionized workers came under the umbrella of the CAW, a move that came directly from the members themselves. For several years in the 1970s while I was active with the union in Windsor, I participated in activities to support various striking unionists who were not CAW members. Often this involved walking the line with them, and over and over again the strikers would tell me how much they wished we represented them. In the early 1980s, during sessions with Bob White, Bob Nickerson, Sam Gindin and others, I began raising the idea of broadening our base and diversifying the union.

We were still part of the UAW at the time, and the U.S. executive insisted on enforcing unwritten rules preventing our union from representing workers in this sector or that sector. Unions in those industries had a reciprocal understanding that they wouldn't try to recruit workers in the automotive sector.

I didn't agree with the idea. Many worker concerns were common across various industries and companies. Why should our union be allowed to focus only on workers in the automotive and associated industries, like aerospace, just because our name included the word *auto*?

Then, in 1983 the Canadian Airline Employees Association (CALEA) asked if they could be affiliated with us. They were a relatively small union that had not gotten along well with other unions in the airline industry. They liked Bob White and the kinds of things we were doing for our members, so we started talking about a merger of sorts.

Things quickly became complicated. Our members, almost by definition, were concentrated in the centre of the country working closely together in large plant facilities. They came together to discuss issues and cast votes when necessary. CALEA members were stretched literally from Newfoundland to Vancouver Island and north to the Arctic. As you can imagine, voting on almost any issue, from new union executives to contract ratification, was totally different and would require changes to our constitution if CALEA were to come on board.

There was some opposition to this idea from the old school guys. The idea of airline workers and auto assembly workers sitting side by side at union meetings was a little difficult for some of our leadership at first, but I kept pointing out that CALEA represented about 7,000 workers who needed strong representation in the workplace. Timing was also a factor; we were in the throes of separating from the UAW, and expanding our member base would help us ride out what we all expected to be a rough and challenging period. In fact, if we had remained in the UAW when CALEA came aboard, we would have been required to obtain permission from the Americans to change the constitution, and they likely would have refused.

We had other concerns to deal with as well. "If they come with us," Bob White and Bob Nickerson said in so many words, "they follow our rules." I disagreed. We could change the constitution to accommodate them and still keep to our basic principles, I insisted, and thanks to my repeated arguments CALEA members became part of the CAW. Within the next 10 years we brought 18 other unions on board, totalling more than 84,000 new members representing miners, hotel and restaurant staff, fisheries and more. By 2008 we had added another 15, raising the union's total membership to about 265,000.

The impact of these new members on the CAW extends well past the numbers. More than the change in size, the union underwent a major change in structure and operations.

These changes included adjusting some aspects of our operations to the new members and the new industries we represented. From a rigid "our way or the highway" attitude where new members were concerned, the CAW began adapting to make the newly merged unions and their members feel welcome from the very first day.

Sometimes the efforts were small but the rewards were substantial. One of my earliest decisions regarding new unions concerned logos. Traditionally a smaller union merging with a larger, more established one would be directed to adopt the bigger union's name and logo design. To members of a union with a long and storied history of struggling for worker rights, this was an affront to their tradition. I understood this and began questioning the old policy. Why insist on it? I asked. Let them keep their name and adapt our logo as part of it, rather than eliminate the union's history entirely. The Mine, Mill & Smelter Workers Union in Sudbury, for example, is known within the CAW as Local 598 but to its members and the community where they live it is still Mine, Mill & Smelter Workers. Keeping their name was not a big deal to us in the CAW, but it was an historical link for the Sudbury workers and they retained it.

Talking about the Mine, Mill & Smelter Workers reminds me of another adjustment made to respect their needs and history. The CAW constitution designates that member dues are calculated as a percentage of wages, cost of living allowance (COLA) and bonuses. This works well, except in the case of the underground mineworkers who receive extra income labelled "danger pay" in recognition of the risk they take every day. The mineworkers call this a "blood bonus." Regardless of its title, under the CAW constitution this income would be subject to union dues payment. To a couple of generations of unionized miners, the blood bonus had never been subject to dues payment, and they objected to the idea when merger talks with the CAW began. Many in the CAW dug in their heels, saying quite correctly that a bonus is a bonus no matter how it's earned, either by working harder or working in a dangerous environment.

I refused to see this as a deal-breaker. "You have to respect their history," I told those who were objecting to the proposal of exempting the danger pay from dues calculations. "The Mine, Mill union is one of the oldest in North America. So this isn't about money. It's about solidarity and support for a union that has a history longer than our own and making them feel at home in our union."

My proposal won them over, leading to a new clause in the CAW constitution that enables the national executive board to exclude certain members from various demands in the constitution as long as there is a precedent or some other factor to justify it. Today Mine, Mill workers are among the strongest supporters of the CAW. They retain their name and logo, and their blood bonus remains excluded from calculations for their dues.

We made similar adjustments for the railroad unions who chose to become part of the CAW. Instead of bargaining units, the railroad workers' union had been structured around lodges located coast to coast, and as long as the members were satisfied with this arrangement and they operated within our general guidelines, this was fine with the CAW.

The more diversified the union became, the more we recognized the need to provide forums within the CAW where shared concerns could be expressed and addressed. One step was to set up sector councils where worker representatives in specific industries could come together two or three times a year and discuss mutual problems such as health and safety issues, bargaining experiences and working conditions. These sector councils operate on behalf of railroad workers, aerospace employees, health care and university workers, and other groups. All sectors, of course, have access to national and worldwide information and expertise, thanks to the size and facilities of the CAW.

This attitude of respect and accommodation continues, enabling the CAW to marry different cultures and bring them together in a unified front. Other unions in Canada have attempted to expand their size and coverage, but none has been as successful as the CAW, due, I'm convinced, to its flexibility. This has not been the case with other unions. The Communications, Energy and Paperworkers Union (CEP) was created through the merger of three unions in 1992, and more than 15 years later the organization still struggles with internal stress, preventing it from being as effective as it should be.

In some cases, unions joining the CAW had a tradition and organization that needed repair rather than preservation. The best example of this occurred when healthcare workers who had been members of the Service Employees International Union (SEIU) chose the CAW to represent them. For many years the SEIU simply permitted contracts to expire and, with their members working under the previous contract, staff of the union handled bargaining with the employers. Neither rank-and-file members nor local leadership provided any input into the process, and the bargaining, such as it was, almost always led to arbitration. We refused to maintain that approach and informed employers of SEIU members— hospitals, nursing homes and homes for the aged, for the most part—that we would begin contract negotiations in advance of contract expiry dates, we would address concerns and expectations of rank-and-file members, and we would not agree to arbitration. We wanted bargained settlements.

And that's what we got for these hard-working employees. In the first six years after becoming CAW members, the union won two consecutive three-year contracts featuring several important improvements in working conditions and benefits, with no strikes.

Another substantial change arrived with the very different membership structure of the new unions within the CAW family. Many of the new members were visible minorities and women, representing ethnic and regional backgrounds new to the CAW. They also brought a different union experience that affected their view of the world and the union's role in it. Where many of the union issues had dealt in the past with primarily male skilled trades workers earning hourly wages well above the national average, now the membership roster included immigrant women performing cleaning duties and being paid wages uncomfortably close to the poverty line.

In 1984, when the UAW Canada split away from its U.S. parent to become the CAW, workers in the automotive sector represented over 80 percent of all members. Thanks to growth provided by members of other unions, and the result of downsizing among the Big Three and auto parts, in 2009 this figure had shrunk to about 30 percent. While it's a little sad to see the auto representation reduced to minority status, in hindsight the move to expand and diversify proved essential in providing the union with the strength to deal with automotive issues in Canada. Without these new members the CAW would be substantially weaker on the shop floor, at the bargaining table and in the halls of Parliament.

When you add it all up, it's clear to anyone who chooses to set his or her biases aside that strong unions foster better communities. Union members tend to be socially conscious and have greater disposable income for community projects. They also—and this is always a revelation to anti-union types—improve manufacturing quality and productivity. Out of the 10 most productive auto plants in North America, four are in Canada, six are in the U.S., and all are unionized.* And guess where the most reliable, quality-built cars sold on this continent are assembled? Not in Japan, not in Germany, not in the U.S. They're built at the GM car plant in Oshawa, Ontario, unionized since 1937.

Sadly, you won't read this kind of news and opinion in newspapers, hear it on radio or watch it on TV.

---

* Or were. As I write this, auto plants are being closed all across North America and the very existence of the industry remains in jeopardy.

FOUR

The Media and the Messages

It may surprise some people to discover that I can be critical of the media in Canada. After all, many of them claim I never met a TV camera or a radio microphone that I didn't like.

It's kind of true. I kept a high profile in the media during my years as CAW president. I did it as a way of trying to strike a balance in the coverage of union and labour issues against commentary flowing across the airwaves and in editorial pages of newspapers in this country. It also permitted me to speak over the heads of commentators and critics directly to CAW members, their families and all Canadians.

To my surprise, my reputation for being accessible and open to reporters spread beyond Canada. During the fall of 2008 and into 2009, I received calls from reporters in the U.S. looking for the union perspective on developments in the North American automotive industry. They couldn't get any response from UAW leaders beyond "no comment," assuming the UAW public relations director even returned their calls, but they could count on me to at least acknowledge the topic. I had to be a little more careful of my words in these instances because I was addressing issues of a foreign country. Still, my words made an impact. As recently as the 2009 Detroit Auto Show, the giant business news organization Bloomberg contacted me for a quote on the state of the auto industry because no one at the UAW headquarters wanted to discuss it.

Most of my comments in Canada were made with CAW members in mind. I learned, first with UAW Canada and later with the CAW, that our people perceived information differently according to where they encountered it. For many years we issued a national union publication and sent copies to every CAW member and retiree, reporting on news and issues within the union. It was an expensive, time-consuming enterprise, and I discovered that few people paid attention to it. In contrast, newsletters issued by individual union locals were carefully read from cover to cover. The lesson was clear: When it came to specific concerns, our brothers and sisters wanted the news close to home, not from somewhere distant in Toronto. When union members wanted news on a broader front, they went to the local and national media. That's where I intentionally made my most provocative comments.

My role as CAW national president was to challenge the status quo. This involved dealing with issues such as workplace safety, unfair trade, excessive corporate profits pouring into the pockets of CEOs, childhood poverty, unfair treatment of First Nations people, high unemployment and a dozen other concerns. So I attacked the issues and challenged the people responsible, but I never tried to do so with malice or mean-spiritedness. I've used a zinger now and then to make a point, and sometimes I tried to inject a little humour into the situation. Such as the time I suggested that the return of certain government regulations on airlines might assist Canadian airlines and save many CAW jobs.

When then-transport minister David Anderson was asked in 1996 by a reporter when he thought regulations might return, he responded, "When pigs fly."

"Hell," I told a reporter when he repeated Anderson's words to me, "I thought the debate was about getting Canadian airlines flying, not Mr. Anderson."

Over time, the media knew they could get a colourful comment from me, but colour often was the only quality they were looking for. Most insights I provided into the plight and concerns of working people were rarely addressed. I often spent hours each day, extending well into the evening, responding to media requests for interviews and comments. Sometimes it worked the other way: I would call reporters and commentators whose newspapers, radio stations, or TV stations had run stories about the union that were factually inaccurate. I needed our members and the Canadian public generally to know the other side, and I would provide it as succinctly and as colourfully as I could. Now and then it helped to balance things. Often it proved a waste of time, but the effort had to be made.

The generally anti-left bias in Canadian media is hardly a surprise, considering that three individuals or corporations control 90 percent of the newspapers and TV channels in this country. By their very nature, the owners of Canwest Global and CTV have little regard and less support for the Left and its concerns. This is demonstrated in dozens of instances every day, from the refusal of national media to cover union charitable activities such as the generous contributions of CAW members to the Asian tsunami relief to the use of the term "union bosses." When I'm interviewed for any topic the media chooses to discuss with me, more often than not I'm introduced as "Buzz Hargrove, former union boss of the CAW." Let me know when you hear Rick Wagoner introduced as "the former corporate boss of General Motors." It will be "the former CEO." I was elected to my post every three years. Most CEOs have the job as long as they want, which usually means until they choose to leave and take their golden parachute and its tens or hundreds of millions of dollars with them

Radio station ownership, especially in smaller markets, is more fragmented, but when they style themselves as "talk radio," it's a virtual guarantee that most commentators and callers, if asked to choose their ideal politician, would select Attila the Hun. Can you name one prominent left-wing radio talk show host in Canada or the U.S.? I can't.

A few columnists and commentators appeared to adopt me as some kind of "go-to" target they could try to skewer. Diane Francis, from the *National Post,* began writing to me a few years ago. Her letters had nothing to do with the economy or job security. Most demanded to know my salary level, my expense account, my assets, and so on. My response was always to scribble "none of your business" alongside her queries, sign it "Love, Buzz," and mail the letter back to her.

In 2004, a CBC producer tried to launch a new television show. The premise was to pit two opponents against each other and watch the sparks fly. For his pilot program, he invited Diane Francis and me as guests. She and I agreed, and as soon as the cameras were turned on, Francis began attacking me as someone who was always questioning the salaries, expenses, and overall income of corporate executives. "I've been trying for years," she said, "to have Buzz Hargrove tell me what his salary and expenses are and he refuses to answer."

The host turned to me and asked for my response.

"Diane is exactly correct," I replied. "Up until today I have refused. But I'll tell you what. I will bring in all of my income tax returns for the past five years and present them on this show if Diane will bring hers in as well, and we'll compare them."

Francis, of course, didn't like that idea. "I'm not going to do that!" she sputtered. "It's nobody's business at all!"

Too bad the show never aired. But it ended those letters from Diane Francis demanding to know my income, expenses and assets. Just for the record: the CAW president's annual salary is set by the union's constitution through a formula based on the wages bargained for skilled trades workers in the auto industry. When I stepped down, this worked out to just under $150,000. I'm still waiting for Diane Francis to reveal her annual income, but my hopes aren't very high.

I have a lot of respect for reporters who work hard at their job, which is to get out and dig up information for readers and viewers, telling them something they didn't know before. That's what they do for a living, often under the direction of some hard-assed editor or producer, and the good ones deserve all the credit they get.

It was the other reporters and commentators, the ones who play guerrilla journalism where unions are concerned, that got under my skin. They ambush their targets, fire a salvo or two, and then disappear into another topic or issue, leaving an impression that often has little connection with reality. They may use the same tactics with corporations and employers as well, of course, but the skew factor applies, and anyone who claims that the media in Canada is left-wing has his or her head someplace where it doesn't belong. I can name enough right-wing commentators and columnists to fill this page, but how many people are covering the other side of the spectrum? A couple of columnists at the *Globe and Mail*, a couple more from the *Toronto Star*, a small number of community newspapers, and damn few others. It's a challenge for the CAW because unionists tend to be more open about their positions than employers, making them an easy target for attacks from the right.

Unlike many employers (and many other unions, too), the CAW invites the media to hear its position on contract negotiations or other concerns. Why not? If you're planning to fly Air Canada or buy a CAW-built car or visit a health care facility or draw upon any of dozens of other CAW unionized operations, why shouldn't you know about a work dispute? The union won't negotiate in the media, but it won't hide its position either.

Let's face it, both sides use the media to their advantage where possible. When contract talks are coming up, management will cry poor and wring their hands over the outlook, suggesting that union bargainers should, I guess, hold a tag day for the employer. We had our own tactics, which usually included a strong statement regarding our expectations and demands. The strategy was always the same: as long as we were in the game we were determined to play hardball. It's the only one that works.

When going into bargaining on any issue, if you announce something like, "Gee, I hope we can agree . . ." you'll never win. You won't win at the bargaining table and you sure won't win in the media. Hoping you agree is the sign of a loser.

Bargaining for a contract with an employer, especially one as large and powerful as General Motors or Air Canada, was rarely a win-win game with me. Lawyers and business people will talk about going into negotiations as though it's two old friends deciding who's going to pay for the beer. "Look for a win-win situation," they suggest. "Find out what the other side wants and look for a way to satisfy both of you."

Standard union contracts based on collective bargaining aren't like that at all. We always knew what the other side wanted. It wanted us to work for minimum wage, limited pensions and reduced benefits while leaving workplace decisions totally up to management. Likewise, the employer knew what we wanted: to maximize income, job security, pensions, benefits and job satisfaction for every union member.

Now and then we managed to persuade the other side to listen to a proposal that would benefit both workers and employers, usually dealing with improved productivity and better use of existing facilities. This wasn't our version of "win-win," by the way; it was just a spinoff of our efforts to do more for our members. And it was amazing how often the union's position benefited the other side and made them look like geniuses.

Here's an example of what I mean.

In the late 1980s Chrysler minivans were selling like crazy. They were good vehicles, well designed and well made, and the company couldn't produce them fast enough to satisfy the demand, even with two shifts at the Windsor plant and a newly opened production facility in St. Louis, Missouri. GM, Ford and the importers were getting ready to introduce their own designs and attract customers who couldn't get their hands on a Chrysler minivan. "If you want to hang onto this market," we suggested to Chrysler management, "you've got to increase production now, and not wait around to build another plant. All you have to do is start a third shift in Windsor and you'll boost the number of minivans you can sell by 35 percent."

We thought it was a great idea. The Chrysler people were appalled. "You can't have three shifts in a car production plant, running it 24 hours a day," they told us. "It's impossible!"

Well, it wasn't impossible. Several parts suppliers making sub-assemblies for the minivans were running their plants on three shifts and they were doing just fine. Why couldn't Chrysler do the same thing? Because, Chrysler explained, it hadn't been done before. Auto assembly plants were big, complex operations needing six or eight hours between two shifts for maintenance, adjustment and other chores. Hell, we knew that. And we knew a third shift would work without causing the problems Chrysler feared. We kept pushing the idea and the Canadian Chrysler people kept rejecting it. In desperation we drafted a letter to Chrysler CEO Lee Iacocca detailing the proposal.

One evening about a week or so after mailing the letter to Iacocca, the chair of the Chrysler bargaining team, Ken Gerard, was relaxing at home when his telephone rang. Ken's wife, Bea, answered, turned to Ken and said, "It's Lee Iacocca. He wants to talk to you."

Ken, who was a big, rough-edged guy, assumed it was a joke. "Bullshit," he replied. "Tell whoever it is to fuck off."

Bea repeated Ken's comment and hung up.

The telephone rang again a minute later. This time Ken barked "Hello!" into the receiver and almost fell over when he recognized Lee Iacocca's voice saying, "Ken, it's Lee. We need to talk."

Over the next few minutes Iacocca told Ken he was intrigued by the idea of running three shifts at the plant, the idea his Canadian managers kept rejecting. Ken went into some details, and the more they discussed it the more Iacocca liked it. A day or two later Iacocca sent Chrysler's corporate jet, with Ken Gerard aboard, to pick up Bob White, Sam Gindin and me in Toronto and take us to New York, where we met a team of Chrysler people in a boardroom on the 37th floor of the Chrysler Building. With the Chrysler managers and executives watching, the four of us drew charts on a blackboard to demonstrate how Chrysler could operate the minivan line on three shifts, turning out vehicles literally 24 hours a day without sacrificing a thing—not quality, not maintenance, not anything.

We couldn't get far with most of them. Chrysler's head of manufacturing, Frank O'Reilly, kept coming up with reasons why it wouldn't work. Most of his objections concerned staff management and maintenance. "We've got 3,500 people in the plant on two shifts now," O'Reilly grumbled. "If we add a third shift that's another 1,500 people, which'll make the plant bigger than most towns in Ontario. It'll be a nightmare!"

We told him he was exaggerating. Plants with 5,000 or more employees were running efficiently all over the world. It might take a little more effort on his part but increasing the plant's production by a third would be worth it.

Maintenance was a different issue. Paint booths had to be cleaned, electric motors needed servicing, and other duties needed addressing. Three shifts left no time for them to happen. "If one of those motors driving the assembly line breaks down in the middle of a shift," O'Reilly grumbled, "we'll lose a whole shift. It takes hours to repair those motors, and if it happens often enough we won't make a cent on this idea."

I knew the plant. I had spent 11 years there before moving into union duties. Ken Gerard knew it as well, and each time O'Reilly objected, we would go to the blackboard and show how it could be handled. He had been correct, for example, about the big electric motors that powered the line. It might take hours to repair them if and when they broke down, but Ken and I knew it took about half an hour to replace them. Each motor cost between $5,000 and $10,000, and totalling the cost of all the critical motors in the plant was still peanuts compared with the profits Chrysler could make in one week with a third shift. The answer was to keep replacement motors on hand and rotate them according to a fixed schedule, doing it when the plant was shut down on weekends.

"If a motor goes down, yank it out and replace it with a new one," we replied, "then fix the old motor and keep it on standby. Or replace the motors at regular intervals on weekends. Keep track of when they've been serviced and you can set up a replacement schedule, installing a new one before anything goes wrong while you're rebuilding the old one."

We had an answer for cleaning the paint line as well, but nothing we suggested could sway the manufacturing people over to our side. The only guy who appeared to see the wisdom of our proposal was Chrysler's chief financial officer. He began calculating the savings and profits it would produce and knew it would be a major money maker. But he couldn't get past the hostility of the manufacturing guys, who were supported by Tom Miner, Chrysler's labour relations director. Miner was a crusty guy who kept complaining that the union wasn't interested in increasing Chrysler's production, saying we were just interested in working fewer hours for the same money. A plant shift was eight and a half hours long, including an unpaid half-hour lunch break. Two shifts meant 17 hours of plant production, so the only way to have three equal shifts would be to reduce total hours per shift by half an hour, meaning seven and a half hours on the line with a paid half-hour lunch break. This seemed reasonable to other people, but not to Miner.

"These guys want a shorter work day with the same amount of pay," he complained. "Once they get it in one plant they'll shove it up your ass in every other plant in the U.S. and Canada."

Thanks to Miner and the manufacturing people, no decision was made. We returned to Canada, the plant stumbled on with two shifts, and GM and Ford launched their own minivan line, stealing sales right out of Chrysler's pocket. In an effort to hold onto their market share Chrysler began scheduling overtime, lots of it.

In 1993 we decided to take a stand at contract negotiations and reduce overtime, the move led by Larry Bauer, president of the Chrysler Windsor local and chair of the master bargaining committee. It took a lot of courage by Larry to do this because many of the local's members liked the extra money they were making from overtime. Others didn't, preferring more leisure time to spend with their families. It seemed that the loudest, most aggressive types supported overtime, and to his credit Larry stood up to them, pointing out that running a third shift would create jobs for over 1,000 workers, many of them friends and neighbours of the people on the lines. What's more, plants making parts for the minivans would also expand, opening up thousands of new jobs for others. Eventually enough workers got past their overtime mentality to agree with the move. "Either you put a third shift on at the plant," we told Chrysler, "or you're not going to get a settlement."

This convinced them to try it, and we ratified the deal in late September 1993 with a deadline of the end of February 1994 to work out the kinks and have the third shift in place and running smoothly. By Christmas, well ahead of schedule, the plant was running three shifts with no serious problems. Production jumped by one-third, employee morale improved, accidents and injuries were reduced, and overall quality was noticeably better. Many of these benefits, I'm convinced, were the result of eliminating overtime, leaving the workers more alert and focused on their jobs.

All the news was positive. Chrysler was getting an enormous upsurge in production with minimal investment in plant and facilities. Not only that, but the fixed costs of the plant—property taxes, utilities, general building maintenance, original investment, all of that—were being divided among more vehicles, which enabled Chrysler to lower its sticker price and widen its profit margins.

It might have happened five years earlier, when Chrysler still dominated the market, if the company had been open to new ideas. They ignored a fact that every worker knows by heart: Nobody in a manufacturing company, not the bean counters or the MBAs in the executive suites, knows how things really work as well as the people who run the machinery and crank out the products day after day. They share their opinions with shop stewards, and good shop stewards listen and take notes from workers. If you want to know the real story about what works and what doesn't work in a unionized facility, talk to a shop steward.

Our people knew a third shift would work, and knew how to *make* it work. Nobody knows how much more profit Chrysler could have earned if they had moved to a third shift policy when we first proposed it. And nobody who was at Chrysler back then will admit it, but a lot of them are still kicking themselves in the ass for not listening to us. I know, because they told me so.

This is just one instance where the CAW, working admittedly toward its own goal of creating more jobs for union members, linked worker benefits to similar gains by the employer. It's also a lesson still to be learned in some places. Many auto assembly plants in Europe and Asia operate three shifts, essentially copying the arrangement we suggested more than 20 years ago. (The Japanese manufacturers still refuse to run three shifts for some reason.) Here in North America the idea took a while to spread. General Motors watched for a time before introducing third shifts to their Oshawa truck plant in 1995 and later the car plant before taking the same step at plants in the U.S. Chrysler moved to three-shift operations at its Brampton car plant in 1998.

Why the slow response? Because every outfit in the automotive business is convinced it's better at making cars and trucks than its competitors. This attitude is especially noticeable among the three North American companies, which may be part of their wider problem. Each company believes it is thinking "outside the box" and perhaps it is, but each also believes it has the best solution.

As president of the CAW, I heard for years that Chrysler's introduction of three shifts was a dumb move. People at GM and Ford claimed Chrysler was being short-sighted, predicted they would have serious quality problems, and believed the move would cost them big bucks before it was over. It took a long time for the people at GM to try it for themselves, and when they did the company began pulling in the same profit benefits as Chrysler.

Surprisingly, although they have tended over the years to be more open to new ideas, Ford was the last to switch to three shifts. Not until 2008 did Ford agree to try a third shift at their Oakville, Ontario, plant. They hired and trained new workers, but just as they were about to launch the new schedule, sales began their slide and the company killed the plan.

Earlier, Ford had tried introducing "quality circles" as a means to improving efficiency and productivity. When CAW members saw the move for what it was, as a means of reducing the number of workers in the plant, Ford switched to something called "employee involvement," which proved an equally dismal failure. Each time Ford tried one of these ideas the company claimed it was empowering workers, and each time the workers saw it as a means of reducing, not expanding, their power to improve quality and productivity.

We agreed with Ford's objectives. We just disagreed with the way they were trying to reach them. "Forget all this stuff you've been trying," we suggested. "Set up union-company committees. Not 'quality circles' or 'employment involvement groups.' Just committees with company and union people looking for ways to improve quality and productivity." They agreed. Soon it was obvious that these groups were much better at reaching their goal than any of the quality circle ideas they were still trying to hammer out in Ford plants in the U.S.

So did the American Ford plants switch over to our system? Not a chance. Ford people in the U.S. continued to believe they were on the leading edge, right up to the day the plants began laying off thousands of workers, with some of them closing their doors permanently.

* * *

In the spring of 2008 I went through the most upsetting experience of my entire adult life in the automotive industry, and as a union member and leader. It was not a matter of GM and I disagreeing on anything. It was, to my mind, a conscious move to betray me, to betray the CAW Local 222 bargaining committee, and to betray every CAW member who was an employee of GM. In response, both of us tried to make the most of the media. GM wanted to soften its bad news through a statement from me, and I wanted to apply pressure on them to treat our members fairly.

On May 15, 2008, we completed negotiations on a new three-year contract for GM workers in Canada, including the Oshawa car and truck assembly plants, which had an excellent record for quality and productivity. A couple of nights later I had dinner in Toronto with Gary Cowger, GM's senior VP for worldwide operations. We talked about a lot of things, including problems with the auto industry generally. Then we said some cordial goodbyes and went our separate ways.

Two weeks later, GM asked our national secretary treasurer Jim O'Neil and me to attend a 7 a.m. meeting in the Bristol Place Hotel, on Toronto's airport strip. Jim and I arrived to find Arturo Elias, GM Canada president, and Troy Clarke, president of GM North America, waiting for us. We didn't know what to expect when GM called the meeting. We thought it might be to cover details about GM's plan to build a new generation of Chevrolet Sierra and Silverado trucks at Oshawa. As part of the new contract they had committed to keep the Oshawa truck plant open, and invest a billion dollars in preparing it to build the next generation of Sierras and Silverados, including the hybrid version. We did the usual greetings and hand shakes, then Elias and Clarke dropped the bomb: GM planned to close the Oshawa truck operation. Initially they planned to do this at the end of the third quarter of 2009, later moving it up to May 2009.

Jim O'Neil and I went into shock. We were both veterans of hard-nosed decisions made by the auto companies, but we had been blindsided. An employer going back on a contract before the ink was barely dry? We'd never heard of this.

Arturo Elias tried to soften things. "We're willing to talk about putting more car production in Oshawa to offset some of the losses in the truck plant," he said. Then he added: "You can use that news publicly, but we're not going to say anything to the press about it. It's too early for us to make any promises."

I couldn't believe Elias's naiveté. Did he really believe I was dumb enough to step in front of our members and the media and claim that GM was planning an expansion of their car production in Oshawa, just to soften the news? Hell, only 14 days earlier I'd waved a three-year contract to the media that included the promise of a billion-dollar investment by GM. Not long before that, GM had accepted $435 million in grants and interest-free loans from the federal and provincial governments, to invest in their Canadian plants. Now I was supposed to say to my members, "Sorry, GM is closing the truck plant, but here's the new deal: more car production some time in the future, but they can't tell us yet"? All while GM kept their mouths shut? Why would anyone believe me?

I don't know if Clarke and Elias thought I would scream, plead, shout or walk out on them. I didn't do any of those things. In truth, I was somewhere between shock and anger, stunned at this turn of events and furious with GM for acting in this manner. I restrained myself and asked a few questions about timing and other details.

GM made the public announcement to close the truck plant later that day. When the media came clambering to me for a quote I said, "I do not believe that General Motors' CEO Rick Wagoner will look across the table at me and say, 'Buzz, we're not going to live up to what we committed to just two weeks ago.' I do not believe it. I think Rick Wagoner will say, 'We're not going to close your plant.' I have that much confidence in the relationship and the trust we have built up over the years."

Did I really suppose this would happen—that the CEO of GM would reverse his decision based on our relationship? I wasn't sure.

I thought that GM would find some way of treating their unionized employees with respect and honouring at least part of the deal that the CAW had signed in good faith, and I made a statement designed to push GM in that direction. "This plant is General Motors' best-quality, best-productivity, lowest-cost producer of half-ton trucks and they're closing it!" I explained to the media. "The decision is unfair, it's unjust, it's unwarranted, it's illegal, it violates our collective agreement, it violates the law . . . and we're not going to allow this to happen."

My goal when I said we wouldn't let this happen was not to see the promise fulfilled, because it was clear that GM was serious. I had no doubt it would happen, but I said those words to draw attention to GM's cynical move of signing a deal and reneging on it two weeks later. I wanted to set the stage for some kind of acceptable settlement for CAW members in Oshawa.

By this time, Local 222 in Oshawa had launched a blockade at GM Canada's headquarters building, forcing almost 1,000 non-union salaried workers to respect our move and GM to close the headquarters office. It was illegal and it wouldn't change GM's mind, but it drew national and international attention to GM's actions and, perhaps more important, helped the assembly line workers vent some of their anger and frustration. I assured the protestors that they had the full support of more than a quarter-million CAW members behind them. High-profile politicians like Jack Layton of the NDP and Stéphane Dion of the Liberals, as well as the president of the Canadian Labour Congress, Ken Georgetti, brought messages of support.

Later that week, members of the Local 222 bargaining committee travelled with Jim O'Neil, Peter Kennedy and me to Detroit to meet with GM's top executives. The group included Chris Buckley, president of Local 222, Keith Osborne, chair of the Oshawa committee, and Greg Moffatt, chair of the truck plant.

Rick Wagoner wasn't there at the beginning. When the meeting began we were dealing with Troy Clarke; Gary Cowger; Fritz Henderson, who had just assumed the president and COO position of GM worldwide; Tim Lee, North American director; Dean Munger, GM's human resources director out of Detroit; and a terribly embarrassed Cheryl Ollila, GM Canada's vice-president of human resources, who had been their chief bargainer at the recent contract talks. Ollila had called me shortly after the meeting at Bristol Place to explain that she had known nothing about GM's plans until after the bomb was dropped on Jim O'Neil and me. "I've been with GM for over thirty years," she said, "and I never thought I would see General Motors waste my time and my credibility doing something like this." It was a risky comment to make to a union leader, but that's how upset she was. I had great respect for Olilla's collective bargaining skills and found her to be a person of integrity, and she in turn enjoyed credibility with our bargaining team.

Concerned about GM's actions and my chances of turning their decision around, I hadn't slept well the night before this meeting. My emotions were running high and the adrenaline was pumping, but I managed to hold my temper. Before leaving for the meeting I reminded other members of the team that the people we were about to encounter did not have to consult anyone. This was the top leadership of GM worldwide, and they could make a decision on the spot. We were damn well going to make sure they did, whatever direction it might take.

Nothing of significance was covered until Rick Wagoner arrived. I addressed my strongest words to him, reminding him I had been telling the media that I did not believe he would look me in the eye and confirm that General Motors refused to live up to commitments they had made in writing during our bargaining sessions less than three weeks earlier.

"Buzz," Wagoner replied when I finished, "I regret to say that we are going ahead with our plans to close the truck plant."

I demanded some kind of explanation, some rationale.

Wagoner shrugged. "Things have changed," he said. "The market has changed."

"I know enough about the industry," I said, "to understand nothing could change between the middle of May and the first of June to cause you to make that decision." I had looked at the sales figures, and GM's were as good on June 1 as they had been on May 15. "What's the real reason?"

His reply was to explain that GM had looked at a number of factors beyond the market and the industry. "We had all these pieces, these facts," he said, "and we put them together to look at the total picture, and the total picture told us we could not live up to the promises we had made during the contract talks."

I asked him to identify these pieces, these facts. He couldn't. He could only say that all of them added up to a decision to kill the deal they had agreed to a few days earlier.

Gary Cowger jumped in to help Wagoner. "When you and I had dinner the night we signed the deal," Cowger said, "I told you how difficult things were for us. You should have seen this coming."

I told Cowger I hadn't just fallen off the turnip truck. "You knew when you signed the deal how difficult things were, and both of us negotiated on that basis," I replied. "You talked about introducing a new generation of Sierras and Silverados, with hybrid versions to boost the market, all to be built in Oshawa. So don't act as though you had warned me about this. Because you hadn't."

I was furious all over again. This was the biggest setback, the biggest betrayal I had encountered in negotiations over my 40 years of collective bargaining with some of the largest corporations in the world.

Disagreements and misunderstandings occur, usually when a new HR person or senior executive comes into the picture, or when one side interprets the language of a deal differently from the other side. This wasn't the case here. This was one side of the deal's showing disregard for the other side's situation. Yes, we made the commitment, GM admitted. Yes, it's in writing. Yes, it's real. But we're changing it. We're not going to live up to it.

I have never known a union to do such a thing, and I had never known an employer to do it either, and when it comes to employers I have dealt with the odd bastard in my time. Yes, we agreed to it, General Motors was saying about our deal, but we're not doing it. We're just not doing it. I don't recall ever being as shook up about anything as I was over GM's announcement to close the truck plant.

"You look pretty nervous," a reporter said when I went downstairs to meet the media.

"If you think I'm nervous, you don't know me very well," I said. "But I'm some goddamn angry."

On the plane returning to Toronto Chris Buckley, Greg Moffatt, Keith Osborne, Jim O'Neil, Peter Kennedy and I discussed our next move. We realized that there was no way we could save the plant, but this didn't mean we were giving up our efforts to get decent treatment for the CAW members, and Local 222 decided to keep the blockade going. I arranged meetings with GM's human resources managers Dean Munger and Cheryl Ollila.

GM applied for a court injunction to lift the blockade and, remarkably, the Canadian judge expressed sympathy for the union despite the obvious illegality of our actions. Judge David Salmers delivered the terms for our handling of the blockade—better organization, a maximum number of pickets on site, a schedule to permit entry from time to time—but he refused to meet GM's demands that the blockade be lifted completely. In fact, his judgment expressed sympathy for the union and distaste for GM's actions. "Contrary to the submission of GM Canada's counsel," he wrote, "I do not find that the June 6 meeting or anything else yet proposed by GM Canada purges, remedies, or excuses in any way [their)] almost deceitful behaviour . . ."*

The judge's decision, added to the media coverage resulting from my declaration that I would not allow GM to do what they announced, generated a tremendous amount of sympathy for our members. We heard from business people, lawyers and the average person on the street, writing to protest GM's actions and asking, "How can they get away with this?"

The total impact was enough to persuade GM to cut a much better deal for our members than they originally offered. They maintained their offer to expand car production at the Oshawa plant, but I refused to bank on that, or even announce it to our membership. GM's credibility was already lost, and I would be damned before I destroyed mine as well.

"We have to find a way to guarantee either jobs or income," I suggested to the local committee. "We need an agreement that says that anyone who is involuntarily laid off would benefit from some sort of income replacement based on seniority." And that's what GM eventually agreed to. The agreement was a combination buyout deal for lower seniority CAW members and "incentive to retire" offer for those eligible to retire.

Much was made about the $435 million in government money that GM appeared to be ignoring. They clearly reneged on that deal, but I'm realistic enough to make a distinction between a plan to build more cars and a contract to continue employing people. You can't force a company to build something it can't sell. No judge in Canada, or in any capitalist country for that matter, will interfere with private enter-

---

* Ontario Superior Court of Justice, Whitby Court File number 55786/08, June 13, 2008.

prise, especially if the corporation makes a good case for not meeting its commitments due to changed market conditions.

Signing an agreement to employ thousands of workers at one facility and then choosing to close that particular facility almost before the agreement takes effect while keeping others open is deceitful. Although Judge Salmers described GM's behaviour as almost deceitful, I'll stick to my own assessment.

Three months later, when the extent of the credit crunch and its impact on the auto industry became clear, GM's announcement to close the truck plant was almost forgotten amid headlines that seemed to get gloomier every day. It was not forgotten by me. The company was contractually obligated to inform and consult us about plans to close facilities and they broke that obligation. And I have yet to hear anyone from GM explain why, if they felt a need to close a truck plant, they chose the one with the best record for quality and productivity while keeping other, less efficient plants making the same vehicle open.

Only one explanation is likely for this last question. These were American executives favouring American locations and, I suspect, bowing to pressure from the American union and perhaps American politicians to favour the U.S.

I'm not offended by that aspect of their decision. I'm a big boy and I've been around business and politicians long enough to know how the world works. I remain offended, however, by the sneaky way GM handled it and by the refusal of anyone in our government to take a stand and say to GM, "You can't do this to Canadian workers!"

The GM truck contract fiasco was one of the few times that the mass media in Canada expressed an understanding, if not broad support, of our situation. It was one battle we managed to win with newspaper and broadcast outlets. In other situations, our position is often skewed to suit an anti-labour and pro-business agenda.

This was proven by a 2003 study reported in the *Canadian Journal of Communication.* In its Labour Day edition that year, the *National Post* published a series of polls on the attitude of Canadians toward labour unions. Given the uncompromising right-wing stance of the *Post,* the evaluations were predictable. The *Post* established the bias of their message when they asked columnist Terence Corcoran, who never met an anti-union opinion he didn't like, to draft a front-page commentary on their supposed research. Corcoran, his hands almost visibly shaking with glee, wrote: "After decades of mythical struggles based on slogans of class warfare, worker oppression and exploitation, the entire union movement shows up in the poll as an ideological sham. Self-portrayed as the champion of downtrodden masses of working men and women, the union movement emerges today as the iron protector of a privileged minority."

Did the poll Corcoran referred to reflect the bias of the newspaper? Silly question. Of course it did. It had to, because it was commissioned by *Labour Watch,* an organization made up of employment lawyers and "open shop" companies that seeks, in its own words, to "restore balance" to an employment situation it feels is slanted in favour of labour.

Labour Watch, which granted exclusive use of the poll to the *National Post* and Global TV, had Léger Marketing design and conduct the study. Anybody who knows anything about polling can spot the angle in the original questions, conducted through telephone calls. Consider this one:

> Citizens charged with a crime are provided with a government funded lawyer. Employees with human rights concerns about discrimination or with employment concerns about working conditions have access to paid government employees to help them with their issues with their employer. Employees who want to obtain a union or keep their current

union have access to the union's paid staff and lawyers to help them. *Employees with concerns about unionization are on their own* with no government or other funded mechanism and they cannot get legal aid. Do you consider this to be appropriate or inappropriate? (emphasis added)

In other words, find yourself in legal trouble, or with a human rights complaint, or with a plan to become unionized, and you have lots of support. If you have a problem with your union, however, you are on your own. It makes the members sound like sheep being led to slaughter by their elected union leaders.

Too bad the people who designed this questionnaire weren't present at meetings when I was spat upon and threatened with hanging. Besides, organizations such as *Labour Watch* and various government bureaus offer this kind of assistance every day.

Even after stacking the deck, the study hardly amounted to a denunciation of unions. When asked how satisfied members were about their relationship and communication with their union, 79 percent said they were "very satisfied" or "somewhat satisfied." Only one out of five respondents expressed dissatisfaction. Could you find one out of five employees in any company, in any industry, who would express dissatisfaction with their employers? It'd be a piece of cake, in my opinion. Or how about this: 56 percent of all respondents said unions were as relevant today as they have ever been, a figure that jumped to almost 80 percent among currently unionized workers.

Other results went back and forth on various issues (50 percent more respondents held unions in higher trust than governments) depending on how far the poll designers went to skew the answers. Despite this, and despite the overwhelming support that members expressed for unionization in their workplace, the *National Post* headlined their coverage of the results with lines such as these:

Poll Finds Deep Divide on Unions

Leaders Out of Step with Members

Non-Union Workers More Satisfied with Their Jobs than Unionized

Unionized Workers Less Happy at Work

Court Rulings Entrench Unions

I don't expect newspapers and the broadcast media to be unbiased. Hell, I'm biased myself, as you may have figured out by now. But I give credit to employers when they do the right thing, and my friendships with people like Gerry Schwartz, Frank Stronach, Rick Wagoner and a gang of other shrewd and tough business people proves that I can see both sides. When it came to expressing the union's view in Canada's primary media outlets, however, it was often like banging my head against a brick wall.

In 2004 David Asper, owner of the *National Post,* asked if I was interested in contributing a biweekly 500-word column to the paper. I agreed, although I was offered no payment for the work, and received none. I thought my views would be something of a balance against comments from Corcoran, whom I actually enjoy having a beer with from time to time.

Writing on labour and social topics, I generated a lot of feedback to the paper, and to me personally from readers. After a year or so, however, I suspect the feedback from their right-wing readers began to resemble a backlash, and without warning or explanation the *Post* dropped the column.

So for several months I sought to balance the neo-con ravings of the *Post* with a few progressive views. Did I change any opinions? I'll never know. But for a while things were perhaps a little less out of balance in the media.

FIVE

Globalization
and Free-Market Follies

Remember globalization? Sure you do. Right-wingers told us it was inevitable and beneficial, the ultimate rationale for closing factories if there was a chance to make an extra buck offshore. Of course, the people who were after the extra buck were never the workers who found themselves thrown out of the factories, or the farmers who were eased off their farms by low prices on imported food. It was the CEOs and the bankers, along with politicians catering to right-wing interests. When socialists like me raised questions and objections, we were told we were out of touch and were lectured about being economic Luddites, or we were charged with trying to protect our own asses. The men, women and children sliding into poverty through no fault of their own were rarely mentioned.

For the first few years of the 21st century, globalization dominated almost every economic discussion. It was unavoidable, its advocates preached, and would lead to worldwide prosperity because, in its purest form, it meant countries A, B and C could exchange goods not only with each other but with countries X, Y and Z, and all would grow wealthy together.

I and other unionists and working people had a different idea. Open globalization wasn't about spreading prosperity, it wasn't about creating new job opportunities, and it sure as hell was not about helping the working class. Globalization was and is about the machine that both drives and creates international business. The money machine, as George Soros put it (and he should know) roared ahead of morality. Everything to do with globalization is driven by the bottom line, and while I know that's the primary focus of all business people, in the case of globalization it's the *only* focus. In almost every country in the world that can't feed its people or can't provide jobs for them, the problem is never economics. It's lousy governments. The way globalization fans talk about it, everything can be solved by open markets, with money flowing like water toward its own level, and if some people are left high and dry (the globalization fans like to babble that "a rising tide lifts all boats," which assumes that everybody *has* a boat), well, too bad.

Some people may charge me with protectionism, claiming that I want to erect trading walls between countries. Well, that's another crock. Canada has built its wealth on trade—more, perhaps, than any other comparable nation. We're much more of a trading country than the United States, for example, and our position as a trader makes us aware and sensitive to the importance of trade. We expect that countries who buy our goods, products and services will want to sell us some of their goods, products and services as well. Hey, that's a good idea. Just don't call it "free trade" when I'm around.

The terms "free trade" and "globalization" are tossed around as though they were carved into stone tablets along with the Ten Commandments that Moses carried down the mountain. Challenging their merit or even their definitions will start name-calling and finger-pointing from business executives and right-wing commentators. The fact is that the world doesn't need more free trade and it sure as hell doesn't need more globalization based on free trade. What it needs is *fair,* or *managed,* trade—agreements that prevent one country from conquering another country's markets while shutting its doors to that same country's exports. If you believe this doesn't happen, you must also believe that a tooth under your pillow turns into a loonie overnight. Trade *can* be beneficial for both parties, but market forces and corporate decision-making will never guarantee that mutual outcome. Only active management of trade flows, to ensure that trade is fair, can ensure that everyone benefits from trade. Ironically, that is exactly the sort of intervention that the free trade agreements try to prohibit.

Trade unionists have railed against globalization for years, refusing to buy into promises of some great golden future when, to use another cliché from that crowd, "all playing fields would be level." The neo-cons refused to listen to our concerns. But as I write this, in early 2009, we no longer have to shout to be heard, because the message has been delivered in the form of the biggest global financial crisis in nearly 80 years.

We've had credit crises in the past, but for the most part they were limited to one country that controlled its own internal banking rules. If a bank in the United States failed, almost nobody in Canada or anywhere else in the world felt a ripple. But look at what happened with the sub-prime mortgage fiasco in the U.S. The gang who lectured us about the inevitability of globalization applied the same rule to securities, and a bunch of financial shysters peddling worthless paper brought down banks all over the world. It was so bad that Iceland, a country hardly known for its risky investment style, practically declared national bankruptcy. *Iceland!*

All those pious lectures about the virtues of globalization are painfully ironic today, with the global economy mired in crisis. Indeed, now the executives of Lehman Brothers, Morgan Stanley, AIG and various U.S. banks are as unemployed as CAW members at the John Deere plant in Welland, the Freightliner plant in St. Thomas, the Navistar plant in Chatham, and dozens of other locations across Canada. Of course, most of those executives walked away from their jobs with multimillion-dollar parachutes. Most of the workers walked away with only memories. Both were victims of globalization, although it's difficult to describe Richard S. Fuld, CEO of Lehman Brothers, as a "victim." According to *Forbes* magazine (April 30, 2008), Fuld was paid $72 million in 2008, bringing his total compensation for the five-year period from 2003 to 2008 to over $350 million. Do not hold a tag day for Richard S. Fuld.

We saw the same thing happen to the big-money people around the world in 2008 that had been happening to CAW members for the past decade. I take no pleasure in watching people for whom I have little sympathy fall on their collective asses. (In the case of Fuld and people like him, at least the fall was well cushioned.) And I'm not the kind of guy to scream, "I told you so!" either. But I honestly hope that, if nothing else comes out of the sub-prime disaster of 2008, it will be a realization that *globalization is largely a fraud, as are all the claims for the benefits of "free trade."*

The members of the CAW didn't need a world financial crisis to prove the truth of this idea. We've been watching this shell game for years. Nobody, I guess, gave a damn when working people were hit by the effects of globalization. It took a few executives selling off their yachts before people noticed.

I think it's interesting and outrageous that we needed the loss of hundreds of billions of dollars spent on lousy investments based on American sub-prime mortgages to draw attention to the same kind of thinking that caused the loss of hundreds of thousands of manufacturing jobs through free trade. The CAW and other unions have been pointing to the fallout of globalization for decades. In response, we were told that protectionism was dead and the world was evolving into a different kind of economy. The hell it was. It was evolving into a form of social Darwinism that said people will fall by the wayside, through no fault of their own, and families will slide into poverty without well-paying jobs.

Over the course of my years in the labour movement, I watched this decline happen. The size of the corporations and dollars involved weren't as impressive as those in the Crash of 2008, but the human misery was just as real and painful and unnecessary. No better example exists than the CAW's experience with the Ste. Anne Nackawic pulp mill, which operated as a successful venture for many years on the Saint John River. It employed 400 people, 300 of them CAW members. Many employees had 40 years or more of employment there. Without warning, in September 2004, the New York-based owners of the mill ceased operations in the middle of an annual maintenance shutdown. The following day, they declared the mill bankrupt.

The timing was more than a little suspect. Surely the owners had seen this coming. Why declare bankruptcy in the middle of a scheduled overhaul, leaving the machinery in pieces with no one to reassemble it after the millwrights moved on to other work when told they wouldn't be paid? One theory was that it made it easier to ship the equipment out of the mill, especially when workers weren't around to protest the move. This idea gained a lot of traction when George Landegger, the CEO of the mill's parent company, made an amazing announcement.

The mill, he noted, had assets of about $35 million, which just happened to be the amount that Landegger had loaned it some time earlier through his own American-based investment firm, St. Anne Industries Inc. Under the terms, Landegger was first in line to be paid when the firm was liquidated. So the guy who pulled the plug gets his money back and the employees of the company, along with the citizens of New Brunswick, who had loaned the mill $15 million, get nothing. The employees and retirees were owed $32 million in vacation pay, pension and health care benefits, and other compensation. After Landegger called his own loan, there was just enough money in the company to offer sharply reduced pensions to the people who had given much of their lives to the company. Everyone, including the retirees, lost their health care benefits.

Thirty-four years earlier, one of the employees had had to choose between joining the RCMP and working at the mill. He had planned to marry soon and the RCMP informed him of its rule at the time that no recruit was permitted to marry within two years of joining the force. So he chose the mill, and worked his butt off for the company, contributing to what he believed was a "gold-plated pension plan." When the plant closed, reality arrived. He was 54 years old, one year shy of the 55 cut-off age. He had worked nowhere else in his life, and would get nothing for a pension. Not one red cent.[*]

Working with CAW Local 219, the national union supported the employees in blocking the company from removing the disassembled equipment, and appealed to New Brunswick Premier Bernard Lord for assistance. Things dragged on for weeks. Eventually, a joint venture between Quebec-based Tembec and a company in India agreed to take over the mill, investing $35 million with provincial help. Not only have

---

[*] "How Safe Is Your Pension?" *MoneySense*, November 2006.

they made the operation a success, they're also modifying its product from a pulp that is used exclusively in paper materials to a pulp that can also be used to make rayon.

Here's something else globalization does: It permits executives in one country to make decisions that are devastating to employees in another country without the executives suffering even the mild pain of public rebuke. In August 1998, back when the G-word was first becoming popular, some CAW executives and I met in Quebec City with the executives of Volvo. The Swedish car company had been operating a plant in Nova Scotia for over 30 years, with other facilities in Quebec. Employing about 300 employees in total, 230 of them CAW members, it wasn't a huge plant compared with most others, but it was extremely important to the province of Nova Scotia, had a long history of success, and was a profitable operation. Volvo's car-assembly operation in Canada was a legacy of the 1965 Auto Pact, which gave tariff-free access to Canadian markets to global companies, in return for meeting Canadian value-added targets.

"How are things going?" we asked the Volvo people, and got nothing but smiles in return. Things were wonderful, they told us. They were doubling their sales in Canada. The company was prosperous around the world. Volvo was happy to be in Canada.

One month later Volvo closed the Canadian plant. There was no quality problem, no productivity problem, no cost problem, nothing of the sort. Somebody in Sweden decided to close a plant thousands of kilometres away, throwing 300 people out of work. Just like that.

It was no big deal to Volvo, but in a city the size of Halifax dumping 300 unemployed workers onto the streets creates one hell of a mess. Things got worse when the bosses in Sweden refused to offer any benefits to the workers. Thirty years on the job and all the workers got was a handshake and "Goodbye!"—or whatever the word is in Swedish.

As a unionist, I believe it makes no sense to get angry at times like this. The only thing that matters is doing what's right for the workers. When we got the news about Volvo's closure, we put together a plan to keep the facilities open, with practical suggestions and options. When this failed to get a response we sent a delegation composed of CAW national and local union leaders to Sweden, where they met with top-level Volvo people and presented their case. Volvo listened politely, then said, "Forget it." Globalization, the Volvo executives explained, meant they could provide their product to any market anywhere in the world from Sweden. They had no obligation to Canadian workers, and no need for them anymore.

We asked our national representative, Larry Wark, and the president of the local to come back to Canada, gather our members, and take over the Volvo plant, barricading it until Volvo agreed to an acceptable close-out deal with basic benefits for CAW members. At four o'clock the next morning that's what happened. Volvo agreed to discuss another arrangement. It didn't give the workers back their jobs, but it provided some assistance until they could find other employment.

That's what globalization does: it permits large international corporations to dispense with employees like scrap metal, throwing them on a heap and walking away until somebody shows up to recycle them. If globalization worked the way its right-wing proponents claim it does, I would have no complaints nor would anyone else. Supposedly, globalization enables each country to buy and sell among other countries with ease. If Country A sells $1 billion worth of auto parts to Country B, it's free to purchase an equal amount of widgets from the same country. Sounds good to me.

But that's not what happens. It's not even close.

Consider Canada's trade in automotive products (both finished vehicles and parts) with Japan and Korea. For every $100 in automotive products Korea sells to Canada, Korea buys all of *58 cents* of automotive products back from us. That's an imbalance of 161 to 1. The situation with Japan is even worse; for every $100 that Japanese auto companies sell in Canada, Japan buys *49 cents* here, a ratio of 187:1. No wonder Canada's combined trade deficits with these two Asian powerhouses reached $8 billion in 2008. Our trade with Korea and Japan is a one-way flow costing tens of thousands of Canadian auto jobs.* That's not trade. Dictionary definitions of "trade" imply that two parties exchange something. Where's the exchange with these two countries?

Our lopsided automotive trade with Asia (which will get even worse as China develops its auto export capacity) is especially painful to Canada because automobile and truck manufacturing represents a larger portion of our GDP than of other countries. So a gross imbalance, such as the one we have with Korea in automobiles, cuts more deeply into our economy.

Compared with business icons south of the border like Freddie Mac, Fannie Mae, Lehman Brothers and many more, Volvo and Nackawic were small potatoes. (Of course, when you're 54 years old and a promise made to you more than 30 years earlier is broken, it's not small, it's massive and crushing.) Volvo arrived at a cold, calculated decision in an office several thousand kilometres away partly, I suspect, just to prove that it could be done. Given the success that the new owners appear to be having with it, the Nackawic experience proves that many of the problems of manufacturers are caused not by changing markets or "excessive" worker wages but by bad management decisions. The claims are based more on covering the asses of financiers than on seeking imaginative and effective ways of adapting to change.

Speaking of "excessive" wages . . .

---

* Data calculated from Industry Canada's Strategis database for 2008.

One of the most common complaints made by critics of trade unions in recent years has dealt with wages. Our contracts for assembly line workers at Ford, GM and Chrysler have been cited time after time as the reason these auto companies have found themselves in deep trouble in recent years. "Greedy auto workers and their union leaders," the chant goes, "are the reason the North American car companies can't make money."

That statement, to put it bluntly, is a load of crap.

CAW members assemble parts and cars. That's all they do. They don't design them, they don't price them, they don't market them, and they don't sell them. They put them together on a fast-moving assembly line where hundreds of parts have to be installed according to fixed tolerances and tight schedules. It's not easy, but they do it at least as well as workers in other countries and better than most—"better" meaning with higher productivity and quality. Where do you think the Buick LaCrosse/Allure models, the North American cars rated highest for off-line quality by J. D. Power and Associates, come from? Not Toyota or Honda. These competitively priced cars come off lines where CAW members assemble them, end of story.

You want to talk greed? Look at the salaries of executives in the automotive business. If CAW workers were half as greedy as many top executives, they'd be on the street. The executives, however, walk away with their pockets stuffed with millions. I don't begrudge Frank Stronach his annual take-home pay in the millions, because Frank built his company from nothing—he didn't walk out of an MBA class and into a corner office suite. Frank is also very good at running his companies. Have we had our differences? Sure, we have. But Frank Stronach's decisions have been good enough long enough to provide well-paying jobs for tens of thousands of people for more than 40 years. Whatever you think of his methods, you have to admire him for that—especially if you compare him with the outrageous antics of the people who ran Delphi Corporation.

Until 2007, Delphi was one of the world's largest manufacturers of automobile parts, with 170,000 employees, most located outside North America. The company began as Automotive Components Group, a subsidiary of General Motors, in 1994. Five years later it was spun off as an independent company, Delphi Automotive Systems, and later Delphi Corporation.

Almost from the outset, Delphi was in trouble with regulators. In 2004 the U.S. Securities Exchange Commission charged it with deceitful accounting practices. The charges were so serious and the evidence so convincing that the company's top executive team resigned and Delphi was delisted from the New York Stock Exchange. Soon after, it filed for bankruptcy protection and began selling off various parts of the corporation. It also began demanding crippling wage cuts of 50 percent or more from its unionized workers, and eventually revealed that it had $1.5 billion in unsecured pension obligations for its employees.

But even as the top executives of Delphi were telling the workers, suppliers, creditors and shareholders of the company to accept severe losses, they were setting up an executive pay package that included $87 million in cash bonuses for themselves when the company exited from bankruptcy protection. "When we finally get some cash together," the top executives' actions said to everyone, "we're gonna have one hell of a party for ourselves. Too bad about you guys." Fortunately, a federal bankruptcy judge ruled that the bonuses were exceptional and undeserved, and cut the deal back to *only* $16.5 million for the top people.

That's an American case to be sure, but Delphi provided parts for GM factories, and other operations, on both sides of the border. Excessive costs, lousy management and greedy executives make an impact on an industry no matter where it is located.

At Delphi greed knew no bounds—not even death. In June 2008, the *Wall Street Journal* reported that some top CEOs had negotiated a deal that transferred millions of dollars into their estates when they died. In one instance, $282 million was to be deposited immediately into a CEO's estate on his demise. On the one hand, you want to make a joke about these guys who defy the adage "you can't take it with you." On the other hand you feel sickened over the obscenity of CEOs who can negotiate a deal like this one moment and the next moment transfer tens of thousands of jobs offshore, in search of fatter profits to fund their golden parachutes—or, in this case, golden coffins.* Meanwhile, people grumble about union wages being responsible for corporate problems in North America. Give me a break.

Union wages on the automotive assembly lines, or anywhere else for that matter, get talked about *because their details are accessible to the media and the public.* If the CAW negotiates a 3 percent wage increase on a new contract, it's in every newspaper and on every radio or TV newscast. "Auto workers get fat new wage hike," the headlines will say. They rarely say, however, that a collective agreement is a two-way deal between the union and employer, and that the 3 percent increase in wages may be balanced with a 3 percent improvement in productivity, or some other workplace changes that benefit the employer. And they never talk about a 5, 10 or 20 percent increase in the cost of brake discs or dashboards or tires from suppliers, and the effect these have on the price of a new car or truck. All anyone hears about are wages paid to union members assembling the cars and trucks.

I sure wish Canadians who blame union workers for the troubles at Ford, GM and Chrysler would spend as much time looking at some of the horrific screw-ups made by the top management of those firms.

---

* "Companies Promise CEOs Lavish Posthumous Paydays," *Wall Street Journal,* June 10, 2008.

Like the $100 million Chrysler invested in a paint shop to produce a new vehicle at their Windsor truck plant before deciding not to make the truck after all. Not one vehicle went through that paint shop, nor will it ever—it's been torn down. I can only imagine the headlines and the hand-wringing that might occur if the CAW or any other union pulled $100 million out of a corporation without returning any benefit to it.

There's no doubt that the Big Three auto companies have faced hard decisions. We all face hard decisions, from cancelling a $100 million project to deciding whether this week's paycheque will be spent on food or on new clothes for the kids because we can't afford to do both. In the CAW I've witnessed both sides of the story, and forgive me if my sympathy lies with the wage earners. I remember Lee Iacocca's shrug when he realized our union was serious about putting money in the pockets of retirees. After all his bluster and complaining, saying the union demands would break the company, he found the money in his "big barrel of cash." And barely two months after Rick Wagoner dropped the bombshell on us in June 2008, reneging on our agreement regarding the Oshawa truck plant contract, the General Motors CEO was in Thailand announcing a $445-million engine plant and upgraded assembly plant to build four-cylinder diesel engines for use by Chevrolet in Thailand and other global markets.

I have no problem with GM investing in a new plant in Thailand or anywhere else. I have a serious problem, however, when those engines and the cars they power start arriving here in Canada, displacing Canadian-made vehicles and the jobs of workers who assemble them. The defenders of this and other aspects of globalization will claim it's part of a growing trend toward free trade. Well, it's not "free"—not when it costs Canada tens of thousands of manufacturing jobs every year.

We don't need "free" trade. We need fair and managed trade, which benefits all partners if designed and conducted correctly, and we proved it with the success of the Auto Pact. As I noted earlier, both the U.S. and Canada gained from the Auto Pact. The Auto Pact benefited the auto companies, helped the workers by creating well-paying jobs, and added billions of dollars to the Canadian economy. Consumers benefited through lower prices for new cars, creating a win for everyone involved. The deal wasn't "free"; it set hard and fast rules that each government enforced—rules that are missing whenever free traders begin promoting globalization.

Want proof? How about this? From 2003 to 2008, car and truck sales in Japan decreased dramatically, down to their lowest levels since the mid-1970s. Did the Japanese car manufacturers lay off employees or close plants? No, they did just the opposite: they announced the construction of new plants and sought workers for them. These new plants are being built on the ocean shoreline—Toyota in Ishinomaki, Honda in Yorii and Ogawa, Mazda in Hiroshima—making it easier to load the vehicles they produce on board freighters for shipment . . . to guess where? Not to Tokyo. They're coming to Toyota, Honda and Mazda dealerships near you, here in North America.

Japanese automakers can do this because they know our market is wide open and theirs is protected from imports. Not just North American imports, either. Japan's closest auto-producing neighbour is Korea, 500 kilometres away across open water, and Korean labour costs are about half those of the Japanese. Yet Korea sells about as many cars in Japan as Ford.

By the way, Japan was among the loudest in protesting to the World Trade Organization that the Auto Pact was unfair, leading to the WTO decision banning the agreement. North America is the most open automotive market in the world, and Japan has some of the world's toughest non-tariff barriers against imports. Do you see the same contradiction I see?

I'm not prejudiced against the Japanese for taking this stand. I almost admire them for it. They're protecting their economy and their workers, which I agree with. I just wish that all those Canadians who preach "free trade" would recognize how hard other countries fight to defend the jobs of their citizens, and push our government to take a similar stand.

SIX

The Political Buzz

In the weeks after I announced my retirement in July 2008, stories popped up in the press speculating that I would run for political office as a Liberal in the upcoming federal election, specifically against Jim Flaherty in the riding of Whitby-Oshawa .

Boy, was that tempting.

Flaherty has been a disaster as a finance minister. Even more galling to me than his incompetence was his arrogance. He cut taxes (especially for corporations) while underinvesting in public programs and infrastructure. He suddenly and surprisingly reversed the government's policy on income trusts, catching millions of personal investors by surprise. Then he told the world that Ontario was a lousy place to invest money, cutting off badly needed financing for the province and insulting its workers. I couldn't believe it. Ontario is our most populous province, our manufacturing centre and still our biggest economic engine, and Flaherty was essentially telling the world to put their money someplace else. Hargrove versus Flaherty would have been a hell of a show but my heart wasn't in it.

The talk about my moving into politics was driven by my political activity as head of the CAW over the years. But I've always been more of a practical guy than a political animal. If something doesn't work, either repair it or replace it. This approach is just as valid, it seems to me, for political philosophy as for machinery, and explains why I took positions that angered various provincial and federal leaders of the NDP over the years.

The NDP is based on the same principles of social justice, fairness for workers and respect for labour as the CAW and other unions. The party, however, has evolved into something very different from the one inspired and led by Tommy Douglas. Meanwhile, the Conservatives are more anti-progressive and free market-oriented than ever. So in 2004, in the interests of at least denying a majority for Steven Harper, I proposed that CAW members practice strategic voting, trying to prevent a Conservative victory by concentrating anti-Conservative votes on the candidate, either NDP or Liberal, who had the best chance of defeating the Conservatives. Hell, at times it was hard to tell the difference between the Liberals and the NDP, anyway.

The traditional union approach to the NDP, in English Canada at least, had been to view the party as an extension of trade union goals and values into the political arena, and for years many leaders from the shop floor to the union executive offices were NDP party agitators. Political action committees in the CAW and elsewhere were considered branches of the NDP.

That's all in the past. Like it or not, trade union members are no more prone to vote NDP than they are to support any other party, from the Greens to the Conservatives. It became very clear to me several years ago that if I were to tell CAW members, "We recommend you vote NDP and if they get elected everything will be fine," they would laugh at me.

CAW members are far more sophisticated and independent now than they were a generation ago. They resist being told how to vote, and they have learned the hard way—especially those in Ontario during the Bob Rae era—that the NDP cannot solve all of their problems.

Unions, I maintain, must be present in the political arena as unions, not as political parties or even as one-party supporters. Their activities must be strategic, deliberate and independent. They should also reflect the long tradition of extending democracy on behalf of all working people by improving fairness in elections, placing limits on corporate funding of parties and candidates, insisting on balanced media coverage and encouraging stronger voter participation. Ultimately, we want more voter control over the way our society and economy evolve.

And something else: CAW political policy must reflect the will of the entire union, not a single individual, and should never be beholden to outside groups, including political parties. Wider participation in the political process by union members remains an important goal. Union members should not be preached at or told how to vote by anyone, and union leaders should expect their members to engage in political activities only when each individual member decides for himself or herself that the issues reflect his or her values, concerns and priorities. This approach reflects the way the CAW and similar unions deal with collective bargaining, which is a model of participatory democracy.

So when Stéphane Dion called a second time after I announced my resignation from the CAW, asking me to run as a Liberal in the federal election expected in the fall, I agreed to discuss the idea with Liberal Senator David Smith, who repeated the offer. Smith and I discussed possible ridings for me to represent. We didn't discuss anything beyond that—no demands from me, no promise from the Liberals. It was simply an idea we tossed around. When we parted I told him I would give it some thought, and talk it over with my wife, Denise.

It didn't take long for Denise and me to quash the notion. I had spent 30 years flying across Canada and to various places in the world, spending an untold number of nights in hotels eating room service food and wishing I were back in my own bed. If I were to win a seat in Parliament it would be an honour for sure, but it would also mean weeks away from our home in Mississauga. We decided not to accept Dion's offer.

Nobody from the NDP made a similar proposal to me. Fat chance—the Ontario wing had booted me out of the party two years earlier, which was about 12 years too late.

My disillusionment with the NDP started in 1993 when Bob Rae, who was then Premier of Ontario, tried to transfer the weight of the province's economic woes onto the backs of its union members. When Rae asked the two largest civil service unions, the Ontario Public Service Employees Union (OPSEU) and the Canadian Union of Public Employees (CUPE), to absorb $2 billion in wage cuts, they told him to get lost. Rae's response was to legislate, via his so-called "social contract," 12 days of unpaid leave for all civil service workers in the province, including teachers, nurses and other professions, the equivalent of a 5 percent reduction in annual income.

The forced implementation of these "Rae Days" helped torpedo the provincial NDP, and in the 1995 election they sank from a ruling party with a majority to the third-place party in the province, opening the door for Mike Harris and his neo-con cronies, including Jim Flaherty, to strut through.

It wasn't just the loss of twelve days pay that was so offensive to the labour movement that had helped to elect the NDP in the first place. Even worse was the government's knee-jerk willingness to force the changes through, with no respect for the principles of free collective bargaining. It's one thing for a corporation or a right-wing government to try to take away workers' hard-won rights to bargain their contracts.

It's quite another when a supposedly "labour-friendly" government tries the same thing.

The Social Contract wasn't merely unfair, it was politically stupid. Ontario may have needed to cut its expenses in order to deal with the challenges it was facing in 1993, but Rae and his NDP members demanded sacrifices from unions, the party's base, while leaving everybody else untouched. One of the first rules in politics says you should never attack your own base. Unions and the NDP had been conjoined twins, sharing in the good times and working together in the bad times. Now Rae wanted a pound of flesh from the unions and nothing from anyone else.

If Rae had gone to all the people of Ontario and said, "Look, we have a major problem here," and made a strong case for taking action by applying a surtax for a specified period of time, he would have made a lot of people upset but his base would have been intact and labour activists would have maintained their enthusiasm for the party. Instead, he put a special tax equal to 5 percent of annual wages on the only people he had power over—the public servants who helped put him in the premier's chair. By demanding pay cuts from union members, and little or no sacrifice from groups identified with other parties, he effectively blew up the foundation of his own house and watched it crumble around him. It was a clear abuse of power, which is how I described it when he brought the idea to me. "Don't do it," I cautioned. "Get the union leaders onside and agree to a temporary income surtax for working people, unionized and non-unionized, and get the unions to support it."

He assured me he wouldn't just pick on the public service employees to cut his expenses. Then he went ahead and did it anyway.

Bob Rae is an intelligent guy, but I have always believed that intelligence alone doesn't ensure great leadership. In fact, it can lead to arrogance and a lack of empathy, two elements that I believe brought about Bob Rae's downfall. The scars of the Social Contract run very deep in Ontario, and although Bob Rae now sits in Ottawa as a Liberal, I wasn't surprised when the party chose Michael Ignatieff as their leader over Rae. It's unfortunate, in a way, because Bob Rae's experience governing during a major recession had prepared him to be an effective leader, especially if you believe in the value of "baptism by fire." But Rae's baggage from his term as Ontario premier was just too heavy. Had he secured the Liberal leadership, each time he stood up to make a speech just two words from his opponents—"Rae Days!"—would have dredged up bitter memories. Few working people in Ontario will forget those forced 12 days of unpaid leave for all civil service workers, the freeze on wages of all provincial civil service workers, and the reopening of collective bargaining agreements with all public sector unions.

I spoke out loudly and harshly against Rae Days and the Social Contract, and watched, with neither satisfaction nor surprise, when thousands of Ontario people, union and non-union alike, washed their hands of the NDP. Rae's attempts to keep unionists on side with Bill 40, introducing anti-scab provisions to Ontario, was too little too late and the NDP in Ontario has been wandering in the outback ever since.

The election of Mike Harris and his Conservatives in 1995 proved the pendulum never stops in the middle when it begins to swing. Harris and his "Common Sense Revolution" were even more of a disaster to union members than Bob Rae and his Rae Days. They had to go. But who would replace them? There was no way, given the fresh memories in the electorate's minds, that Harris and the Conservatives would be booted out in favour of a refreshed NDP party. So in 1999 I suggested that the CAW set a goal of defeating or at least restricting Harris's policies. Since an NDP victory was clearly out of the question, our main goal became limiting the Conservatives.

Let's get something straight: I'm not a knee-jerk kind of guy who immediately pigeonholes somebody based on political affiliation or any other quality. Bill Davis, who served as Ontario premier through the 1970s, was as Tory-blue as any politician in our history, but he was also sensitive and astute enough to introduce progressive ideas like work- place closure protection, laws requiring employers to issue a notice of layoff, early retirement pensions and pension benefit protection for workers. I sure didn't agree with all of Davis's policies, but I recognize and thank him for these and other achievements, including his support for CAW jobs in the auto industry.

I'm not trying to demonize Mike Harris, either. I dealt with him in various ways while his government was in power. In fact, we almost had Harris and his caucus as paying guests at our CAW Family Education Centre in Port Elgin, Ontario. The centre began as a rather rundown lodge purchased by the union in 1958 with plans to develop it as a place for local union leaders and executives to gather for strategy sessions and conduct official business. Over the years it expanded into a major edu- cational and recreational centre for members and their families, with banquet facilities, rooms for meetings and presentations, and accom modations for 180 people.

One day I encountered Harris at the Sutton Place Hotel in Toronto, and during our conversation he asked if we would consider renting accommodation and facilities at the centre for the Ontario Conservatives to hold a caucus meeting. It would be perfect for the occasion, Harris noted. Just the right size and located far enough away from Toronto to get the isolation they wanted, but near enough to reach in an after- noon's drive. It was also close to Paisley, Ontario, where the International Ploughing Match was taking place that year, and Harris could slip down to the event during the day and mingle with many of his high-profile rural supporters.

I thought it was a great idea, especially after learning that Bob Rae and his NDP cabinet had been holding meetings in non-union hotels in Niagara Falls. When challenged, the NDP explained that they chose not to use the Education Centre because it left them open to charges of being too close to the labour movement! Go figure.

When I brought Harris's idea to the CAW executive for approval, nobody else agreed with me. Have Mike Harris and the hated Tories eating, sleeping and strategizing on CAW property? Some members acted as though we would have to fumigate the place when they left, and I had to call Harris back and suggest he go elsewhere.

What a shame. TV coverage of Mike Harris, Jim Flaherty, Tony Clement and the rest of the gang emerging from a CAW building would have been something to see.

I was never outraged by Conservative Party philosophy as expressed by Bill Davis, although I obviously preferred a left-wing agenda. But Harris was no Bill Davis. Mike Harris went beyond traditional Conservative philosophy and injected the values and goals of the Reform Party into Ontario politics. The divisive and mean-spirited policies of the Reform Party have no place in Canadian society, and I was determined that neither Mike Harris nor anyone else was going to introduce them into Ontario under another name.

The attitudes and actions of Mike Harris and his Tories justified, in my mind, a new approach to politics by the CAW, and that's what I recommended to the union leadership. In past elections, the NDP at federal and provincial levels across the country could always count on the unions to back them every time and everywhere they ran candidates. This meant that we supported NDP candidates in ridings where they didn't have a hope in hell of winning. For the most part, these people deserved our assistance in principle, but in practice, a vote for an NDP loser would split the anti-Tory vote in many ridings, and help a Harris Conservative gain a seat over a Liberal candidate.

I did not propose abandoning the Ontario NDP. In fact, in 1998 with an election looming, I supported the CAW national executive board's decision to contribute $100,000 to the NDP, and to encourage individuals and local unions to offer their support as well, but instead of concentrating on the overall election, we addressed the problem riding by riding. If the NDP candidate had a realistic chance of winning, we backed him or her. Otherwise, we encouraged our members (and all voters) to support the candidate with the best chance of defeating the Conservative. We also purchased billboards at strategic locations in Ontario, identifying the Harris government as the most anti-union, anti-worker, antisocial, insensitive government to ever serve in any jurisdiction in Canada.

This is basic strategic voting, and it's a fact of life in any first-past-the-post parliamentary system. Past analysis of Canadian voting results shows that Canadians vote strategically anyway, whether anyone encourages them to or not. Canadians aren't stupid. They don't like to throw away their votes. Yet I was attacked for even suggesting the concept.

All political action is strategic and always will be, but when I talked about strategic voting you would think I was suggesting a return to the divine right of kings. The most painful criticism came from other unionists. "The problem with Buzz Hargrove," I began hearing from various union sources, "is that he appears to have forgotten what the word solidarity means."

Hey, I know the meaning of solidarity among union members when it comes to the pursuit of fairness and justice. But without a hope of attracting enough voters to move government policy to the left, we had a solidarity of silence, a solidarity of no challenge to the status quo. Where was that getting us? Where was it getting Canadians, especially those concerned about a struggling health care system, the loss of our manufacturing base, the deteriorating environment, the unfair treatment of our First Nations people, the absence of a national daycare policy, the endless cycle of poverty and a host of other issues?

In June 1996, Howard Hampton replaced Bob Rae as Ontario NDP leader. I didn't know Hampton well before he assumed the leadership, but I expected he would take the party in a new direction away from Rae's stubborn approach, perhaps starting by patching things up with the party's base. Well, he didn't. Nothing changed, except that Hampton proved even more sensitive to challenge or criticism than Rae.

I commented in the media on Hampton's failure to restore some goodwill with the socialist base in Ontario before the 1999 election, Hampton's first as leader, was called. My opinion of Hampton was mine alone, and not everybody within the CAW agreed with me. That's fine. We live in a democracy, after all. I expressed my opinion and moved on, assuming Hampton would as well.

Before the election was called, I had invited Hampton to speak to our council. They deserved to hear his side, and Hampton deserved a chance to make his case. Hampton agreed to speak, but Harris called an election just prior to the council meeting date. That's when I decided to push the idea of strategic voting to prevent another four years of Tory rule, even if it meant not supporting NDP candidates where their cause was hopeless. Following the election, with Harris leading his second majority government, someone in the media asked Hampton about coming to speak to the CAW council. Hampton replied, "It would be theatre of the absurd for me to go to a podium and speak with someone who has spent the better part of the last two years trashing me and trashing the party."

I thought it was a silly comment to make. He wasn't invited to speak to Buzz Hargrove. He was invited to speak to 800 independent-minded delegates, 80 percent of them from Ontario. I have never asked to see the comments made by speakers to the delegation before delivery, nor would I try to influence their remarks, and I certainly wouldn't have done so with Hampton. He could say whatever he wanted about me or any other topic, and maybe score some votes inside and outside the CAW with his comments. His tantrum was an opportunity missed, and it revealed a fatal weakness in the NDP leader. Hampton stood to lose nothing by making his case to people representing hundreds of thousands of voters, the very base of the NDP's support. He almost certainly would have gained a great deal by his courage to appear, at least. Yet his only response was to label the opportunity "theatre of the absurd."

I will never understand politicians who do not understand politics. Effective leaders take every opportunity to broaden the base of support of their political party. In this case, Hampton chose to step aside. As I might have predicted, his tenure as leader of the Ontario NDP was a record of one failure after another.

I kept proposing a two-prong voting policy for CAW members and other supporters of social justice. Prong one: help the left wing win where possible. Prong two: where this was not possible, prevent the right wing from succeeding. Some people misread my intentions and began asking if I was planning to move into politics and maybe form a new political party. My answer was always no. "If I wanted to form a new political party," I would explain, "I'd target the people who don't participate in our elections. Nearly 40 percent of the electorate don't bother to vote or take advantage of the opportunity to reach out to support their principles. Whoever appeals to these people can't lose. But it won't be me."

Even if we had a political party or a political leader who perfectly echoed the labour movement's ideas and policies, the union could not simply rubber-stamp that party or leader and give them, in essence, a blank cheque. We have to retain our right to act independently as a union, rather than blindly endorsing any political party. The moment unions pledge support without conditions is the moment political leaders start taking unions for granted, no matter how well-intentioned those leaders may have been in the first place. This commitment to maintaining an independent political voice for the union was the common thread linking all the CAW's conflicts with the NDP from the days of the Social Contract until my expulsion from the party.

* * *

In the end, you play the hand you are dealt, and in late 2005, with the federal Liberals in trouble over the Sponsorship Scandal and the Tories feeling their oats under the leadership of Stephen Harper, we decided to test the waters of the right wing. Chris Buckley, Whitey MacDonald and several other CAW leaders from the auto sector came with me to Ottawa, where we met with the Tory auto caucus, asking their support for our members' jobs at Ford, General Motors and Chrysler. We weren't alone in our request. The federal Liberals and NDP, along with the Ontario Liberals under Dalton McGuinty were backing us up.

The Tory response was a flat refusal to assist the auto industry. James Rajotte, Tory MP for Edmonton-Leduc and the industry critic at the time, told us, "We are opposed to corporate welfare," proving he and his party just didn't get it. Auto plants were closing in Canada even while new plants were being built in southern U.S. states, attracted by tax breaks, cash grants and other federal, state and local incentives totalling hundreds of millions of dollars. Rajotte didn't care. Of course, he had no auto plant in his riding. His focus was on petroleum production and it didn't matter to him where the cars that burned the gasoline were built.

We managed to convince Paul Martin's Liberal minority government to establish a $1 billion fund in support of new investment for the auto industry, something that would not have happened a few months later with Harper in power.

Back home, I renewed the call for strategic voting to ensure that Stephen Harper did not become prime minister. "Make sure you don't send any more Tories to Ottawa," I appealed to CAW members and their families. When Paul Martin spoke to our CAW council meeting and urged CAW members to vote for his party, he was supporting the same idea. "I know many of you in this audience have backed the NDP," Martin said, "but I also know this: Liberals or Conservatives, one of us will form the next government."

This comment, plus a photo in the newspapers of me slipping a CAW jacket over Martin's shoulders—something I had done for other guest speakers in the past—was enough to make Jack Layton's hair stand on end, if he'd had any. "Mr. Hargrove," Layton said when asked his opinion of the news reports, "is well known for having his opinions and expressing them, and he's entitled to them." Despite Layton's fuming, later that weekend CAW Council delegates overwhelmingly endorsed the union's strategic voting strategy, in an effort to prevent a Stephen Harper victory.

A few weeks later, when it appeared that Harper's party might gain enough seats to form at least a minority government, I stirred things up a little more at a Liberal meeting outside London, Ontario, where Paul Martin was also speaking. In a conversation with a group of reporters, I suggested that supporters of the Bloc Québécois could help prevent a Tory victory by voting strategically, and their actions would do more for national unity than a victory by the Harper-led Tories. I was being intentionally controversial, but I was not really stretching the truth. To those who asked how the CAW could promote cooperation with a separatist party, my response was that the Conservatives were, in essence, separatist too; they just weren't as open in their promotion of separatism as the BQ and they used different tactics. "Stephen Harper is playing into the hands of the separatists," I said, "because he would promote the loosening of federal institutions, programs and powers." My point was that while Harper might declare himself a federalist, his policy of awarding more power to the provinces and making obvious efforts to turn them against each other serves to weaken federalism, not strengthen it.

As expected, my identifying Harper as a closet separatist kick-started comments among both politicians and pundits. Paul Martin was clearly upset about my statement, telling reporters, "I have large differences with Stephen Harper, but I have never doubted his patriotism." Harper almost lost his legendary cool over my comments. "Right in the presence of Paul Martin," Harper blustered to the media, "one of his most prominent supporters, Buzz Hargrove, said that people should vote for the Bloc rather than have a new government. Mr. Martin and his people will say anything to stay in power," Harper went on, ignoring Martin's disclaimer about my comment. "They will even say people should vote to break up this country."

Which, of course, had been my point about Stephen Harper and his calculated moves to undermine federalism and create division among the provinces. Let's be clear about this: Buzz Hargrove is the last person in Canada who wants to break up this country, and the first person to stand up and suggest that this may be the result of Stephen Harper's policies, including his disingenuous decision to pass a resolution in Parliament declaring the Québécois to be a "nation."

Paul Martin is a bright guy and a smooth politician, but even the best of us can make serious errors, and Martin's handling of the Sponsorship Scandal effectively ended his career. Inheriting the situation from Jean Chrétien, Martin made a decision that his predecessors, including Mulroney, Trudeau and other astute politicians, would never have made. He permitted himself to be goaded by Stephen Harper and his Tory attack dogs into launching the Gomery inquiry, and suddenly all the dirty linen was flapping in the breeze for everybody to see. It's clear to those who studied the evidence that neither Martin nor his inner circle was involved in the scandal, but it didn't matter to voters once the Gomery inquiry got started. The Tories made the most of their opportunity, as expected. Then during the election campaign, the RCMP announced, with the complicity of the NDP, that it was investigating the federal finance minister and other officials for bungling a public announcement regarding the government's withdrawal of its proposal to tax income trusts. It was a phony "scandal" but support for the Paul Martin Liberals dropped like a stone, and Harper got his foot into the door of government with a narrow minority victory.

What would Chrétien and the others have done about the Sponsorship Scandal? The same thing any organization should do when criminal acts are suspected: call in the cops, cooperate with the investigation and leave it to law enforcement professionals. If the police found laws had been broken, charges would be laid and justice, as such, would take its course. The investigation would have been carried out by the RCMP. It would not have turned into the political circus of the Gomery Commission.

Strategic voting helped make the most of a bad situation. The concern Canadians felt about handing Stephen Harper the power of a majority government, supported by the efforts of the CAW and others to deny him those powers, was crucial in preventing him from winning a majority, a fact confirmed in a post-election analysis of the results performed by Decima Research, which highlighted the significant number of Canadians who voted strategically.

Nevertheless, the combination of the sponsorship inquiry, criticism of strategic voting from some quarters and public announcements by the RCMP all weakened the strategy I proposed. Too bad. It might well have succeeded in keeping Harper out of office. Unfortunately, Harper squeaked in with the narrowest minority government in Canadian history. It was better than a Conservative majority, but still opened the door to Harper's painful, regressive policies. Thus the January 2006 federal election changed the country's political face dramatically. But it was close.

Consider this: In 11 federal ridings, 10 of them in Ontario, the NDP had little or no chance of winning and the Conservatives managed to squeak past the Liberals by a total plurality of less than 9,000 votes— about 800 votes per riding. In one riding, the NDP candidate took a three-week vacation to Ireland in the middle of the campaign and still managed to suck enough votes away from the Liberals to permit the Tory candidate—Tony Clement, one of the most reactionary guys from Mike Harris's right-wing cabinet—to gain a seat in Ottawa.

If strategic voting had swung a majority of those 800 votes per riding onto the Liberal side of the ballot, Harper would have been denied his minority win, Paul Martin would have had a chance to solidify his position, Stéphane Dion would not have stumbled through his disastrous leadership experience, Jim Flaherty would not have gained a platform for trashing Ontario, and Canada would look very different today.

But when the dust of the 2006 federal election settled, the country had a minority Tory government, and within a few days the NDP had its revenge. Mike Shields, the CAW representative on the executive board of the Ontario NDP party, called me at home one Sunday morning in February 2006 to say the Ontario NDP executive had considered suspending the membership of four people. In the end, only one person was dropped from the party roster, and it was me. According to the party, which announced its decision to the media but not directly to me, I had violated its constitution by suggesting that CAW members support Liberals in ridings where the NDP had no hope of being elected. Losing my Ontario NDP membership also cut my ties with the federal party. Politically speaking, I was out in the cold.

That's how my 41 years as an NDP member and supporter ended, with a telephone call from a friend. No one from the party officially informed me of their decision, which would have been the classy way to do things. Nor did the party note that my proposal for strategic voting had expressed a democratically adopted policy confirmed at a CAW council meeting the previous December.

It was not a lifetime banishment. The NDP executive noted that I could regain my membership if I wrote a letter of apology and promised not to endorse candidates for other parties in the future. Fat chance. I refused to grovel, and I had nothing to apologize for anyway. And maybe I should be relieved that expulsion was all I got. Sandra Clifford, Ontario president of the NDP, told the media that some ridings had called for worse punishment. Worse punishment? What more can a political party do than expel a member? Tar and feather him? Draw and quarter him?

More than two years later, the federal election of October 2008 revealed how much our federal political scene had disintegrated thanks, in large part, to the shallowness of the party leaders and the influence of American election tactics on this country.

In an age of neo-conservatism and the disasters it spawned, Canada needed a strong voice from the left as a counterbalance, a forum for those who knew there was an alternative to the policies of Mike Harris, Stephen Harper, George W. Bush and their cronies. Jack Layton should have been that voice. Unfortunately, Layton has proved that he is a man who will say and do almost anything if it means he can tuck another vote in his pocket. I call him Get-a-Vote Jack, which gets me in trouble with my loyal friends who remain in the NDP.

Layton loves being in the public eye, and that's fine with me. Anybody who aspires for political leadership had better be comfortable with the spotlight because it comes with the job. To my mind, however, Jack Layton invests more energy in promoting Jack Layton and the NDP logo than in promoting progressive issues.

During the 2006 election, Layton trained the NDP's guns on the Liberals and mostly ignored the surging Conservatives. His logic was simple: the NDP takes votes from Liberals, not Conservatives. This might help the party win more seats (they picked up 10 in the 2006 election) but it can do grave damage to the country if it makes it easier for people like Harper to get a foot in the door.

Then, in the 2008 federal election, Layton did it again. He spent more energy attacking Stéphane Dion and the Liberals than challenging Stephen Harper and the Conservatives, despite the fact that Harper was proving to be the most insensitive and extreme right-wing leader in Canada's history.

Stephen Harper not only does not understand the concerns of working people and the political values of the left; he has no interest in the subject. Over the first three years of Harper's tenure as prime minister, I met him on just two occasions. One was a session with six other labour leaders that lasted about half an hour, meaning each of us enjoyed an average of five minutes in which to discuss our concerns. The other was in November 2007, almost two years after his election, when Harper agreed to meet with me and CAW economist Jim Stanford to hear our concerns about the automotive manufacturing sector in Canada. It was another half-hour session, but at least we had an opportunity to focus on one sector.

Jim Stanford and I made our case, I believe, but Harper's behaviour bordered on bizarre. In an effort, I assume, to suggest he was just one of the boys, a guy who could relate to blue-collar workers despite his political record, Harper managed to say "fuck" two or three times, none of them in what might be called a normal context. As we left the meeting, Stanford and I looked at each other and asked, "What the heck was *that* all about?"

Harper did not disagree with our position on the trade issues with Japan and Korea where the auto industry was concerned, and he claimed to understand the need to install clauses of the now-defunct Auto Pact requiring each country to strive for equal dollar value in bilateral trade. His objection to our proposal was the possibly negative reaction from the Americans. "I don't believe we can get them to buy that," he offered.

I suggested he at least make it a public issue to show that he and the rest of Canada were concerned about it. He wasn't interested, partially because he and his cabinet were itching to sign a free-trade deal with South Korea that would include no protection for Canadian jobs, proving he is out of touch with the entire subject.

The only time Harper and the Tories pay attention to manufacturing generally, and the auto industry in particular, is when they go trolling for votes. In late 2008, when everyone was waiting for Harper to drop the writ and call a general election, I began hearing about Tory plans to support the auto industry through public funding. The timing and execution of these proposals were so cynical and sloppy that I didn't know whether to laugh or cry over the Tories' incompetence.

Did I want to see the Tories support new jobs? Damn right I did—the Conservatives had been ignoring the industry and CAW members since they took office more than two years earlier. Government assistance would save jobs, save plants and, in the long run, save money. But since January 2006, auto workers in Canada had been invisible to Conservatives. Now they wanted to be our buddies, at least until the election was over. So the Tory machine went to work with all the subtlety of a runaway train.

In August, while I was still in the CAW president's chair, I received a call from a contact at Ford asking if I could assist with the Tories' offer to fund a Windsor operation. "The feds and we both want this deal closed right away," he explained. "But it's a joint federal-provincial deal and the province is holding things up. Can you help get this done?" A similar call from our St. Catharines local union asked the same thing. Ottawa wanted to back a new GM engine program there, with Ontario's participation, but the province wasn't cooperating. What could we do?

I called the office of Sandra Pupatello, Liberal MPP for Windsor West and Ontario's minister of international trade and investment, hoping she could loosen whatever log jam had developed. Flavio Volpe, her assistant, explained that the province wasn't the problem. The problem was the near-panicked insistence of Harper's Tories to announce the deal before the election was called. "They want us to sign our part of the deal," Volpe said, "without giving us a chance to read or evaluate things." The whole operation was a pig in a poke just to enable Harper, Jim Prentice, Jim Flaherty and the others to boast they were supporting Canadian workers.

Incredibly, Harper's government also tried to take credit for "saving" GM's Oshawa plants. The company already had been given significant financial support from the federal and Ontario governments as part of the "Beacon Project." By closing the Oshawa truck plant and taking other downsizing measures, GM was violating the terms of that project, under which GM was required to meet certain thresholds for investment and employment. Harper allowed GM to take other actions, such as announcing new model allocations at its plants that remained open, and then claimed credit for somehow "saving" those plants. What hogwash!

Harper and his team then informed GM that, as a result of the announcement to maintain production in Oshawa, the company did not have to pay back over $200 million in government loans. "We did not spend any money to get this deal," Harper boasted. Really? If I loan my buddy 200 bucks and tell him a few months later that he doesn't have to pay me back, I've spent 200 bucks, like it or not. Harper spent $200 million but claimed he received GM's assurances, for whatever they're worth, by not spending a penny of taxpayers' money. Maybe we should all tap Harper for a loan until payday.

If anyone had doubts about Harper's reputation for being a control freak, his handling of the September 3, 2008 public announcement of the new engine project at Ford Windsor, which ended up receiving an $80 million interest-free loan, should dispel them once and for all. Completely ignoring the CAW's role in fighting for and eventually winning the financial backing, his party informed Ford that they wanted to use the company's premises to make the announcement, but they did not want either Ford or the CAW to be present or even to comment on the deal.

To its credit, Ford told them to get lost. If the Tories wanted to use the company's site to make an announcement affecting its operations in Canada, Ford insisted on the right to comment. They also reserved the right for the union to comment if it wished to.

Harper's people weren't happy, but they finally agreed, on condition that they could approve the company's and the union's statements before they were released. For the entire night before the announcement, statements were faxed back and forth between our union and Tory officials, with my assistant Bob Chernecki and the people at the Ford local in Windsor handling our side, until we had a wishy-washy piece of text that Harper could live with.

At my suggestion, CAW Local 200 president Mike Vince called a press conference at their union hall later that day and, while acknowledging the value of the loan, blasted the timing for what it was: a calculated election gimmick.

For almost three years the federal Tories had demonstrated neither understanding nor sympathy for the auto industry in this country and the plight of its workers. Then, two days before calling the unnecessary election of October 2008—an election based entirely on Stephen Harper's hunger for power—they attempted to portray themselves as saviours of the working class, with no opportunity for anyone else to comment.

The federal election denied Harper the majority government he sought, but it also failed to advance the fortunes of the NDP and its followers. The goal for the CAW and the left generally is to find a way of standing up to Ottawa without dividing the country. This strategy has proven effective for Newfoundland and Labrador, Nova Scotia, Saskatchewan and Alberta. It has also, of course, proven effective for Quebec, especially for the Bloc Québécois, who don't give a damn if their policies break up Canada—that's one of their goals.

Danny Williams rallied the people of his province around him in his battle over the issue of transfer payments, when Ottawa suggested they would be reduced according to the amount of offshore oil royalties Newfoundland and Labrador earned. He did a few "un-Canadian things," in Paul Martin's words, such as removing Canadian flags from public offices, but he forced people to pay attention. Williams not only won the battle for Newfoundland and Labrador, he earned a similar agreement on transfer payments for Nova Scotia. Sometimes confrontation works. Over the years Saskatchewan and Alberta have also managed to defy Ottawa and achieve at least some of their objectives. From the 1920s when the Prairie provinces were concerned about tariffs on farm equipment, through the 1970s conflict over domestic energy prices to periodic squawks from the Alberta Separatist Party, the West is very good at yanking Ottawa's tail to get attention. And it's usually effective.

Can Ontario do the same thing? I don't believe it can. Ontario's role in the past has been the glue that holds Canada together through its influence in many areas—economic, social, cultural and political. If the province were to follow the same extreme measures that worked for Danny Williams, it would divide the country terribly.

Stephen Harper and his gang know this. That's why Jim Flaherty, as federal finance minister, can make outrageous statements such as the one he made in February 2008, criticizing Ontario's higher rate of business taxes. "It discourages investment in the province of Ontario," he said. "If you're going to make a new business investment in Canada and you're concerned about taxes, the last place you will go is the province of Ontario." Making such a claim in any other province would be political suicide, and he knows it. This wasn't just a wild assertion by Flaherty alone. It had to be a Harper-approved Tory tactic. Does anybody really believe that Flaherty made those and other statements without the approval and probably even the encouragement of Stephen Harper?

Ontario politicians realize that a down-and-dirty fight with Ottawa would prove disastrous for Canadian unity. The best solution is to rise above Harper's outrageous positions and find a way of changing the government in Ottawa to one that is less confrontational and more responsive to the needs of Canadians.

When Flaherty doesn't kick Ontario in the backside with insults he does it by other means, usually finding a way to target the manufacturing sector in general and the auto industry in particular. Flaherty's riding includes many people who work for GM in Oshawa. I know Flaherty may make foolish moves but he's not stupid, so I can only conclude that many of his decisions are born in the brain of his boss, Stephen Harper. But not all. When he's left on his own, Flaherty can find his own ways to screw things up. Like this one:

In September 2006, I and several other auto industry people met with Flaherty, then-environment minister Rona Ambrose, Minister of Natural Resources Gary Lunn, and others. Among them was then-industry minister Maxime Bernier, who, unfortunately, did not bring girlfriend Julie Couillard with him.

Flaherty had announced that the Harper government would introduce its version of California's Clean Air Act to Canada, just weeks after celebrating GM's decision to build a new Camaro in Oshawa. If the Act were introduced as written, however, the Camaro and many other made-in-Canada vehicles would face strict limits on their sales in Canada because of Flaherty's Made in California emissions targets. We all agree that the auto industry needs to produce more fuel efficient and less polluting vehicles. But the way to facilitate this evolution is hardly to shoot your own industry in the foot with regulations punishing their products while enhancing market opportunities for imports.

When I drew this to Flaherty's attention, he shrugged and noted that the cars couldn't be sold in California either. He missed the point: California doesn't have an auto industry. Not a serious one, at least. About 2,000 people in California have jobs associated with the automotive industry. At the time, we had 150,000 jobs in that industry in Canada.

"Buzz, I come from Durham Region," Flaherty said when I pointed this out to him. "Do you think I'm going to do something to harm the auto industry?"

Well, no. Would a smart bird would foul its own nest?

I found out the answer a few weeks later when Flaherty introduced his budget. In 2006 Ford, General Motors and Chrysler collectively lost more than $15 billion. They would have lost even more except that their sales of SUVs and larger cars remained strong. They didn't sell nearly as well in Canada as in the U.S. but their sales benefited us because many of the parts are produced here.

It didn't matter to Flaherty. His budget slapped a tax of $1,000 to $4,000 on dozens of larger vehicles (most of them made in North America). But one kick in the backside wasn't enough. While slapping a tax on Canadian-made cars and trucks, Flaherty gave a gift to foreign automakers when he announced tax incentives on smaller fuel-efficient or hybrid cars, most of them built in South Korea or Japan. Both of these decisions were made without any consultation with, or reflection about, the hundreds of thousands of Canadians who depend on this country's auto industry for their livelihood.

The only Canadian-made Big Three vehicle that qualified for the "green" tax incentive was the flex-fuel Impala. And why did he exempt the Impala? Because it was capable of using E-85 ethanol fuel which, in Flaherty's mind, made it sufficiently fuel efficient. Sure it does—except when the budget came down you could purchase E-85 fuel at just *two locations* in all of Canada, one in Kitchener, and the other in Ottawa. Buy an E-85 Impala in Victoria, B.C., or Gander, Newfoundland, or anywhere in between and when you're out of E-85 fuel you're SOL.

I support the Kyoto Accord, and I believe the Big Three North American automakers could have done a better job developing fuel-efficient vehicles and bringing them to market earlier. We need to reduce petroleum consumption and greenhouse gas emissions in Canada and around the world. But before crafting their knee-jerk response on large cars and SUVs, Harper and Flaherty needed a lesson in history and a dose of reality.

The history lesson deals with the Auto Pact. Under the Auto Pact, the number of cars and trucks sold in Canada had to equal the number of vehicles manufactured here. Participating companies, in return for tariff-free access to Canadian consumers, had to maintain a proportional manufacturing presence in Canada. A second test imposed under the Auto Pact, called the "value-added" test, made sure Canada got a fair share of parts and power-train jobs, not just assembly line jobs, by demanding that the total value-added produced in Canada had to equal 65 percent of the total value-added sold in the country.

To meet the value-added test it made sense for the auto companies to manufacture larger cars and trucks in Canada. This ensured that their production value would easily meet or exceed the sales value of smaller cars sold here. Nobody could argue with the wisdom of this decision over 40-plus years, and in Canada we became very good at building larger vehicles. So it wasn't an accident that the plants and capital equipment in Canada were all oriented toward producing large rear-wheel-drive cars, minivans and trucks, and it wasn't because Canadians didn't "care" about the environment. It was a fact of life that reflected hard economics.

The reality is that the bulk of our automotive production focused on these kinds of vehicles—the same ones Flaherty slapped with one hand while the other hand gave bonuses to foreign automakers whose governments effectively bar Canadian-made vehicles from their own markets.

In time, I hope our automotive industry will adapt to new environmental standards with products produced in unionized plants. Until then, the industry is being hammered on all sides, and the livelihoods of tens of thousands of families depends on the kinds of cars we have turned out for almost half a century. Dealing with them in the brutal manner that Flaherty demonstrated, with the support if not the direction of Harper, proves the prime minister and his cabinet are out of touch, out of tune and out to lunch where working-class Canadians are concerned.

I don't enjoy bashing politicians, believe it or not. Some people think I get pleasure out of doing it, but I don't. I admire anyone who devotes his or her life to public service, and Lord knows it takes a lot of something—guts, ego, sacrifice, all of it—to open up your private life and accept humiliation from time to time just to satisfy your political ambition. But when hard truths need to be said, they need to be said.

Remember my comment to Stephen Harper at our meeting, when I told him that nothing would have given me more pleasure than to announce to the media that he had joined the CAW in taking steps to end unfair trade with Asian automakers? He said this would not be possible. Big mistake. If he had taken action back then, I would have praised him and the Tories in front of the whole country. I did this when Ernie Eves took over as Tory premier of Ontario and set up a $500 million investment fund for the auto sector. I joined Eves at the GM Oshawa plant when he made the announcement, and in front of the media I praised Eves for his dedication to working people in Ontario, especially those in the automotive business. I took some flak from CAW members for saying good things about a Tory premier, but why not? If you hammer them when they screw things up, you have to congratulate them when they get it right.

Meanwhile, the NDP staggers from election to election, becoming less relevant each time. Why? Because, I suggest, it has become less associated with the ideas that appealed to its base from the beginning, and less successful at selling them to the electorate at large.

Since my dust-up with Bob Rae back in 1993, the entire relationship between labour and the NDP has changed. Many of the unions that disagreed with my criticism of the party and my support for strategic voting have come to recognize that the old model of strict affiliations to the party is out of date, and even the attitude of the Canadian Labour Congress toward the NDP has cooled noticeably.

Some of this change is due to the leadership, or the lack of it, in the party. Much of it, I believe, links back to the NDP's apparent abandonment of long-held principles. Whatever happened to using public ownership as a tool to achieve social goals? When applied with restraint, isn't this an effective means of dealing with the periodic traumas that threaten to shatter raw unfettered capitalism? In fact, given the chaos that has resulted from the current global financial crisis, there is a huge political opening right now to rejuvenate the idea of public ownership. The old assumption that the private sector always does it better than the public sector is in tatters. All we need is creative, inspiring leadership to show that public ownership, in certain areas, can play a constructive and efficient role in rescuing the economy.

A rare example of showing creative leadership to make the most of the political opportunity was shown by all three opposition leaders, including Layton. Just weeks after the 2008 election, Finance Minister Jim Flaherty tabled an incredibly inept economic update that essentially denied the existence of the financial and economic crisis that Canadians could see unfolding around them. Layton, Stéphane Dion and Bloc Québecois leader Gilles Duceppe seized the opportunity and proposed a coalition government involving all three parties that would seriously address the coming recession. In fact, the CAW had proposed this very idea way back in 2004, after the Liberals' minority victory. We argued it made sense for progressives from all three parties—Liberals, NDP, and Bloc—to work cooperatively to advance progressive policies. Unfortunately, Governor General Michaëlle Jean gave Flaherty and Harper a second chance by proroguing parliament, and the coalition didn't last. But the basic idea of building bridges across party lines to promote ideas of common interest is valid, and is practiced regularly in other multi-party democracies. Layton, Dion and Duceppe were on the right track.

Sadly, however, this was an exception. More often, NDP leaders respond too cautiously and conservatively to opportunities to challenge the power of private business and right-wing ideas. For example, time and time again, when I proposed that a provincial or the federal government assume control of a company that chooses to move out of Canada, leaving an entire workforce without jobs and with no pension benefits just so the owners can add a few percentage points to their profit statements, I was told we were beyond that. Socialism of that kind is dead, people lectured me. Sure, it would preserve jobs and help us retain our manufacturing base, but the idea would never fly.

Really? How do they explain the American government's decision to acquire the private mortgage lenders Freddie Mac and Fannie Mae during the credit crisis? How do they account for the same government finding $700 billion, give or take a few billion, to bail out investment bankers? How do they deal with the wave that swept literally around the world, when capitalist governments suddenly became socialist in their outlook? Do jobs matter only when the workers wear white collars, not blue collars?

It sure seems that way when you look at the way workers at places like Versatile Manufacturing were treated. Located in Winnipeg, Versatile achieved international success building a line of farm tractors and other agricultural equipment specially suited for western prairie conditions. When John Buhler acquired control of it in 2000 he gave the Versatile employees, members of the CAW, an ultimatum: Accept a deep cut in their wages and benefits or he would move the company across the border into North Dakota. It wasn't a matter of saving the company; Versatile had always made money, and its products were top-quality. It was a means of lining the pockets of the new owner with a few more bucks and to hell with the Canadian Versatile employees who had invested much of their working lives with the company.

I suggested to Gary Doer, the NDP premier of Manitoba, that he tell Buhler Versatile was to stay put. "Take over the company," I said. "The province can invest in it and save the jobs."

Doer didn't like the idea. "The Manitoba government," he sniffed, "is not in the business of purchasing private businesses." Maybe it damn well should be if it can guarantee jobs and fairness for the people who elected it. That was my point and I still maintain it. As it turned out, an 80 percent controlling share in Buhler was purchased in 2007 by a Russian company, Rostselmash. The shrunken Winnipeg facilities have been operated without a union since a bitter nine-month strike and lockout in 2001. The federal and Manitoba governments actually facilitated this Russian takeover by forgiving past loans that Buhler owed them. Premier Doer was unwilling to use public ownership to protect a key economic asset and stood idly by while yet another Canadian company fell under foreign control. Why is public ownership considered completely off-the-wall, yet another foreign takeover hardly raises an eyebrow?

It's clear to me that the western world, in the early years of the 21st century, has two types of economic systems: capitalism for the working class and socialism for the rich. It's time to spread the socialist idea down the economic ladder, now that we have precedents like Fannie Mae, Freddie Mac and various bank bailouts around the world. Maybe there's an NDP leader somewhere who can make it happen.

With or without the NDP, the labour movement in Canada must remain politically alert and active because, in many ways, it represents the most effective bulwark against reactionary right-wing thinking that seeks to eliminate many social and economic advances. The disgraceful record of former president George W. Bush may spell the end of the right-wing domination in that country, but it continues to set the pace for Canada and Britain.

Canadians demonstrated a little independence from that trend, refusing to grant Stephen Harper his much-wanted majority for two consecutive elections. But it was close. Imagine if Harper and his Conservatives had held a majority back in the spring of 2003 when George W. Bush and his pals were claiming Saddam Hussein possessed weapons of mass destruction, supported al-Qaeda and threatened the security of the West. Harper would have sent thousands of Canadian troops into Iraq, many of whom would have returned to Canada racked and torn with their bodies in coffins.

We may be tied to the American economy in ways that both benefit and harm us, but we can and must follow an independent course in seeking peaceful solutions to reducing international tensions, protecting the environment, maintaining social programs for our citizens and making other choices that reflect Canadian values and tradition. I'm not suggesting that the left has all the answers to these problems, but it's the best damn one available right now.

SEVEN

Border Glitches

I don't know what kind of country Canada would be if it weren't cheek by jowl with the United States, but we all know it would be very different from what it is. Much of our social, political and economic life is intertwined with the U.S., so it's something of a miracle that Canada has managed to create such a distinctive character under those conditions.

Many of our efforts to separate ourselves from American policies and actions have been risky, especially when the administration of President George W. Bush ruled Washington. I remember the ridicule hurled at Prime Minister Chrétien when he refused to join Bush's "Coalition of the Willing" in the invasion of Iraq in 2003. Many Canadians on the right side of the political spectrum hurled charges of anti-Americanism at anyone who, as I did, questioned the existence of Saddam Hussein's weapons of mass destruction and noted that no one associated with the September 11 attacks was proven to have ties to the Iraqi dictator.

Even while Jean Chrétien stuck to his guns and refused to commit Canadian soldiers to the Iraqi adventure, Stephen Harper, Ontario Tory Premier Ernie Eves, Alberta Premier Ralph Klein and a gang of others harangued him for his decision. They seemed especially horrified when George W. Bush cancelled a planned trip to Ottawa in early May 2003 as punishment for Canada's acting like a sovereign nation instead of following Washington's lead, as though we were America's fifty-first state.

The grovelling to American interests by these politicians and business leaders was insulting to me and most Canadians. Not supporting the war, we were warned, would cost Canada investment and jobs. Even if it were true, was that reason enough to get involved with the killing and maiming of Iraqi civilians and the destruction of a society? Shouldn't moral judgement, fixed principles and accepted values dictate the conduct of world nations, and not greed for the almighty dollar?

Five years later the world turned its back on Bush and his policies and the U.S. was looking for ways to extricate itself from Iraq with some degree of honour. Our economy was clearly outstripping our southern neighbour's and Jean Chrétien, on the topic of Iraq at least, was being praised for his wisdom and courage. President Bush, as history will confirm, and historians will shake their heads in wonder over, squandered an incredible amount of international goodwill during his term. He tossed away sympathy and support for his country following the attacks of 9/11. He also came into office when the U.S. boasted a substantial budget surplus, and two terms later left with a deficit that is almost beyond comprehension, measured in trillions of dollars.

The effects of these blunders spilled beyond his country's borders, much of it splashing, as usual, onto Canada. Our closely linked economies mean that we benefit when times are good in the United States and suffer when times turn bad. Today, however, Canada is suffering in frightening new ways that go beyond economics to include our civil liberties and our traditional tolerance for varying views and cultures.

Our close relationship with the U.S. brings both concerns and benefits, and much depends on balancing one against the other. This has caused problems with Canadian unions. The creation of the CAW, which split from the UAW in 1984, is the most dramatic example, but it's not the only one.

The decision to launch a Canadian auto workers' union independent of the American organization generated amazement and anger in some quarters. The Auto Pact had unified the industry, critics noted; why would we want to split the union? Bob White and I, along with other union leaders who put their careers and necks on the line, were criticized inside and outside the union movement for suggesting a split with the UAW. We risked (and actually gave up) tens of millions of dollars in union funds held in UAW coffers to strike out on our own.

Was it an ego trip on our part? No, it was a necessity. The UAW was trying to impose U.S. strategies, U.S. policies and even U.S. laws on Canadian workers. We needed a union that reflected our own needs, circumstances and culture. That's why we had to launch our own union, subject to Canadian law and dedicated to the rights of Canadian workers. It didn't make a damn bit of difference who owned the plants that employed our workers. Americans owned and ran the plants, but so what? Did that mean the workers were subject to American rules? If so, workers at Honda and Toyota plants in Canada would have been subject to rules made and enforced in Japan, and how far do you think that idea would have flown?

The story of the creation of the Canadian Auto Workers union is well known by anyone who has seen the National Film Board of Canada movie *Final Offer* (1985) that tracked the back-and-forth exchanges between the American UAW leadership and UAW Canada, led by Bob White. The break with the U.S. parent union still stands as one of the most dramatic and successful actions taken by any trade union to achieve its own goals.

It all came down in 1984, but five years before the split happened I knew it was inevitable. In late 1979 Chrysler went to the U.S. Congress looking for financial assistance to get through the recession. The government agreed, but only if the union accepted wage concessions, which UAW President Doug Fraser promised to do. The concessions, Fraser informed us, had to include Canadian workers as well.

This was a load of crap, and all of us in Canada tried to explain to Fraser why he couldn't do this. For one thing, the American workers could vote against any representatives or senators who opposed the union and its members. Canadians couldn't; we were told to shut up and accept an American-made law that hit us right in the wallet. Plus we had universal free health care, while American employers were paying large insurance premiums for medical coverage for workers and their families. We had different labour legislation, different conditions for legal strikes and on and on. Yet Congress, with UAW support, was telling us to fall into step and accept the same non-negotiated unratified deal as the American workers.

We refused, and I participated in negotiations with Doug Fraser and the rest of the UAW people from Detroit, who were putting enormous pressure on us to accept the same concessions as their American members. Fraser, who up to this point had been a good friend of Bob White and the Canadian union generally, wrapped himself in the American flag. Trying to explain our position, Bob White said we would discuss any demands from the Canadian government to make wage concessions but we'd be damned if we would let the U.S. government dictate them to us.

This set the Americans off on a tirade. Solidarity? Brotherhood? Not around that table. "Well, fuck you, Canadians," one UAW executive member said. "If you're not going to make the sacrifice with us, then we're going to demand that all the jobs come over here to Detroit, and Chrysler Canada will be gone." Another UAW leader added, "If the American Congress had meant to exempt Canadians, it would have said so. It didn't, so the legislation includes Canada"—as if the U.S. Congress were empowered to pass laws applying to Canada.

We held our ground, the Americans made their concessions, and eventually things between us and the UAW in Detroit were patched over. But I knew from that day forward something else would come along that none of us in Canada could ignore unless we chose to give up our claims to be citizens of a sovereign country.

Through the early years of the 1980s the UAW began backtracking on many aspects of their agreements with the Detroit automakers. Their negotiations involved concessions on wages and benefits that we in Canada could not and did not agree to, yet we were instructed to accept them regardless. Instead we struck GM in the fall of 1984 in pursuit of a wage settlement more in line with the situation in Canada than the one that the UAW had earlier accepted. The American union ordered us to rubber-stamp their deal. We refused and won a better contract for Canadian workers, making our eventual separation from the UAW inevitable.

On a tour of Japan that Bob White and I made some time after our split with the UAW, Japanese union and management representatives expressed amazement that we had been under the direction of a union headquarters outside of Canada. Unionized workers in Japan would never agree to take direction from leaders in Korea, and vice versa. Canada is the only country in the world whose organized workers belong to unions headquartered in another country. Half of all union members in this country's private sector report to headquarters in the U.S. The way I see it, we may have a branch plant mentality when it comes to business, but we neither need nor should have one when the rights of workers are involved.

When Bob White, Bob Nickerson, Sam Gindin and I, backed by the overwhelming majority of staff and local union leaders, severed our ties with the UAW to launch CAW/TCA, we expected the animosity to fade and the two unions to create a mutually beneficial relationship. We were different entities in different countries, perhaps, but we did similar work for the same employers. Why not share our knowledge and strategies to benefit everyone? Bitterness remained between Bob White and his American counterpart Owen Bieber for a long time, but when these two men moved on, I expected the hostility to dissolve. It didn't. The Americans still had a burr under the saddle.

For a period of time under new UAW President Stephen Yokich, the relationship improved to the point where I invited him to speak at a CAW collective bargaining convention in Toronto. Without any advance notice, he made a plea to CAW local leaders to rejoin the UAW. I was furious, as was the total leadership, and our relationship cooled even more.

There has been too much political insecurity among the top executive of the UAW for them to discuss co-ordinated efforts on international trade and other related concerns. Current UAW President Ron Gettelfinger has been reluctant to take an international view of auto workers' concerns. I suggested, for example, that each union send delegates to sit in on the other union's corporate council meetings, conferences and conventions, enabling both organizations to gain a wider understanding of the needs and concerns of the other's members, but the invitation was ignored.

The Americans may still be licking their wounds over the split, but the CAW has had its own beefs. We've been critical of some UAW decisions, in particular their acceptance of a two-tier wage system and abandonment of retiree health benefits. The two-tier wage system seems to have caught on in the U.S. and could all too easily be adapted by Canadian employers. Under the system, current workers continue to receive the previously negotiated wage levels while new employees are paid wages that are half or even less than those of senior workers performing the same job. The CAW rejected the two-tier system completely.

The two-tier wage system in American auto contracts started at Michigan auto parts supplier Delphi Corporation. When General Motors spun off its auto parts operations, leaving the company primarily an assembler of vehicles and core components such as engines and transmissions, Delphi became the largest auto parts manufacturer in the world, yet from the outset it struggled to make a profit. Its American operations lost billions of dollars while elsewhere in the world Delphi proved profitable.

In 2005 Steve Miller was hired as the new CEO of Delphi and quickly took the company into Chapter 11 bankruptcy in the States. Under Chapter 11 protection, the company began negotiating new contracts with the UAW, which led to the two-tier wage system. I soon predicted that the Delphi settlement, which I referred to as the "Delphi Disease," would spread through the rest of the auto parts industry and eventually to the Big Three.

Sadly, I was proven to be correct as two-tier wage settlements began to be adopted in new UAW agreements with auto parts companies. In response, our union called a meeting of CAW auto parts staff and local union leadership in St. Thomas, Ontario, where I recommended a resolution clearly stating that the CAW would not accept two-tier wages in our bargaining.

The two-tier concept did eventually spread to automakers, and in fall 2007 the UAW ratified a system for new hires that reduced wages for some jobs in GM plants to half the level earned by current employees. The CAW refused even to discuss the idea for Canadian workers. There are other ways for automakers to save money than by taking cash out of the pockets of employees on the line. Let's remember, by the way, that parts suppliers and auto assembly plants in Canada already enjoy a saving over their U.S. counterparts because they do not have to cover most health care costs for employees.

We were critical of decisions made at the UAW head office back when we were the Canadian arm of the union and we resisted orders to report to the UAW leadership. This was a union, after all, not a dictatorship. Today, the CAW remains open to comments on its decisions by the UAW, including whatever criticism they may wish to make. They choose to remain silent, although they have made it clear that they have little or no tolerance for CAW criticism of UAW leadership decisions.

By 2008, more than criticism was flowing out of the UAW. I began receiving a regular tide of requests from members of the UAW asking and sometimes imploring Canadians to start pressing our influence on the UAW leadership. We had no influence on the UAW, yet many American unionists wanted the CAW to somehow change the direction of the UAW because they believed in our philosophy. A Canadian union setting terms for American workers—wouldn't that have been a stunning turn of events?

Cross-border union challenges have not been restricted to the CAW versus the UAW, of course. Any time an American-led union finds a reason to disagree with its Canadian office, it feels it can act with impunity, even firing an entire executive board that has been voted in and supported by Canadian union members. That's what the Washington headquarters of LIUNA, the Laborers' International Union of North America, did in 2007. A representative flew from Washington into Toronto and fired every executive member and all staff members except one of Local 183, one of LIUNA's biggest and most active locals. It was done without recourse, and the Ontario Labour Relations Board approved the slaughter.

Can you imagine the CEO of a corporation arriving in town, making claims of impropriety and kicking its entire executive group out the door without hell being raised and an enormous severance agreement paid? Yet LIUNA Local 183 President Tony Dionisio and his staff were gone in an instant. He had disagreed with head office and would not toe the U.S. leadership line. Tony Dionisio and his colleagues learned very quickly how far the Washington leadership of LIUNA would go to exert control over its Canadian members. After firing Dionisio and his colleagues, American LIUNA leaders then harassed and charged them with various offences, costing them thousands of dollars in legal fees. The charges were false and later dropped, but the victory came at huge personal cost to Tony and his associates. Rubbing salt into the wounds, LIUNA used money from Local 183 to fund its actions, money that Tony and his team had earned for the union while building Local 183 into one of the most powerful and financially stable LIUNA locals in Canada and U.S.

Tony and some of his colleagues decided to establish a Canadian construction workers union to give Canadian members of LIUNA and other unorganized construction workers the opportunity to join a Canadian-based union. I recommended, and the national executive board authorized, a $1 million loan from the CAW to the new union effort and wished Tony, who has done wonderful things for the Portuguese community and for disabled workers, the best of luck. The Americans didn't like the idea, and let us know. Later the CAW national executive board, supported by CAW council delegates, authorized an additional $5 million loan to assist the Canadian union. Terence O'Sullivan, the American LIUNA president, went ballistic.

"We must ensure," O'Sullivan sputtered, "that anytime, anywhere an organization takes us on it feels the power and the fury of our proud, strong and united international union." O'Sullivan expressed his union's "power and fury" by telling all 800,000 members of LIUNA to boycott every CAW-made vehicle, and he listed 20 models from Ford, Chrysler, GM and Suzuki (ignoring the fact that some models were assembled both in the U.S. and Canada). LIUNA lease agreements for CAW-made cars, O'Sullivan fumed, would not be renewed.

O'Sullivan's tantrum did nothing except demonstrate both his dictatorial style and his general ignorance of the auto industry. Even if LIUNA members followed his orders and refused to purchase one of the models he listed, this wouldn't prevent them from buying American-made cars and trucks assembled with parts made at CAW-certified plants. The only effective way for O'Sullivan and LIUNA to boycott the CAW would be to order its members to drive nothing but Toyotas, Hondas, Nissans, Mercedes-Benzes and other non-North American-owned cars—and wouldn't that create an interesting response from U.S. workers?

When asked to comment on O'Sullivan's outburst, I replied that I had no control over anything the LIUNA president said or did, and left it at that. I continue to support any plan by Tony Dionisio to give workers an opportunity to join a Canadian union, and my recommendation was fully supported by over 800 elected CAW council delegates. Given a truly free choice, I believe, a majority of LIUNA members would cross over to the Canadian union, assuming they could do so without losing a substantial portion of their pension and health care benefits. The American union's power in this area was substantially more effective than its childish boycott of CAW-made vehicles. LIUNA held an estimated $1 billion in pension funds, much of it earned by Canadian members. Leave the union, O'Sullivan and his cronies warned, and we keep the billion bucks. In an industry with as many employment gyrations and economic uncertainties as construction, that's a very threatening weapon.

Here's my take on the entire subject: *Canadians should be responsible for their own destiny.* Who is going to argue with that? But many Canadian unionized workers lack this fundamental independence. When a Canadian union or executive group expresses serious disagreement with a ruling coming out of its U.S. head office, they are reminded that the U.S. head office controls the workers' pension benefits, strike funds and other assets. That's the weapon used by some American unions to ensure that Canadian workers follow their rules, even when those rules either infringe on the rights of the workers or conflict with Canadian law. The common response from an American union to complaints from its Canadian arm is "Shut up and sit down." Bob White and I and the leadership of our union in 1984 refused to accept that kind of order from the UAW, and the success of the CAW serves as a model for other Canadian union leaders to employ, if they choose.

I have nothing against so-called international unions, although they have proven time after time to be simply American unions with branch offices in Canada and subservient to the U.S. leadership. I have already pointed out that unions anywhere else in the world would never agree to have their headquarters in another country or to submit to decisions made outside their borders. Nor would unionized workers in other countries allow their dues payments to be deposited in the accounts of their affiliated union in another country and have to ask approval for any significant expenditure to support these same workers, including expenses for strike defence. Yet that's exactly what happens in Canada, again and again.

I strongly believe that when the elected Canadian leadership of an American-based union makes a democratic decision, supported by their members, to establish an independent Canadian union or to join an established Canadian union, this decision should be acceptable to the labour movement generally and be supported by the Canadian Labour Congress.

Before anyone hangs an "anti-American" sign around my neck, let me make a few things clear. I enjoy working with Americans and I am an admirer of many of their historic achievements. My most serious criticism of the country relates to policies of the George W. Bush administration, which hardly makes me either unique or anti-American. After all, when Bush left office three out of four Americans felt the same way toward him as I did. The war in Iraq, launched without any evidence to justify the invasion, will mark, I believe, one of the most disastrous decisions undertaken by the leader of a democratic nation in history. Saddam Hussein was a brutal dictator who killed thousands of his own people and needed to be dealt with by the international community. But we in the West have tolerated brutal dictators for decades without launching an all-out invasion based on trumped-up charges, twisted half-truths and outright lies.

The full impact of the Iraq war has yet to be measured. We can count the bodies, including over 4,000 American soldiers killed and many thousands more wounded physically, mentally and emotionally. Of course, the toll on the Iraqi people has been much, much greater. Official estimates cite 100,000 Iraqi deaths since the U.S. invasion, while some human rights watchers peg the toll much higher, at perhaps over 1 million dead. We can count the financial cost: hundreds of billions of dollars that have deepened the enormous debt carried by the U.S. government. We can speculate about the damage the war created internationally, on the weakened power of the United Nations and on the damaged international prestige of the U.S. And it all adds up to disaster.

The CAW opposed the Iraq invasion from the beginning, which at the time put us in conflict with union members on both sides of the border. No one on the CAW executive was more outspoken in his opposition to the war than my successor Ken Lewenza. In rallies and debates throughout the Windsor area, Ken stood his ground against those who believed in the weapons of mass destruction, and that Bush and Cheney were correct in claiming that Saddam Hussein supported the terrorists associated with 9/11. "Our union's history is about peace," Lewenza kept repeating, "and we're going to defend peace in the world no matter what."

Afghanistan is similar to Iraq in some ways and different in others. As I write this, Canadian soldiers are in their seventh year of war in Afghanistan; more than 100 have died and several hundred more have suffered injuries. Sometimes you don't have to read about these horrific events. Sometimes they happen very close to home. The son of Hemi Mitic, my former assistant, lost both his feet to a land mine in Afghanistan. Multiply this tragedy a few hundred times, add up the misery that conflict is causing the Afghans, and the entire exercise appears futile and catastrophic.

I supported assisting other countries under the auspices of the United Nations in rooting out terrorist camps in Afghanistan, and I support the young men and women in the Canadian forces who risk life and limb over there. But if we believe that a few thousand soldiers can change a tribal culture that is ruled by warlords, and that has repelled foreigners for more than 1,000 years, we're crazy. Thirty years ago, the Russians tried the same thing using much more power than is being applied now, and the Afghans sent them home with their tails between their legs. In my opinion, the longer we remain in Afghanistan the more we'll foster hatred for the West in that country—the same kind of hatred that spawned Osama bin Laden and the fanatics responsible for 9/11, the explosions in Madrid and London, and the suicide bombers intent on killing Canadian troops and aid workers.

* * *

It's on the subject of trade policies that I have the most serious problem with both Americans and their critics here in Canada.

On one hand, I become as furious as most Canadians when the U.S. takes a tough stand on importing our steel, wheat, softwood lumber and other products. When the subject comes up, people wring their hands and say, "Isn't it terrible? The Americans pretend to be free traders and here they are working like hell to protect their market," and they're right. On the other hand, I admire the Americans' determination. They're choosing to support American businesses and save jobs in their country. What's wrong with that? They may push the limit and go over it from time to time, but eventually things settle down and we all get on with our lives. So good on them.

Why can't the political leadership in this country take a similar stand? We're told again and again that it's not the Canadian way, that good relationships depend on quiet diplomacy, and if we push too hard the Americans could retaliate. I love the kinder, gentler Canadian way, but I was never taught that being Canadian involves acting like wimps whenever we're challenged. And while relationships may indeed depend on diplomacy, they also depend on mutual respect. Retaliation? I don't believe the Americans will retaliate to the extent that we fear. Will they stop buying our oil and gas, to which they have guaranteed access under NAFTA?

One of the keys to improving our international trade performance is to reduce our dependence on a single trading partner. The U.S. market still accounts for more than 75 percent of Canada's total exports.

We're fortunate to live next to a dedicated democracy and the world's largest, most dynamic market. But surely we are all free to criticize our neighbour from time to time without the risk of being tarred with a brush out of a pail labelled "anti-American."

The biggest difficulty in handling trade problems with the U.S. stems from their willingness to ignore or rewrite the rules of the game, whenever it suits their national interests. Once again for the record: I'm fully aware of the role that trade can play in improving the economy of all nations, but it cannot be left entirely to the unregulated decisions of global corporations. That's why I want *managed trade* that recognizes the responsibility of all trading partners to respect the position of others in the game.

We saw an example of American trade policy in action and the usual ineffective Canadian response in February 2009 when the U.S. Congress attached "Buy American" conditions to the massive economic stimulus bill that President Obama was proposing. Provisions in the bill could limit Canada's steel exports to the U.S., supposedly protected under NAFTA.

Prime Minister Stephen Harper and his cabinet, who were still babbling about Canada's strong economy when the whole damn system was crumbling around them, had no idea how to handle this situation beyond sending Mike Wilson, our ambassador to the U.S., to say, in effect, "Hey, guys, take it easy on us, okay?" But it was too late to shut the barn door. The horse was already galloping down the lane. Harper and his people, and most of the federal politicians before them, have done a lousy job of positioning Canada in the overall U.S. economy. They were still naively pretending that the provisions of NAFTA would protect Canada from the effects of U.S. protectionism. That didn't happen with the softwood lumber fiasco, did it? And it sure won't happen in this case, either. It would be much better for our officials to fight fire with fire: they should enact strong "Buy Canadian" policies to guide our own public procurement. Then we would have a little bargaining power. That would be far more effective than simply hoping that everyone else in the world will finally start "playing by the rules," just like the Canadians always do.

This is not an easy problem to solve, I know. Other countries besides the U.S. are taking action to cover their own economic butts. When U.S. politicians were waving flags and demanding protection for their iron and steel industries, countries like India, Russia and China were slapping high tariffs on the same materials crossing their borders. It's only Canadians who insist on behaving like the Boy Scouts of world trade, always following the rules no matter what.

Former Air Canada CEO Robert Milton, a self-declared "intensely proud American," once described his view of the U.S. and Canada: "The difference between Canada and the United States is that Canada plays for a tie . . . and America plays for a kill."

Maybe our relationship with the United States would be more successful on various fronts if we all bore that difference in mind.

EIGHT

Up in the Air:
Canadian Airlines and Air Canada

"The thing I like about working with airline people," I said to Bob White many years ago, "is that even when they're mad at you they're incredibly polite."

I was a little premature.

This was before Gerry Schwartz tried to buy Canadian Airlines and Air Canada, before I tried to solve problems of seniority among unionized employees of the two amalgamated airlines, before Air Canada filed for bankruptcy protection, and before any checked baggage with my name on it risked being flown to China when I was flying to Toronto.

The people who work for airlines are still incredibly polite, especially given the stressful circumstances they work, and the often-rude customers they have to deal with. And the difference I had with some of those workers, through the tortuous and seemingly endless course of airline restructuring, have long since been resolved. But my encounters with the endless complications and crises of the airline business remain fresh in my memory. As with all complex problems, there was a lesson to be learned in settling the matter.

One lesson? Make that a dozen or so.

* * *

Years after the takeover of Canadian Airlines by Air Canada in 1999, complaints about various aspects of the deal were still being tossed back and forth. Some people involved in the process continue to harbour resentment against me, the CAW, Robert Milton and a gang of other participants. The near-bankruptcy of Air Canada in 2003 launched a whole new series of charges, many directed toward employees who happened to be members of the CAW.

At times, I wondered what I had gotten into when dealing with airline people. My background was in auto parts and auto assembly before I was selected to become Bob White's assistant at the UAW. What the hell was I doing with airline schedules and in-flight service issues? Later, when I became immersed in the industry as CAW president, I stopped asking what I was doing there and began wondering why so many airline people were angry with me. By this time I was caught in the middle of a takeover battle between Gerry Schwartz and Robert Milton over who would control the two airlines, and in trying to be fair to both CAW members and their employers, I made an error in judgment.

As I mentioned earlier, when serving in the role of union representative and bargainer, I never gave a damn about who owned the company I was negotiating with. Ownership was irrelevant. I focused on wages, pensions and benefits, workers' rights and job security. Those are the important concerns for representative unions, and as long as management bargained in good faith and lived up to its side of the contract, I didn't care if the owners were in Toronto, Thailand or Timbuktu. Much of this attitude, of course, grew out of my automotive background. When you know the shots concerning Canadian workers will be called in Detroit, ownership becomes a non-issue. Did they live up to the collective agreement? That's all that really mattered to me.

By the summer of 1999, it had become obvious to all that Canada could not support its two flagship airlines. Canadian Airlines International (CAI) and Air Canada were dividing international destinations in a manner that made it difficult, if not impossible, for either to establish financial stability. The weak sister was clearly CAI. Despite repeated sacrifices by its union members, the company could never get its footing. Some of its unions went through multiple sets of concessions, accepting lower wages and tougher working conditions, and giving up long-held benefits. Nothing seemed to work.

In 1996 Kevin Benson, the newly appointed CEO of CAI, demanded an across-the-board 10 percent wage cut from all unionized workers on top of previously agreed concessions. This was unacceptable, and I joined Anne Davidson, president of Local 1990, and her bargaining committee, in debates with other CAI unions, pointing out that the airline could not survive by constantly demanding that its unionized employees reduce their wages. The problems at CAI had practically nothing to do with labour costs. "If wage cuts were the solution," I argued at one point, "Canadian Airlines would be the most successful company of its kind in the world, because it has substantially reduced the size of its payroll three times already!"

My argument made no impact on the other unions. Starting with the pilots, followed by the machinists and flight attendants, each of the CAI unions gave in to management demands, taking yet another cut in wages and benefits, and agreeing yet another time to work longer hours and accept fewer benefits.

At the CAW, we held firm. Unionized employees have given enough, we said. Our wages, benefits and productivity were not the problem. The problem was both deeper and wider, starting with top management and including the enormous amounts of money paid to American Airlines for the use of its reservations system—American had been using its investment in CAI as a cash cow for years—and the duplication of services with Air Canada.

Standing your ground in the face of threats from management is never easy. Standing your ground against fellow unionists who are siding with management is agonizing.

In the eyes of some of those union members, the CAW was consciously attempting to bankrupt Canadian Airlines, which was nonsense. We *were* consciously trying to force management, employees and the government to acknowledge what everybody knew to be true: the airline's crisis had nothing to do with employee pay, but deep wage cuts was the only solution management could come up with.

Things turned vicious. CAW leaders soon learned not even to try flying on Canadian because the airline reservation clerks would say the flight was booked solid. If they obtained a reservation and arrived at the departure lounge they would be asked to step aside for other passengers, then told that the flight was full. And if they actually made it aboard the aircraft, flight attendants would make them feel unwelcome. It was all a concentrated effort to punish the CAW for doing its job—representing workers against unfair treatment by management.

My worst moment occurred when some CAI pilots listed my address and telephone number on the Internet. They were wrong; it was actually the home of my former wife. We had been separated for five years, but the phone listing in Pickering, Ontario, remained under my name. After the address was posted, tires on three cars parked in the driveway were slashed in broad daylight. When a threat was made to bomb the home where my children and grandchildren lived, local police took it seriously enough to provide surveillance and protection. The CAW's efforts to do nothing more than negotiate the best deal for employees, no matter which side won, triggered a storm of ill will and a distortion of our goals. Even the federal government got into the act by tabling a bill in Parliament that would force our members to vote on the airline's offer whether they wanted to or not.

I stood my ground, but after several weeks Anne Davidson came to me and said, "Buzz, I believe it's time to face facts. Other union members have given up the fight. Now, instead of demanding a 10 percent cut, CAI is willing to reduce it to a 3.6 percent reduction in wages for everyone, including the other unions, if CAW will sign the deal."

I agreed to submit the idea to the members, who ratified it overwhelmingly. Other Canadian unions benefited from our position, but we all knew the contract was a band-aid. As long as the airline industry had excess capacity from two competing operations, pointlessly duplicating half-empty flights, another crisis was inevitable. It arrived in the spring of 1999, when CAI executives began publicly admitting that the country could not support both airlines, and CAI could see no end to its financial problems.

With CAI slipping toward insolvency yet again, we drafted a program that called on the federal government to purchase a $300 million equity position in Canadian, leave foreign ownership restrictions in place, and take steps to end the destructive competition between CAI and Air Canada. We presented it to David Collenette, the federal transport minister, in early May, stressing the need for immediate action. Collenette agreed that something must be done, and fast.

Nothing happened for four months, proving that while the federal government may have been dealing with a jet-powered industry, their own operations were hitched to a horse and buggy. To be fair, one of the hurdles to be overcome was the federal Competition Act, which made it difficult, if not impossible, for the airlines to merge. Also, when Air Canada ceased its status as a Crown corporation 10 years earlier, one of the directives of the deal limited any single individual or entity to owning no more than 10 percent of the airline. In addition, foreign ownership of a Canadian airline was limited to 25 percent. So there weren't many options available.

Collenette finally took action in mid-August. With a single stroke of the pen he lifted the rules of the Competition Act for 90 days, opening the door to merger talks.

Gerry Schwartz and his group at Onex, who saw an opportunity to purchase and combine both airlines into one money-making company, had anticipated this move. Almost as soon as Collenette's decision was announced, Schwartz asked for a meeting with me and my assistant, Peggy Nash.

I liked Schwartz right away. Bright, affable and low-key, he was not the brusque insensitive entrepreneur I expected. He asked for my input on the situation, wanted to know the mood and attitude of the employees we represented in both companies, and actually enlisted my assistance in making things work. My involvement was critical because Schwartz had been closely associated with the federal Liberals for many years, and he needed outside support to counter charges that the whole takeover deal by Onex was the result of backroom discussions in Ottawa. He also needed to know, of course, that possible resistance from unionized employees would be one less issue to worry about.

My concern was to avoid layoffs where possible when the two companies got together, and to deal with the thorny question of seniority. When two firms merge, it's rarely a battle of equals. One company invariably has more money, more employees or more weight to throw around than the other, creating a winner-and-loser situation. When it comes to determining seniority, the "winner" takes the same position vis-à-vis employees of the other company as Roman generals took after they defeated their enemy on the battlefield: We won and you lost, now accept your fate. This means that employees on the "winning" side line up in order of seniority, and those on the "losing" side fall in behind them. In this scenario a "loser" with 30 years' service can find herself behind a "winner" with less than a year's experience.

The CAW had never accepted that formula. In a merger of this kind, we argued, the employee lists should be merged. The only criterion to determine seniority should be the hire date of each worker, regardless of which company he or she worked for. Otherwise a basic principle of the labour movement would be violated.

When I told Schwartz of our stand, he shrugged and said, "I can live with it if you can." Then he added: "But you'll take a lot of hell from some of your own union members when this goes through."

Beyond the question of seniority, as important as it was, we had other concerns. We wanted a commitment to no forced layoffs, and assurances that none of the work performed by our union would be moved out of Canada, that wage parity would be achieved among CAW members at the new company, and that retirement and severance agreements would be enhanced. Schwartz agreed in principle to all of these demands.

After settling with Schwartz we went to Montreal for a breakfast meeting with Air Canada CEO Robert Milton, who brought along Patrick Heinke, his senior director of labour relations, and Claude Saillon, another executive. Before the session started, we agreed with Milton and his crew that some things would remain confidential between us while other topics could be discussed at a media briefing afterwards. The "confidential" tag would be hung on any specific proposals regarding CAW wages, benefits, employment contracts and similar subjects that Milton floated during our meeting. Milton and his PR department had agreed to this going in, but afterwards when I talked to the media about other matters Milton hit the roof, accusing me of breaking a pledge and revealing confidential data, which was totally untrue. I discussed only the things we had agreed upon.

Using a system that enabled him to leave messages on every Air Canada employees' company phone line, Milton howled that I had intentionally betrayed a promise not to discuss these matters publicly. Why would he make the claim? I saw it as a means of undermining me and the CAW with the airline's unionized employees.

Over much of that autumn, while Schwartz and Milton polished their offers to shareholders and made their pitches in the media, the CAW team tried to nail down each airline's stand on our demands for wage parity, combined seniority, job security and other matters. While Gerry Schwartz always seemed to find time for me, Robert Milton refused to take my calls, constantly referring me to Patrick Heinke. By early November, we had negotiated a settlement on all outstanding issues with Onex except the commitment not to send union work out of the country. I informed Heinke that we were close to an agreement with the Onex group and that we wanted a similar agreement from Air Canada.

In situations like this one, if you're not prepared to play hardball you shouldn't be in the game, and I applied a little pressure in my conversation with the Air Canada executive. "I'm prepared to hold a press conference to say we have reached an agreement with Onex," I informed Heinke. Revealing this would benefit Schwartz, since it would indicate that he faced no serious labour problems if he succeeded in acquiring both airlines, which would encourage shareholders to sell him their stock. "But if Air Canada agrees with the Onex deal," I added, "I'll inform the media that both sides have promised to uphold our concerns. Then the decision will be in the hands of the shareholders and the Government of Canada without labour being an issue."

Heinke said Air Canada could meet our concerns, and he would send me a letter by noon the next day confirming this.

I couldn't believe it. "That's crazy," I said. "How can you send us a letter agreeing to a deal when we haven't met to discuss the issues yet?"

"We think we can put something together you'll be satisfied with," Heinke replied.

The letter arrived as he promised, but it included neither a complete review of the issues at hand nor any sign of commitment from Air Canada to solve our differences. He might as well have sent a blank piece of paper.

I immediately called Gerry Schwartz. "If you sign a letter that your new company will not move any CAW work out of the country," I said, "we'll hold a press conference to announce that Onex and the CAW have reached an agreement." I had just handed Gerry Schwartz a gift, because the news would pave the way for success in convincing shareholders to accept the Onex deal. We met, signed the letter, and I walked directly from there to a press conference.

This was dicey stuff, I knew, and I chose my words carefully. "As national president of the CAW," I said, "I am endorsing the Onex proposal to purchase Air Canada and Canadian Airlines International." Based on negotiations that had taken place, I went on, the union had bargained to protect CAW employees at Air Canada, Air Canada's regional carriers, Canadian Airlines International and Canadian Airlines' regional carriers.

It was a complex arrangement, negotiated in the midst of many other activities being carried out by Onex and the Air Canada group, and I listed the terms one by one:

- no forced layoffs at any of the airlines, including the regional carriers
- no forced relocations at Air Canada or Canadian Airlines
- minimal forced relocations at the regional carriers, if we couldn't work out an arrangement that would allow them to move to the national carrier
- wage parity between the two carriers to be carried out in two stages: 50 percent by January 2001 and the balance by January 2002
- no union work to be moved out of Canada
- combined seniority lists
- enhanced retirement and severance benefits

The document, I pointed out, took effect if Onex became owner of the two airlines, and only after it went back to the respective bargaining committees with CAI and Air Canada and was ratified by members of the combined airline.

Why go public with the statement at all? Why not hold onto it and let Schwartz and Milton and their teams battle it out? These were the questions fired at me later. My reasons were basic to our negotiation strategy. We told both sides from the beginning that we would go public as soon as one or the other provided a signed document. It was a means of leverage, and we hoped other unions involved would do the same thing if they managed to get a signed agreement.

The deal also represented a major breakthrough for labour in mergers of this scope. Thanks to the leadership of Peggy Nash, CAW Transportation Director Gary Fane, Jo-Ann Hannah from our research department and other members of the CAW team, we were able to elevate the concerns of workers to those of shareholders on both sides.

This was important. Shareholders of both companies wanted to protect their investment, and were vocal in stating their objectives. Workers in both companies wanted to protect their jobs, their seniority and their hard-won benefits. Both sides had equally valid reasons for looking out for their interests. In previous situations similar to this one, the shareholders' concerns were always given more priority than those of the workers. The companies made a big deal out of driving up the price of the shares, trying to get shareholders on the other side to sell out for a better profit. Well, if management was working to earn shareholders and themselves billions in profits, we could work equally as hard to protect the most important asset the workers had—their jobs.

To his credit—and I don't believe this has been revealed until now—Gerry Schwartz offered the same deal that he and I had negotiated to the other unions at both CAI and Air Canada. Leaders of those unions did not reveal this offer publicly because, unlike me, they wanted to see which side won out before celebrating. If Schwartz won, they, not Buzz Hargrove, would be the champions of their own membership. Why give Buzz Hargrove credit for doing the job they were paid to do?

Gary Fane and I discussed an outline of the deals with the respective bargaining committees, noting that most of our concerns appeared to be satisfied. We had signed a tentative agreement with Onex, we explained, conditional on Schwartz taking control of the airlines and subject to a secret ballot ratification vote by CAW members. In any case, I said, there was no sense taking the proposals to the union members until we learned who was going to succeed in bringing the two companies together, Schwartz or Milton.

I assumed employees of both airlines would welcome news of the deal. Big mistake. During an interview on CTV, I was asked about ratification of the agreement. "This is not subject to ratification by the membership," I responded, "unless and until Schwartz owns the airline." It was an important point. You can't ratify something, I explained, based on possibilities; you need a deal with somebody in a position to make it stick, and until Onex acquired both airlines everything was supposition, even with Schwartz's signature on the paper.

"I'll offer the same deal to Robert Milton and his group," I added, "and if Air Canada agrees, I'll tell the transport minister that we don't care who assumes control because our members will be protected either way." But Air Canada refused to discuss the deal with me. They were determined to win the struggle with Onex their way, without any commitment to unionized staff.

Despite my assurances that I expected identical deals from both partners and thus didn't care who "won," Air Canada members of the CAW believed I was solidly in Gerry Schwartz's camp, helping him and his Onex partners take over Air Canada. Remember that nobody at Air Canada, especially Robert Milton, wanted to discuss any aspect of the deal in detail. So how could I work with them? Schwartz would talk with us, so we talked. When we had an agreement with CAI, I took Patrick Heinke at his word that Air Canada would match anything Onex proposed, and assumed they would. This wasn't playing favourites; it was just good negotiating.

But Air Canada employees saw a serious problem. Or at least some of them did. I suspect others were pushed in that direction by Robert Milton and his team, who used our negotiations with Onex as a lever in their takeover strategy. The fact that Air Canada employees would benefit equally if their employer agreed to the same terms as CAI didn't appear to carry any weight. Within a day or so of my announcing the arrangement with Schwartz, some Air Canada employees were sporting buttons declaring "BUZZ OFF!" And when a small group of Air Canada employees staged a demonstration at CAW headquarters, which is several miles away from the airport in Toronto, I saw the hand of Milton at work. The perception was strengthened when the demonstrators began chanting, "Robert Milton, he's our man! If he can't do it no one can!" They sounded like a high school football crowd, and the demo smelled to me like a corporate stunt. Somebody organized and paid for buses to carry the demonstrators there, for the signs to be waved, and for the pro-Milton chant, and I will never believe it was the workers alone.

On an Air Canada flight to Edmonton a couple of days later, the flight attendants and even the pilots let me know how unhappy they were with my apparent favouritism, sometimes with words, sometimes with an unpleasant attitude. This didn't bother me much, but when we landed it became clear that the Air Canada pilot had radioed ahead, announcing my arrival. As I walked into the terminal a crowd of Air Canada employees waved signs and called me every nasty name in the book. I stood and talked to them, explaining my position and how they might benefit. The pilots and crew on my flight came by, saw the group, and started the name calling all over again. I did my best to explain my position, waited for emotions to cool down, then went on my way.

Coming home the next day, I encountered a cabin crew who were just as frosty. All I could do was relax and accept it. When we arrived at Toronto and the door from the aircraft to the jetway opened, a CAW employee approached to inform me a large crowd was waiting for me in the terminal and they weren't there to wish me good luck.

There was no reason to subject the rest of the passengers to all the vitriol I expected to encounter, so I sat back in the seat and waited for everyone else to leave. Finally I rose and walked into the jetway, where a maintenance worker approached me. "The crowd in the airport is pretty mean," he said. "You can go up there and encounter them or, if you'd rather, follow me down these stairs outside and I'll drive you off airport property in one of our emergency vehicles."

Discretion, I recalled, is the better part of valour. I followed him down the stairs and rode off in his vehicle. I never learned his name but he was a warm, bright guy who happened to approve of my handling of the matter, agreeing that it didn't matter who owned the company as long as the workers' needs were met.

He wasn't alone, by the way. From time to time I met other Air Canada staff who shook my hand or even demonstrated on my behalf. For a few days, however, I was a pariah with most Air Canada workers, including some members of the CAW.

A few days later Peggy Nash and I attended an open meeting with Air Canada employees at an airport hotel in Toronto, drawing more than 500 people determined to lynch me, and almost as many media representatives, it seemed, to watch the execution. Each time I tried to explain my reasoning I attracted shouts of "Who the hell do you think you are?" and "You can't sign a deal without our vote!"

These people ignored the point that there was no deal until it was ratified, but most of those attending saw Gerry Schwartz as their enemy and Robert Milton as their saviour.

Did their hostility bother me? Of course it did. I prefer to be praised rather than pummelled. But it did not deter me, nor did it make me question my decision. Leadership is not about trying to make everybody happy, which is a recipe for failure. It's about examining, debating and evaluating the issues before reaching a decision, and the decision should deliver the greatest gain with the least sacrifice. If using the competition between Onex and Air Canada to bargain up the standards for all workers in the combined company, no matter who owned it, would accomplish this, so be it. That's what I believed and once the decision was made I moved on. I never looked over my shoulder. I had taken steps to protect the needs of our membership. That was my job. That's what I did. If some people failed to recognize the value and intent of my actions, this didn't make my decision wrong. Not in my eyes it didn't.

So I stood my ground. For several months, however, I chose never to check my luggage when I flew Air Canada.

Eventually it was all academic anyway. On November 5, 1999 when a Quebec court ruled against Onex on a technicality, Gerry Schwartz threw in the towel and the entire mess landed in Robert Milton's lap.

Had I bet the wrong horse? There was no bet and there were no horses. There was only my determination that, amidst the action and confusion about shareholders' rights and earnings, somebody pay attention to the rights of CAI and Air Canada employees who would be depended upon to keep things flying. Where CAW members were concerned this became my job, like it or not.

The biggest lesson I picked up was that members who express loyalty and even affection for their union can feel similar emotions for their employer, even when their employer is at odds with the people representing them. It's a "team spirit" kind of thing, I suppose. In this case, the Air Canada team swung their loyalty from the union to the company. I later learned that most of the airline union leaders had been looking for a solution that required no decision on their part.

This position was the safe one, but it showed no leadership. I preferred an attempt to influence the outcome so that, regardless of who won control of the company, our members' jobs, income and seniority based on date of hire were protected.

In the end, Air Canada management, led by Robert Milton, was forced to match the no-layoff agreement we had reached with Schwartz. So despite internal divisions, and Robert Milton's apparent efforts to manipulate his employees' loyalty to Air Canada, we were able to win an important victory.

Leadership of any kind, in any organization, is not always comfortable, nor should it be, yet difficult decisions must be made. In the case of CAI and Air Canada, seeking the best deal for union members should have been the position of every union leader involved. Unfortunately, most union leaders took the easy way out at what I believe was great expense to their members and their families.

When the dust settled, Robert Milton and his team led the way in merging the two airlines. The "one big family" mentality that Milton had cultivated (and exploited) during the takeover battle quickly disappeared, as Milton got back to the nitty-gritty business of squeezing his workers to maximize profits. Corporate executives always pretend that their workers are their most valuable asset—until it comes time to pay them decently. Once Milton's tactics became clear I expected the loyalty of Air Canada's unionized employees to swing in the other direction, back toward the CAW. And it did.

As expected, Air Canada workers took a "We won!" attitude, which meant Canadian Airlines employees were on the losing side. So why, the Air Canada employees began asking, should anyone from Canadian get ahead of us on the seniority list? There were other concerns, of course, but the seniority issue remained thorny for months after the official merger of the two airlines, especially among pilots. Reportedly, an Air Canada pilot and a former Canadian Airlines pilot almost got into a fistfight over seniority on the flight deck of an aircraft during preparations for takeoff. And throughout the spring of 2001 I received a torrent of e-mails, letters and telephone calls from former CAI pilots, whom I hardly counted among my closest friends. They were asking me to help settle the seniority debacle even though they were not members of the CAW, which represented passenger agents and maintenance workers. All I could tell them was that I fully agreed with their concerns. Beyond that, the situation was in the hands of an arbitrator. Eventually things were sorted out, but not before a flood of emotions spilled into every corner. Auto workers often live up to their image of being outspoken and volatile, but in terms of raw emotion nothing I saw in the auto industry was as explosive as the rage that dominated our airline unions during the Canadian Airlines/Air Canada merger.

Just as things settled down at the end of that summer, the world was stunned by the events of September 11, 2001. When the footage of aircraft hitting the World Trade Center was aired, the bottom dropped out of airline travel. Even with 80 percent of the domestic market, Air Canada could not handle the impact of 9/11, and in the spring of 2003 when world news channels began covering the SARS outbreak in Toronto, Canada's international air travel practically vanished overnight.

At the end of March 2003, Robert Milton calculated that the company needed a 22 percent across-the-board pay cut to stave off bankruptcy. Once the crisis was past, Milton promised, they would begin looking for a 22 percent improvement in productivity and restore the lost income. On March 31 he called our office and the offices of all the other Air Canada unions, explaining that he needed support from them to stave off bankruptcy. "If we can restructure the company, we can save the pensions and try to maintain income levels," was his message. "But if we slide into bankruptcy, it will be a feeding frenzy by the creditors. They'll carve up every asset in the company, including our pension fund reserves."

I had my differences with Milton, goodness knows, and I've never favoured assisting management to do their job, especially when it includes finding ways to meet its financial obligations. But 9/11 and SARS were exceptional circumstances. Canada 3000, the country's second-biggest airline, collapsed soon after 9/11 and several U.S. airlines, including giants American and United, were barely keeping their planes in the air. Air Canada approached all of its unions with a desperate appeal to "help" the company by accepting wage concessions and other measures. At CAW we were willing to show some flexibility (including forgoing a wage increase we were contractually entitled to in March 2003). But we knew full well that still more labour concessions could never save this company, given the horrible deterioration in the underlying fundamentals of the airline business. On April 1 Milton announced that Air Canada was seeking protection from its creditors under the Companies' Creditors Arrangement Act (CCAA). A company under CCAA protection loses a good deal of control over its financial situation. The objective of CCAA is to provide time for the firm to reorganize itself and keep operating free of the demands of creditors.

It took a full year for Air Canada to stumble through various financial solutions, bouncing back and forth between potential investors like a ping-pong ball. Opportunities and offers came and went, and whenever a major source of investment funds dried up, Robert Milton would find a way to blame the unions. The most notable example was Li Ka-Shing, a Hong Kong billionaire who kicked around the idea of becoming Air Canada's saviour through his Trinity Time Investments, but changed his mind when an impasse was reached over employee pensions.

In his offer, Li Ka-Shing insisted on cutting pension benefits to retirees and changing the company's pension plan from the long-established defined benefit structure, where pension responsibilities lie with the employer, to a defined contribution arrangement, which transfers the risk and responsibility to the employees. This was a deal I refused to accept, and my decision received a boost from the judge assigned to oversee the union negotiations under CCAA. "My dad was a retiree," Judge Warren Winkler said, ruling in favour of the unions, "and I do not know what would have happened if someone reached into his pocket and took money out of it." When he heard that, Li Ka-Shing closed his briefcase and walked away.

A furious Robert Milton blamed the unions for torpedoing the idea. It also can't have helped that he and lawyer-turned-airline-executive Calin Rovinescu wouldn't be receiving a promised $20 million payout from Li Ka-Shing based on the deal going through. And it should be pointed out that Li Ka-Shing had no intention of owning an airline. He publicly stated that he planned to hold Air Canada, if he won out, for a few short years before dumping it and pocketing a profit. Let's be up front about this: When global investors arrive on the doorstep of a troubled company pulling a trunk full of cash behind them, they're not motivated by humanitarian instincts. They're looking for profit opportunities, and that's fine—that's their business. The business of unions is to provide a balance by addressing the issues that don't interest the financiers, such as job security, pensions and benefits, equality and so on. Unions have as much right to pursue their goals as potential investors. The CAW's position was aimed at establishing equilibrium between two different motives, and despite what Robert Milton and others may feel about unions, both sides are essential to a civilized society.

When Li Ka-Shing pulled out, I was pummelled with e-mails, faxes and phone calls from hundreds of airline workers, accusing me of forcing the liquidation of Air Canada. Pilots, flight attendants, machinists and their spouses began threatening me all over again. On some occasions, I almost believed I was back at the McDonnell Douglas or Hiram Walker union meetings with members flicking lit cigarettes my way and others saying I should be lynched.

Having been through all this before, I didn't get too excited about the threats, although I became a little more cautious in my everyday activities, looking over my shoulder from time to time and avoiding being alone on the streets of Toronto at night. I remained under constant attack by other unions and by the media, who accused me of trying to destroy Air Canada. What would be the logic of that? I had spent my entire adult lifetime fighting for job security and an improved standard of living for working people. Now I supposedly wanted to be responsible for throwing thousands of workers out of a job? Not likely.

The best way of handling things, I believed, was to get involved in finding a solution, and I approached an old adversary with a request for him to put some money on the table and save Air Canada. Gerald Greenwald, whom I knew from Chrysler bankruptcy negotiations in the early eighties, headed up an investment firm out of New York City called Greenfield Investments. I had dealt with Gerald when his firm bought out the locomotive division of General Motors, which included the CAW-represented facility in London, Ontario. I had a lot of respect for Gerald and hoped he would be interested in investing in Air Canada. As it turned out, he was.

Greenwald agreed to become involved, and he permitted me to tell the media that I knew a number of investment firms interested in Air Canada, which reduced the impact of Li Ka-Shing's decision. The media challenged me to divulge the names and I refused, but I mentioned that one firm was headed by a guy whose first name was Gerald. As expected, the media became convinced that I meant Gerry Schwartz and that the "Buzz and Gerry Show" was about to start all over again. I let them speculate and never denied the story.

Meanwhile, people from GE Capital Aviation Services, Cerberus Capital Management, Deutsche Bank and other investors were flying in and out of Montreal, making pitches to Milton and Calin Rovinescu. In the middle of all this talk between big money and big business, I began asking who was looking after the interests of the employees. It appeared nobody was. We and the other Air Canada unions were kept in the dark for the most part, except for periodic announcements from Milton's office threatening that the airline would not survive unless its employees gave up another substantial cut in their earnings.

More than a year after filing for CCAA protection, Milton announced one last opportunity to save Air Canada remained. Deutsche Bank would provide $850 million in financing if Air Canada's unions would agree to $200 million in cuts. Without the cuts, Milton threatened, Air Canada would lose the Deutsche Bank deal and totally collapse.

Robert Milton had cried wolf! on several occasions before, and I remained sceptical about his claim. Li Ka-Shing and several others, I believed, were waiting on the sidelines to close a better deal than they had turned down earlier. If that didn't work, I suspected, the federal government would take whatever steps necessary to save the airline. Either way, the chances of Air Canada being liquidated, as Milton claimed, were pretty damn slim. Still, the bankruptcy trustee's offer was on the table and I had to at least examine it in detail.

According to the trustee appointed to oversee Air Canada's restructuring, $45 million of the cuts would have to come from CAW members. The other Air Canada unions agreed to the demands, which left the CAW to determine the airline's fate, according to the trustee. I suggested we calculate the amount of cuts we were willing to support on behalf of our members, and proposed $18.3 million.

We held our ground while the other six unions did their deals. When their agreements were reached we were the only holdouts, and neither Milton nor the CAW would budge. After several days without progress, Judge Winkler took charge and instructed Milton and me to meet with him at the Toronto Hilton. Confined in a hotel suite with the judge and a couple of assistants each, we had one full day to hammer out a deal. I had a lot of respect for Judge Winkler based on his comment regarding the pension situation, and looked forward to going head to head with Milton in pursuit of a solution.

As you might have gathered, I'm not a big fan of Robert Milton's management style or his general attitude toward unions. He is undoubtedly, however, immensely knowledgeable about airline operations and responsive to honest, down-to-earth negotiations. We spent a very long, uninterrupted day going back and forth with proposals and counterproposals, bargaining in the classic manner. By dinnertime we had a deal Milton could live with and that I could take back to the members. It involved sacrifices by CAW members, including the loss of a paid lunch, one week less vacation, and other changes, but it didn't add up to anywhere near $45 million in concessions. So the company's number-crunchers added a new line called "productivity savings" to their calculation of total CAW cost reductions and said we had reached the target. Our willingness to push negotiations to the limit resulted in substantially reduced pain for our members, and unlike those accepted by all the other unions the deal contained no permanent reduction in base wages. We shook hands and agreed that I would go downstairs and break the news to the media, who had been hanging around the hotel lobby all day.

"I'm elated to say we got this done," I told the press, adding that I had been impressed with Milton's sincerity and his commitment to reaching a solution acceptable to our union. Milton's office issued a press release stating, "The CAW faced some difficult issues, and we are pleased to have reached an agreement in time to meet the conditions of both the Deutsche Bank and [GE Capital Aviation Services] agreements." Later, he commented, "Unlike other union leaders I have encountered, [Buzz Hargrove] knows what he wants for his members, knows how to negotiate toward that goal, and knows when to stop talking and start working to obtain a satisfactory result. More important, he knows how to conclude a deal."

It was almost a love-in with Milton and CAW members at Air Canada. But it didn't last long.

After the Air Canada bankruptcy proceedings were launched, we kept thinking about all the creditors submitting claims for losses they had suffered as a result of the airline's financial status. We had a claim for forgone wage increases and the value of other concessions we had made. CAW Transportation Director Gary Fane asked, "Why couldn't we join the list and recover funds for our members?"

It sounded like a reasonable idea so we looked into it, only to be told it wouldn't work because the courts traditionally didn't recognize employees as creditors. Why not? I asked. Why couldn't workers make the same claim as anyone else who lost money due to a company's financial difficulties? Our lawyers submitted a claim and much to their surprise it was accepted, which prompted the other unions to follow suit. We were awarded a share of equity in the new Air Canada as compensation, which we promptly sold for $24 million to a group of investors hoping to make a quick buck off Air Canada's reincarnation. As far as I know, it was unprecedented for a union to obtain a decision like this.

I'll admit I was pleased with myself as well as everybody else involved in the legal challenge, including CAW staff, its legal department, and the local union leadership at Air Canada. Besides defying all the so-called experts who said it couldn't be done, we had obtained some much needed money for union members who had given up so much to save the airline. This was a real achievement with a significant payoff to our members. Memories of the hostility directed my way during the Canadian Airlines/Air Canada merger remained fresh in my mind, and I expected that our success at putting money in the pockets of employees who survived the CCAA period would add lustre to my image and soothe some old wounds from the days when Onex was trying to win Air Canada. They're gonna love me for this, I told myself. Boy, was I wrong.

When the cheque arrived at headquarters I contacted Sari Sairanen, then-president of CAW Local 2002, which represented our members at

Air Canada, along with Gary Fane and other members of the committee assigned to handle the settlement. "I don't care who gets the money," I instructed them, "or how you divide it, as long as it's fair and equal. Just get it into the hands of the members." The committee decided that every Air Canada employee, including those currently on layoff, should receive a share of about $3,000 each.

This was a heck of a deal. Air Canada people who had assisted in helping the company survive CCAA protection would be getting an unexpected $3,000 cheque in the mail. I felt great, and moved on to other things. A few weeks later I was in line at the airport for an Air Canada flight. As I approached the customer service agent who would check me in, I noticed her eyes shooting daggers at me. Uh-oh, I thought, what now?

"Where's our money?" she barked at me when I reached the counter.

"What money?" I asked, totally confused.

"The money from that settlement you said you got," she snarled.

I assured her that I didn't have it.

She not only refused to believe me, she refused to issue my boarding pass, leaving the woman in the next kiosk to hand it over.

Under the circumstances I decided not to check my bag, assuming it stood a good chance of spending a week or so in Shanghai, and began walking toward the boarding gate. The agent who issued the pass closed her kiosk and walked quickly to catch up with me. "Do you know what that's about?" she asked.

I told her I didn't but I'd sure like to hear it. So she told me.

It was all related to taxes. Before the CAW could disperse the funds, Revenue Canada insisted on withholding a portion as income tax, and instructed us to place the $24 million in escrow. We challenged the ruling, claiming that Revenue Canada had no right to withhold tax from our members, who would declare it on their individual income tax returns. The arguments were going back and forth, with the CAW working to help the members, but they were blaming the delay entirely on the CAW. Which, of course, meant me.

I knew the reason for the delay, but I assumed that our members would be patient. I guess when someone dangles a few thousand dollars you didn't expect to receive, patience flies out the window. The tax issue was eventually settled, the funds were dispersed, and I started receiving smiles at Air Canada counters. And resumed checking my bags.

A few weeks after the incident with the angry customer service woman, I attended a dinner meeting with Robert Milton. Air Canada seemed to be on its way to recovery by this time, and Milton was feeling rather smug and relaxed. During a friendly conversation about the airline industry and our experience under CCAA terms, I asked if he thought Li Ka-Shing had any regrets about walking away from the Air Canada deal instead of agreeing to our proposal to maintain defined benefit pensions for union employees.

"Sure he has," Milton said. "He probably lost a couple hundred million dollars by not going ahead with the offer on your terms."

After all we had gone through on the labour side, it sounded like a small bit of justice to me.

That's not quite the end of the story, of course. Air Canada's exit from CCAA protection turned out to be just another in the series of unending crises at the airline. Robert Milton spent four years accumu-lating quick cash for the company by selling off Air Canada's various sub-businesses, including the regional carrier Jazz and the Aeroplan loyalty program. Next, he took advantage of a rising stock market to float new issues of these subsidiaries, which also had the effect of net-ting him a juicy profit from each spinoff. (Milton himself took home close to $40 million in the years after Air Canada's exit from CCAA.) But when the global financial crisis hit in 2008, it became suddenly apparent that what was left of Air Canada was completely unprotected against the economic turbulence, and the company lost more than $1 billion in 2008. Today, my old nemesis Calin Rovinescu is filling the chair as Air Canada's CEO. Rovinescu is a legal hired gun who specializes in handling financial crises, not an airline manager.

Rovinescu's return to Air Canada coincided with another ironic episode in labour relations at the airline. The CAW's collective agreement, implemented in 2004 after the CCAA restructuring, was set to expire at the end of May 2009. CAW negotiators (led by Leslie Dias, new president of Local 2002, and Peggy Nash, assistant to President Ken Lewenza) could see the storm clouds gathering as the world economy slipped into recession. So in January they bargained a modest three-year deal, one that contained small annual wage increases. Not great, but not bad given the tough times coming. However, anger in the ranks at Milton's actions during the airline's short-lived recovery was overwhelming, and the deal was voted down by 78 percent of the members.

Rovinescu was appointed CEO in March, and warned immediately that the company would re-enter CCAA protection unless it got quick deals with its unions to freeze wages and defer required pension contributions. The federal government was so worried it appointed a retired judge (James Farley, who had overseen the company's first CCAA restructuring) to mediate the talks. The CAW got the deal first: a stand-pat contract, this time with no wage increases. Ironically, with Air Canada teetering, this deal was ratified by 76 percent of the members.

I hope our members at Air Canada learn from this experience that they can trust their union. When their bargaining committee told them in January that a modest deal was good, given the circumstances, the members didn't believe it. In the end, they settled for a deal that was less appealing than the one they had turned down five months earlier.

The deregulation of the airline industry and the privatization of Air Canada, which the Conservative government of Brian Mulroney brought us in the late 1980s, has been a never-ending tragedy for airline workers, investors and customers alike. Since privatization in 1989, Air Canada has lost a cumulative total of over $6 billion. Who knows how much more will be lost in the future? But now it's up to my successor, Ken Lewenza, to deal with the mess, working with our still determined local leaders at CAW Local 2002.

I just hope Ken's bags don't end up in Shanghai on his next Air Canada flight to Montreal. . . .

NINE

Fighting for Fairness, From Coast to Coast

Some of the most challenging and rewarding experiences of my career grew out of assisting unionized workers to enjoy more job security and better working conditions. Unfortunately, so did some of the most disturbing—like the shocking events that occurred at the Navistar truck plant in Chatham, Ontario, in the summer of 2002.

Navistar had maintained a heavy truck plant in Chatham dating back to 1912, when the original facility was created to build vehicles for International Harvester. For decades the Chatham truck plant was a model of quality and efficiency at producing large transport trucks. Assembling these massive vehicles is very different from building cars and pickups. Truck parts are much heavier, and the process is far more complex. At full capacity a heavy-truck assembly line would still produce less than one-tenth the daily production of a typical automotive assembly line.

CAW employees at the Navistar plant in Chatham were outstanding in their work. That's not just my opinion; that was the opinion of Navistar executives, who boasted in their 2002 annual report that the Chatham facility had achieved higher quality and greater productivity than any other Navistar assembly plant. And it got better: During that year, Canadian workers delivered a labour cost advantage over their U.S. counterparts of $11 per hour. Cheaper labour costs, higher quality, greater productivity—you might think the top bosses at Navistar valued the Chatham plant as a model facility and looked for ways to ensure its long-term operation.

Well they didn't. In fact, they wanted to close it.

This intention became obvious to our bargaining team in the spring of 2002 when Navistar management demanded that CAW workers accept a new contract shaving $20 million from the Navistar payroll. Navistar was insisting on a cut of $6 per hour in wages for assembly line workers, a $4 hourly cut for skilled trades workers, an extension of the compulsory work week, reduced vacation time, increased benefits cost to employees and more mandatory overtime. Without those changes, Navistar warned, the Chatham plant would be closed and its operations moved to Mexico as soon as the current contract expired. Even if a deal was reached, we were told, the company would not commit to keeping it open for more than another year.

Why close an almost 100-year-old plant that outperforms other plants in the company on every level? In a word: NAFTA. If Navistar's move to Mexico could fatten their profit picture enough to bump its share price up a buck or two and add a dime to its dividend, they would damn well say "adios!" to 1,000 workers, almost a century of history, and an entire city. The rules of NAFTA encouraged them.

The Mike Harris/Stephen Harper crowd, who swear that raw capitalism can solve every problem, defend the freedom of capital to move anywhere at any time. They declare that the profit incentive must not be hindered and that capital must be permitted to flow wherever it yields the greatest return. That's hogwash. There is a price to pay for everything, and the price for the Navistar move would have been economic and social devastation for thousands of families, and for the city of Chatham. Remember, this wasn't a problem plant, a sinkhole of inefficiency and labour strife. It was a model plant where many of the workers had built up 20-plus years of service.

When talks broke down and Navistar refused to consider mediation, we called a legal strike. On June 1 our people walked off the job and began to picket the plant, supported by CAW members from elsewhere in Ontario. Management's response was to hire scabs to fill many of the CAW workers' jobs, and enforcers from London Protection International, a private security firm, to escort them through the picket lines.

Few things ignite anger in a union worker more than the sight of someone crossing a picket line to fill his or her job during a legal strike. Add the general inexperience of the security people from LPI, and you had a recipe for disaster. I grew concerned enough about the situation to write to Brad Clark, Ontario's labour minister, to take "immediate intervention in order to avoid someone getting seriously hurt [at the Navistar facility]. There is absolutely no justification for the actions of management, and should someone get hurt the blame will rest squarely with your government who, under Mike Harris, brought in legislation giving the right to draconian management like Navistar to hire scabs. This must be changed."

No one was listening. Three days later, on June 24, a van manned by security people from LPI was driving back and forth videotaping a demonstration on Bloomfield Road in Chatham, just off the 401.

The demonstrators, mainly from Windsor, were determined to express concern about the hiring of scabs by Navistar. The demonstrators saw the video camera and moved onto Bloomfield Road to find out who was taping the demonstration and why. Seeing several dozen workers approaching, the driver panicked and suddenly accelerated the van at full speed into them. Three CAW strikers were run over by the van, which sped off toward the offices. Among them was 38-year-old Don Milner, the father of two children ages one and three. Milner was dragged under the van and spent six months in hospital being treated for a shattered pelvis, ruptured bladder, crushed right elbow and compound fracture of his left arm. While Don was recuperating other complications arose, including an intestinal infection causing permanent damage to his liver, bowel and lungs. A year after the incident he was still undergoing corrective surgery, living with a catheter connected directly to his bladder through an incision in his abdomen. The impact on his life has been nothing less than horrific, and after enduring more than 40 different surgical procedures he has emerged from the experience permanently disabled.

Keep in mind that Milner was doing nothing illegal. He was engaged in strike support and obeying the province's labour laws. He was not a threat to the driver and passengers within the van; his only weapon was a cardboard sign declaring the unfairness of Navistar management.

The incident sparked outrage from all sides. The van driver was charged with three counts of dangerous driving. Chatham Mayor Diane Gagner, who had been unsympathetic to the union until then, demanded a meeting with Navistar management where she expressed surprise that the employer had rejected mediation and ordered Navistar to cease bringing busloads of replacement workers into town. Following the Milner tragedy, the company stopped transporting scabs into the plant but they did not abandon their efforts to break the union; they just changed their tactics.

In one of their most foolish moves, Navistar's American managers began insisting that the federal government bring in the "National Guard" to escort buses carrying scabs into the plant. The *National Guard?* Can you imagine a U.S.-based multinational corporation operating in Canada for almost 100 years and not being aware that Canada does not maintain a national guard? It was sad and amusing at the same time. Even if Canada did have a national guard, how could a foreign privately owned corporation demand that army personnel enforce actions to extract concessions from its workers?

Eventually a series of meetings was held between Dan Ustian, CEO of Navistar, and me. The sessions led to a return to the bargaining table, where an agreement was reached and ratified by our members.

A lot of historic firsts occurred during this difficult dispute. It was the first time a large-vehicle assembler had tried to scab one of our plants, and the first time a labour minister for the province of Ontario refused to get involved in a substantial labour dispute. Brad Clark refused even to call a meeting of the parties, which led me to demand just what he believed his role as minister of labour was. I received no answer.

It was also the first time the leader of our union asked every member of CAW Ontario locals to be ready to put down their tools and head for Chatham to support our Local 127 members at Navistar, and the first time we used an airplane to monitor and report on the movements of a "scab bus." And of course I cannot forget that it was the first time a member of our union suffered life-threatening injuries while peacefully picketing.

The Navistar strike will be forever marked by the terrible injuries suffered by Don Milner, as well as by the inexcusably aggressive and unfeeling attitude of the company. The entire event placed enormous strain, physically and emotionally, on everyone in the CAW, and it is important that I acknowledge the courage, commitment and sacrifice made by the union's leadership, its staff and its members in supporting our position.

Even after the strike was settled, there were still more twists and turns on the road ahead. In October 2002, a few months after Don Milner suffered his horrific injuries, Navistar announced plans to close the Chatham facility and shift production to Mexico. We still refused to give up, and I contacted Dan Ustian and suggested that we engage in one more round of cost-saving negotiations. We also moved to draw the Canadian and Ontario governments into the process. We had been calling loudly for them to actively work to protect our auto plants, because we had seen a southward migration of the industry to places like Mississippi and Alabama. Most had been lured there by a combination of government subsidies and the most anti-union labour laws on the continent. Canadian officials, we demanded, should start doing their bit to protect existing auto facilities and win new ones instead of sitting on their hands.

In time the Navistar plant became the first success in our efforts to re-engage government in protecting Canadian automotive industry investment and the jobs it provided. When we reached a cost-saving agreement with Navistar, Ottawa and the Ontario government proposed a package of investment assistance that included R & D work by Navistar to be completed in labs in Windsor, aimed at developing more environmentally friendly heavy-truck engines. The total government support of $65 million, combined with savings contained in the new CAW contract, were enough to convince Navistar to change its mind. They reversed their decision to close the Chatham plant and began pumping tens of millions of dollars into modernizing it.

It is not often that a union is able to overturn a plant closure decision, but the CAW was able to do exactly that. A combination of picket line strength (symbolized in Don Milner's bravery), savvy bargaining, and political influence allowed us to save the plant and the jobs and community that depended on it.

Within months of the agreement, the Navistar plant was working multiple shifts, turning out more trucks with a higher quality level than ever. Navistar's Chatham plant became a gold mine of profits for a company that had complained it would go out of business unless it could move lock, stock and barrel to Mexico.

Given the cyclical nature of the automotive industry, things have changed since then. They always do, and the problems are industry-wide, not specific to Navistar or their Chatham facility. The lesson remains the same, however: some manufacturers will toss history, tradition, productivity and workers' lives out the window in pursuit of promised opportunities for a few bucks' more profit. The effort to deal with this attitude, to represent the values of workers against the cold and calculated pursuit of ever-increasing profit, never ceases.

A new twist to Navistar's approach to doing business in Canada was added in January 2009, when the company announced layoffs for 500 workers and predicted another 200 would follow within a few months, leaving barely 200 employees at the plant. That news was bad enough, but incredibly Navistar managed to rub salt in the wounds.

The Harper government had just awarded a $254 million contract for Navistar to build 1,300 medium-duty trucks for delivery to the Canadian forces, enough to ensure that some of the layoffs would not be necessary. Then Navistar announced that the trucks would be built not in Chatham but at its plant in Garland, Texas.

When Bob Chernecki, my former assistant, demanded to know why Canadian taxpayer money was being sent to a U.S. plant while the company appeared ready to mothball a highly productive Canadian plant, Navistar claimed the vehicles were too small for the Chatham plant's heavy-truck line, which was nonsense. The Chatham line could easily be adjusted for an order that large. In fact, Navistar could have paid for the line adjustment with over $30 million in financial assistance that the federal government awarded the company in 2003, plus another $35 million provided by the Ontario government. Or the government could have insisted that the vehicles must be assembled in Canada, giving the opportunity for other truck manufacturers such as Freightliner in St. Thomas, Ontario, and Paccar, in Sainte-Thérèse, Quebec, to build them.

Tory Defence Minister Peter MacKay's justification for the contract was so ludicrous I almost fell out of my chair laughing. Okay, maybe the trucks will be built in Texas, MacKay admitted, but their tires would be built at the Michelin plant in Waterville, Nova Scotia. Oh, yeah—and the trucks will burn Canadian gasoline.

We're sending Texas more than $250 million for trucks that could be built in Canada just so we can mount Canadian-made tires on them and fill their tanks with Canadian gasoline? And this fiasco occurred while Finance Minister Jim Flaherty was trumpeting plans to boost the country's ailing economy through infrastructure jobs.

* * *

I understand the ups and downs of economies and markets. I certainly do not expect any business to keep operating if it lacks demand for its products or services, or if the company finds it impossible to continue operating under certain circumstances. Nobody owes anyone a living, and that includes CAW members.

My major concern, over the 40-plus years of my trade union activity, was ensuring fairness for working people. Is it fair, after declaring bankruptcy and leaving workers without jobs, benefits, severance pay or hope, for a CEO of a large public company to walk away with $50 million, $100 million or more as his or her settlement agreement? That's not just unreasonable, it's criminal—or should be. Yet it happens over and over.

Fairness extends beyond the dollars-and-cents aspect. It often includes basic courtesy, or not treating people as though they were disposable parts to be tossed away when no longer needed. Even in our supposedly enlightened society workers continue to be treated in this manner.

One day a few years ago I was working at home when a newspaper reporter called and asked me to comment on the layoff of 3,000 unionized workers from CN Rail. I told him that the figure must be wrong. Barely six weeks earlier, CN Rail President Paul Tellier had assured me the company was doing well and planned to expand, meaning it would soon begin hiring new workers. The reporter should check his facts, I said. Perhaps Tellier meant 300 people would be on temporary layoff.

But it really *was* 3,000 employees. They learned about their jobless status through the media, who were faxed a press release from Tellier. Tellier and his people didn't have the foresight to wait until the company identified the positions and communities where the layoffs would take place before making the announcement. Instead they were prepared to say that 3,000 men and women, most with families to support, would have no income soon, and everyone will just have to wait to find out who they are. For days, every CN employee feared his or her job was in jeopardy, creating unnecessary anxiety among employees and their families. You call that fairness?

Seeking fairness for workers is the primary goal of the CAW, as it is for every effective trade union. As I noted earlier, the CAW is exceptionally diverse, supporting workers in hospitality, tourism, health care, mining, shipbuilding, casinos, aluminium and fast food. Despite the union's identification with the auto industry, the CAW's principal focus is on simple fairness for workers. Business owners have access to legal minds and government leaders who look out for their interests. Unionized workers have the support of unions to look out for theirs.

That's the balance that unions provide, and without them the whole idea of fairness would be a fraud.

Among the occupations that the CAW represents are fishery workers, and I can think of no better example of their need for union support than a dispute we had with Highland Fisheries. The firm, which also operates as Clearwater Seafoods, is owned by John Risley, one of the wealthiest men in Canada. I don't object to Risley's wealth, but I do object to his attitude where workers are concerned.

Risley gets fish for his Nova Scotia processing plants through a government-licensed quota system. Without his quota of fish, awarded to him by representatives of the people of Nova Scotia, Risley would be left with a boat and a fishing pole and not much else. The top hourly wage was $12.25 per hour at a plant where the average worker's seniority was about 25 years. That's not a hell of a lot of money to earn, yet, with his government-granted quota in his back pocket, Risley told CAW unionized workers at his plant in Cape Breton that he wanted a cut of $2.25 per hour. Without it he would shut down the plant and move its operations out of Canada.

Meanwhile, across the water in Newfoundland and Labrador, Fishery Products International was planning to ship more than half their catch of yellowtail to China for processing. Picture this: Newfoundland and Labrador fishermen catch the fish, FPI ships it to China, Chinese workers process the fish, and the stuff is shipped back to Canada for consumption—all of this from a company headquartered in a province with the highest unemployment rate of any region in North America. You call that fairness?

The actions in 2004 of the Irving family and the federal government are another instance of Maritime workers being treated unfairly. Allan Rock, who was federal industry minister at the time, gave the Irvings $60 million of public money to assist them in decommissioning their shipyard in Saint John, New Brunswick, part of a rationalization program to reduce capacity in the shipbuilding industry. The Saint John yard at one time had employed more than 3,000 CAW members. Initially, employees were not offered an additional penny for severance pay, retraining or improving their pensions. When enough people raised enough hell, the Irvings generously agreed to keep only $50 million of public money and divide the remaining $10 million among the 4,000 employees who were out of a job. In return, they demanded that the workers decertify their unions. In effect, the company ordered its workers to give up their union membership or they wouldn't get the money. If the workers failed to kick out their unions, the only effective protection they had against management bullying, Irving would keep the $10 million. You call that fairness?

Five unions were involved, four building trade unions plus the CAW. On the day before the deadline, the four construction unions agreed to decertify themselves. The CAW told the Irvings to go to hell. If work came back to the yard some day, the CAW members said, they'd rather have the union than a lousy few thousand dollars. That's how much they valued their union membership. In the end, we bargained a compromise close-out agreement that won our members their share of the money.

The CAW is also active in the gaming industry, representing 6,000 casino workers across the country. One of the last recruiting efforts I was involved in before retiring involved Casino Niagara, the largest non-unionized gaming operation in the country. Recruiting drives can be exciting events, often involving a hostile reception from management and a sympathetic response from employees. Casino Niagara was a difficult challenge for CAW recruiters who had to perform their duties among blackjack dealers and slot machine addicts. Management did everything in their power to intimidate employees from agreeing to union participation. One of their tactics included dedicating an entire wall in the employee area to news clippings of companies with CAW membership that had closed for various reasons. They did not, of course, post clippings of closed companies that were not unionized because they'd never have had enough space—those firms would out-number the unionized shops about 10 to one.

Demanding fairness for workers is not a means of squeezing con-cessions from employers. It's a way of improving productivity and secu-rity for both sides. Workers who are not treated fairly are, almost by definition, unhappy workers. Those who feel the employer values them as human beings as well as a source of productivity are content, and contented workers do more for the company.

A few employers recognize this fact, as I witnessed during some bargaining sessions. This doesn't mean they were pushovers, by any means. That was fine with me. I always went into a bargaining session determined to stand toe to toe with the other side, giving and taking until both of us were satisfied. Perceptive employers understood this and, while not every issue was solved completely through bargaining, many major steps were taken to benefit both sides.

Sometimes the benefit of union representation goes beyond nego-tiating wages and benefits to include the preservation of entire com-munities. When Rio Tinto assumed control of Alcan Aluminium, the CAW negotiated an agreement leading to a $2 billion investment in its Kitimat, B.C., plant, ensuring job security for workers and the contin-ued prosperity of the community. Canada would have lost hundreds of jobs and Kitimat would have become a ghost town without Alcan's presence.

Also on the west coast, the CAW represents workers at more than 50 Kentucky Fried Chicken outlets in the Vancouver area. Their 2007 contract was ratified by 97 percent of the members without any job dis-ruption, proving that workers in the service sector can use an effective union to improve their standard of living and working conditions. This could work just as well at Starbucks, Tim Hortons, Burger King and other fast-food employers if workers were willing to organize themselves and boost their collective power. If anyone needs a union, surely it is the people flipping burgers for minimum wage.

As proud as I am of the many ways the CAW achieved success in its goal of improving conditions for unionized workers, I am also pleased that we managed to influence government and industry to take steps that benefit all Canadians. One of these achievements happened during bargaining with VIA Rail in 2007.

It became apparent that VIA was unable to achieve everything it wanted, because the federal government was failing to provide the financial and political backing it needed and deserved. In response, the CAW placed billboards and distributed pamphlets urging Canadians to demand more government funding for VIA and the country's railroad system generally. The country was not even close to realizing all the potential benefits of an updated and efficiently operated passenger rail system, and the campaign generated a good deal of interest and discussions.

Contract bargaining extended over several months; eventually we reached a settlement ratified by more than 80 percent of the members. A few weeks after the ratification vote, the Harper Tories announced $700 million in financing to update VIA's equipment. This was an amazing announcement from a federal government that usually believes government should own nothing, an announcement made more gratifying when both Paul Côté, the CEO of VIA, and Federal Transport Minister Lawrence Cannon stated that the CAW campaign at least partially motivated their decision.

"We argued the importance of VIA Rail for the unity of Canada," I said when the funding announcement was made. "For working-class people who don't have a lot of money, the only means they have to travel this country and see its vastness and beauty is by rail. It's an effective way for people across Canada to experience this beautiful country and get to know one another."

Among other things, the government's action was proof that a strong union can make headlines without sending their members out on strike or upsetting politicians.

The Hard Reality
of Collective Bargaining

The most common complaint I hear from anti-union people concerns the bargaining process. Especially in manufacturing situations, unionists are accused of bargaining according to their own exclusive agenda, and of ignoring the concerns of management and shareholders.

Let's put the record straight: These people are absolutely correct.

I don't mean that unions don't give a damn about the people who run the company or invest in it. They share an interest in the firm's success. After all, a union worker's standard of living depends on the company's financial stability and its prospects for future growth. They need the security of a financially stable job to pay for the homes they live in, the clothes their families wear, the vacations they hope to enjoy, the vehicles they drive, the education they plan to provide for their children and so much more.

When union bargainers adopt an adversarial attitude with management, it simply means that the business school model of "win-win" negotiating doesn't apply when it comes to collective bargaining. And let no one accuse CAW members of being selfish or insensitive about others, especially those less fortunate than themselves. As I mentioned earlier, members of the CAW have a record of supporting charitable organizations such as the United Way far more generously than most Canadians. To the surprise of some people, we also cooperated with management to address common concerns, giving and taking where it benefited one side as much as the other. We just didn't buy that win-win philosophy.

Business people, especially those with MBA after their names, will lecture that a perfect deal occurs when both sides get what they want out of a bargain. They call it "interest-based bargaining," where both sides work toward shared interests. Then, I suppose, they walk arm in arm to the bar and sip martinis. Maybe that works for the country club set, but it never has and never will work for union-management negotiations. True, I've shaken hands and had a drink or two with the other side after a long bargaining session produced a deal. But that was out of respect for the process and the people on both sides of the table who participated in it, not because we suddenly became equal partners.

Or think of it this way: Do you suppose that before a hockey game between the Toronto Maple Leafs and the Montreal Canadiens the captains and coaches get together and say, "Let's find a way we can both come out of this as winners"? Like hell they do. Both sides go in to win. Any other approach would be a betrayal to their supporters.

That's the model for union-management negotiations, not the phoney win-win arm-in-arm strategy of the MBA crowd, which I think is a lot of hooey anyway—some of the most intensely competitive people I ever met have sat across the table from me wearing Armani suits and kick-ass expressions. I suspect they act the same way in every business situation.

And while executives openly talk about win-win, they practise something very different behind closed doors. They have a vested interest in reducing labour costs to the minimum, in order to fatten the return to their shareholders and pad their bonuses. When their workers are no longer needed, they kick them out onto the street.

Don't get me wrong. I'm not saying unions and employers can't work together. They have to, because one way or another each relies on the other for survival. But I find that unions do their job much better when they understand clearly what their role is: to advance the interests of the workers they represent. End of story.

Union-management collective bargaining is all about workers making progress. That's how I saw it, and that's the goal I set for every bargaining session. I wanted to achieve progress for the people I represented. It's also about recognizing the imbalance between the power of a corporation and the power of an individual employee when it comes to defending the employee's rights. After all, every job embodies an inherent asymmetry between the boss and the worker. The worker is desperate to have a job in order to put food on the table. The boss does not feel the same way about any individual worker. Yes, the employer needs all the workers to show up and do their jobs; otherwise, no work gets done, and no profits are pocketed. But the individual worker is always more vulnerable than the boss, and that's why unions were invented.

Collective bargaining remains a democratic process, and of all the actions a union can take on behalf of its members, this is the one that most engages the total membership and their families. Debates about the union's position occur in the workplace, at the union hall, in the pubs and around the family dinner table. What should the union's priorities be? members and their families ask. Should we expect a strike? Should we set aside some money just in case? What are we looking for in wages, pensions, benefits and time off the job? All of these questions are raised and discussed long before the bargaining begins. The workers see the union as an important and relevant part of their working lives, balancing the power of the employer.

This is another reason why the corporate "win-win" philosophy doesn't work in union/management negotiations. The MBA approach suggests at least some equality of power between two sides. If Company A and Company B want to do a deal together and Company A doesn't like the smell of things, it can walk away from the entire arrangement and stay in business. If workers are similarly unsatisfied, what's their choice? Sure, they can walk away as well. But if they can't walk directly to a new job with similar income and benefits, they're basically *out* of business.

The process is important in understanding the difference between a union-management negotiation and two corporate groups doing a deal together. The union's position is dictated by members who identify and endorse the demands, and the union represents a balance of power between individual workers and the corporation. The members who established the demands either accept or reject any deal negotiated by the union. That's ownership of the process by the union; the members provide their demands and the union provides the power to express them. I was constantly surprised that many employers did not understand the way things operated. They assumed, I guess, that Buzz Hargrove and a bunch of his union buddies got together over a case of beer and said, "Let's see how much we can squeeze out of the SOBs *this* year!" That's not how it works at all.

So the union collectively delivers the expectations of its members to the other side, whose representatives arrive at the bargaining table with their own list of demands gathered from workplace supervisors, managers, shareholders, business writers, maybe the CEO's wife, and who knows who else.

Many management demands that I dealt with concerned issues related to productivity, work rules and other operational matters. When these were on the table, the CAW tried to adopt a thoughtful, effective approach. On one hand, it is a core responsibility of the union to protect its members against the negative impact, including health and safety consequences, of efforts to speed up production. On the other hand, we also had to recognize that running a high-performance, highly productive workplace is a precondition for the employer being able to pay the wages and benefits we aimed to achieve in bargaining. So on the whole, the CAW was constructive about efforts to enhance productivity in the workplace. It is a blatant stereotype to complain that the union is always a barrier to productivity. In many ways the union actually improved productivity. Here's an example.

I always listened closely and responded to management charges of featherbedding, the practice of giving a few union members some high-paying but less demanding jobs, because it is essentially unfair and undermines union solidarity. Everybody should work as hard as everyone else on the same job, and nobody should expect that the world owes them a living. This is why the CAW refused to accept a proposal from the auto companies to set up "job banks" in Canada, a concept that American managers had negotiated with the UAW. Job banks meant that surplus workers would not be laid off but instead would show up every day and sit in the lunchroom playing cards, receiving almost full pay for just hanging around. I argued that our members wanted to work, not to receive money for doing nothing. If the employer had no work to be done, I said, lay the workers off with adequate income support until they can be recalled or have found work with a different employer.

The U.S. media had a field day with job banks, pointing out that the auto companies were losing billions of dollars while paying people to play cards. They were right, I suppose, although given the option of no job and no income or showing up to be paid to play cards, what choice did the workers have? These men and women preferred working for full pay to wasting their lives dealing cards. The job bank concept, in my view, was an insult to people who wanted to be productive and to be paid well for their efforts. It was an insult to their pride and a weapon for anti-unionists to wield whenever they chose. By fostering the old stereotype of union members being greedy and unproductive, it did more harm to our image than it was worth.

I also listened to any legitimate argument from management that would improve quality or productivity without placing unacceptable demands on our members. Our union always proposed ways to build better-quality products and to be more productive because we knew it was the best way of ensuring the company would succeed and the jobs would be secure. When management's suggestions made sense and added job security for our members, I backed them. When the demands flew in the face of our principles, I resisted them.

One frequent demand from management concerned job posting opportunities. Management wanted the authority to place any employee it chose into any job function available. This conflicted with the union's principle of seniority, the idea that long-term employees deserve first consideration in those situations, and we consistently rejected the idea.

One way or another, the bargaining process unfolded, sometimes through give and take, sometimes through arguments and threats. In the majority of sessions we finally agreed on a deal, signed the papers, shook hands and moved on. After the completion of a successful bargaining session with one of the automakers I would announce the major terms of the deal at a press conference. When you have 10,000 or more employees eagerly awaiting news of their job security, income and working condi-tions, why wait to tell them? Inevitably, after hearing about our side of the deal someone in the media would demand to know what Ford or GM or Chrysler got out of it. I would reply, "They get the best workforce in the industry, producing the best quality in the most productive manner. That's why our plants always lead in quality and productivity, and signing a new contract represents a great victory for the company."

Achieving success in bargaining without a strike requires planning that begins long before the first sit-down with management. My strat-egy was based on getting to know the people on the other side of the table—not just what they wanted but who they were. Months before the first session I would arrange to have lunch or dinner with the chief negotiator for the company, just a casual couple of hours of breaking bread and talking in generalities. I would schedule a similar get-together with the head of the local union bargaining group to gather a sense of his or her expectations.

These sessions were more than get-acquainted times. They were opportunities to test certain attitudes and ideas, and choose where and how to set priorities in our bargaining. I also acquired the skill of read-ing people, absorbing the things that make them tick, understanding the actions that either gratified or annoyed them, and figuring out how to make it all work in the union's favour.

A good example of this occurred a few years ago when union lead-ership, being open-minded about these things, wanted the automakers to provide benefits to same-sex couples. We had chosen Ford as the first company to negotiate with, setting the pattern for Chrysler and GM to follow. Ford had a record for being the most progressive of the Big Three when it came to social issues, but I learned that Don McKenzie, their vice-president of human resources, was a devout Catholic vehe-mently opposed to the idea of same-sex relationships.

Whatever Ford's corporate policy may have been about same-sex benefits, we knew we'd be facing a roadblock with McKenzie over the subject, which was only one of many issues to be addressed. Why insert something we knew we'd have a hell of time winning compared with other equally important goals? So we backed off same-sex benefits with Ford. A few weeks later, we managed to sell the idea to GM. This is very unusual in the pattern-bargaining approach agreed upon between the auto firms and the CAW, where the first company to settle establishes the broad contract provisions for the industry. But it happened, and three years later when we came back to Ford for a new contract, same-sex benefits were in the pattern and Ford had to accept it. Don McKenzie had no problem at this stage, because his conscience was clear: he'd opposed the idea when it was brought to him new, and had to accept it when the pattern was fixed.

Pattern bargaining enabled the union to focus on negotiating a deal in one location that could be applied to other workplaces, usually, but not always, in the same industry. When bargaining at GM, Ford and Chrysler, an agreement reached with the first company selected—it became the "target" company—would be put in place by the other two companies. On the surface pattern bargaining appears to make things easier for union negotiators during subsequent bargaining sessions: they can point to an existing contract as a precedent, and suggest that if one company can afford to reward its employees in a certain way, the others should as well.

But there was more to it than that. The overriding goal of pattern bargaining was to take labour costs out of the competition between the rival firms by establishing similar wages, pensions, benefits and workplace standards in comparable industries. I understand the basis of competition, and I reject the idea of a monopoly in the marketplace as much as I reject a monopoly in government. Choice is good, and competition tends to produce better products and value for consumers, but I draw the line at companies looking for a competitive edge by cutting wages and benefits to their workers. Competition should be limited to better design, improved service, low pricing and other qualities that benefit the customer without penalizing the workers. That's the basis of pattern bargaining.

In my experience bargaining with the Big Three, I usually found Ford to be the most open and flexible. Overall the company was more responsive to new ideas than GM or Chrysler. This corporate approach was reflected in the nature and attitudes of the people I dealt with as well. In 2005, for example, Ford named Stacey Allerton-Firth as its chief negotiator. Stacey was the first woman vice-president of human resources of any of the Big Three in Canada, a tribute to her intelligence and ability. Also the first woman to head up major auto bargaining with the CAW, she has a good sense of humour, she's knowledgeable about the company and the industry and, when necessary, she's as tough as any negotiator I've encountered across the table.

The most important factor in these sessions is communication. Openness and honesty by both sides creates trust, and trust is a critical quality in negotiations, even when each side sees the other as an adversary.

To the surprise of many people who think of automobile manufacturing as a dirt-under-the-fingernails business, Stacey and I established an immediate rapport, helped along by the presence of my assistant Peggy Nash. A former passenger agent with Air Canada, Peggy is a working mother like Stacey. Maybe that's what made the process go more smoothly. Whatever it was, the sessions went so well that we concluded a deal nine days ahead of schedule. Two women got the job done well, proving that the old notion of union and management negotiators facing each other like a couple of tough guys in the ring is obsolete.

Another key element of the bargaining process is knowing how and where to apply pressure. In most union-management negotiations, of course, the ultimate pressure point is to launch a strike or a lockout. Strikes hurt both sides, however, and although they enable workers to blow off steam, a price is paid one way or another. Disputes may also involve binding arbitration, which both sides tend to avoid. In some ways, negotiations are like a family dispute: as loud and nasty as both parties get with each other, the concept of a third party stepping in to solve the matter is rarely welcomed. From the union side, arbitration removes the concept of the union owning the process, and an arbitrator can ignore all the hotly debated goals and demands made by members. The companies, of course, make the same argument from their perspective although, as we'll see later, in some circumstances both sides can agree to accepting arbitration.

Some employees, such as certain health care workers, are not permitted to strike, which makes the application of pressure more challenging. That's when you have to get creative. When members of the Service Employees International Union (SEIU) decided to join the CAW, one of their main issues was the SEIU's history of always accepting binding arbitration to settle their contracts. We agreed to change the system. When we didn't have a contract, my assistant Bob Chernecki would organize demonstrations in front of nursing homes and hospitals, a tactic that proved effective at drawing attention to the dispute. Listing the excessively high salaries of health administrators on placards displayed by the demonstrators, and comparing them with the low wages of the protestors, applied enormous pressure on the employer and helped the workers reach a settlement.

Even when strike action is available, pressure on the employer can be applied by other means. Back in 2002, Ford Canada was making healthy profits thanks, in part, to the remarkable productivity of CAW workers at their plants. When contract time came around the workers naturally expected to share in some of the earnings. Ford had other ideas. The company's first proposal, submitted to our bargaining committee, was worse than miserly; it was an insult.

With a potentially long and trying process ahead of us, we decided to apply pressure that would reduce time and effort. We could have kept the details confidential within the bargaining committee. But in this case the offer was so bad we knew it would enrage the rank and file members. So we did something we had never done before. We copied the Ford proposal, which was printed on official company stationery with the Ford logo prominently displayed, and distributed it to our members in the workplace. When the Ford workers read the offer in the same manner as the bargaining committee first saw it, they went nuts. Ford never had so many outraged workers in the workplace, and within 48 hours we had another, more acceptable offer in hand.

The only way to be a good union negotiator is to rally deep and widespread support from rank-and-file members, and let management know you have their backing. If word gets to the other side that rank-and-file support is weak, or that some kind of conflict or disagreement exists between the workers and their bargaining committee, the union's position is doomed. In my opinion, a union negotiator who is not confident of solid rank-and-file support yet chooses to apply pressure by threatening a strike is doing the workers a disservice. Putting workers on a picket line in those circumstances means cutting their income and creating hardship for their families with little chance of success.

In the CAW, we tried to avoid this by insisting that any bargaining group planning to call a strike in response to failing negotiations must get prior approval from the office of the union president or from the secretary-treasurer. When this happened the issues were reviewed, the attitude of the rank and file was assessed, and a conclusion was reached. If it was clear that support for a strike was weak, the proposal got shelved. This procedure avoided a lot of unnecessary strikes while ensuring tough bargaining on behalf of workers.

Some unnecessary strikes are the result of too much enthusiasm and too little realism on the part of the union members. Hemi Mitic used to call these "nickel strikes." You went into a bargaining session looking for a wage increase of 50 cents an hour, and when the dust settled management was offering 45 cents an hour. The strike deadline loomed, management stood pat, and that's when the workers started shouting, "No goddamn way—we wanted 50 cents and we're going to get 50 cents!"

So what do you do—shut down the operation, throw everybody on the streets, and suffer through a strike for a lousy nickel an hour? If the strike lasted a week and workers finally got their nickel, how long would it take them to earn back a week's worth of lost wages? If they were making $35,000 a year, or about $675 a week, the extra nickel put maybe $100 a year in their pockets. So it would take nearly seven years to earn back the salary they lost while on strike for one week. That didn't make any sense at all, yet some hotheads would insist on doing it, saying it was a matter of principle. Still, the union had to be ready to walk out if the company's offer was truly unacceptable. Otherwise, the next time we started bargaining the company would give a dime less, then a quarter less, then a dollar less on the assumption that the union won't bother striking over such a "small" sum.

Another union tactic that became a familiar CAW policy was "deadline bargaining." Bob "Nick" Nickerson, the first secretary-treasurer of the CAW, was a big promoter of deadline bargaining. "If you've got a midnight strike deadline, you don't settle until the last minute before midnight," Nickerson would preach, "because you might miss something. There could be something left for the other side to offer but you don't get it because you settled early."

I disagreed with Nick that it is always a mistake to settle early. In some cases deadline bargaining can prove an effective strategy, but not always. You have to recognize that every contract negotiation is unique. There are times when you just keep hammering, times when you know a strike is not inevitable, times when a strike deadline is not effective, and times when you can wrap things up and everybody goes home early. It all depends on the company you're dealing with, the issues to be resolved, and the prevailing economic conditions, among other things.

Sometimes the strategy chosen was based on the industry involved. For example, settling early became important when negotiating with auto parts manufacturers. Operating on "just-in-time" delivery sched ules, auto assembly plants cannot and do not warehouse their parts. Within days, sometimes within hours, of a part coming off a supplier's line it is being installed on a vehicle assembly line at Ford, GM or Chrysler. In this way, the workers at a parts supply company control the assembly line almost as much as the assembly line workers themselves. When the just-in-time philosophy was implemented, the auto companies laid down the law with parts suppliers: If a supplier's union contract expired in May and the supplier did not have a contract by February, the auto company would remove its tools and dies from the supplier and hand them off to someone else.

"That's better for us than a strike deadline," I argued when the auto companies announced this policy. "We don't need to threaten a strike and have our members face losing a paycheque. Ford, GM and Chrysler will put the pressure on the supplier for us, so who needs deadline bargaining?" After the introduction of just-in-time parts supply we did a lot of early bargaining with suppliers and came away with excellent agreements for our members and their families.

The widespread perception of trade unionists as people who welcome or enjoy striking against their employer is nonsense. Sure, there are hotheads everywhere who look for a chance to blow off steam now and then. You don't have to be a trade unionist to know that. But most union workers are family people with children and spouses who depend on their income for food, clothing and shelter. Why would they throw away even a week's wages for the so-called joy of marching on a picket line in a blazing sun, a chilly rain or a freezing snowstorm? It ain't fun, believe me, despite all the camaraderie that strikers show to the TV cameras.

A good example of our practical approach is the contracts we settled with the Big Three automakers in the spring of 2008. For the first time in our history, the CAW reached deals with the automakers months before the previous contracts were set to expire. So much for the idea of pushing the talks to the limit, waiting until one minute before midnight to extract the last possible concession from the employer. Why did we change our strategy? We had enough foresight to see the major storm clouds gathering around the industry as a result of the global financial crisis, and instead of waiting for the storm to swamp us, we became proactive.

We settled on a contract with Ford in late April, following a couple of weeks of off-the-record discussions. The contract was modest, no doubt about it: no base wage increases, an 18-month suspension of our cost-of-living protection, and the loss of a week's time off. We estimated the deal would save $300 million per year for the auto industry, once fully implemented, and would have the effect of freezing our hourly labour costs over that period. Given the looming economic catastrophe, holding our own was not a bad outcome at all. At the news conference where we outlined the deal, a reporter asked what my strategy was. "It can be summed up in five words," I quipped. "Get in and get out."

The tentative deal we signed was a good one, given the times, and it received endorsement of the Ford master bargaining committee led by

Mike Vince, the president of CAW Local 200 in Windsor. When the Ford members received the offers, some suggested the bargaining committee return to the table to see what else might be available, but the majority were happy to have an early settlement and the deals were ratified.

Those who wanted the union to apply deadline bargaining with the auto companies were not happy about the early settlement, and they let everyone know about it. That's not news. Some members in every democratic organization are looking for a way to get attention, maybe with an eye to being elected as executives, and unions are no exception. But let's face it: when it comes to backroom deals, conspiracies and personal attacks, unions are probably amateurs compared with political parties—just ask Jean Chrétien, Paul Martin, Stéphane Dion, or how about Stephen Harper and Peter MacKay?

Following our pattern bargaining system, similar deals were reached with GM and Chrysler. The talks were wrapped up by the end of May, three months early. This was a big departure from our past practice. But it was the right thing to do, given the circumstances. Then, on September 15, just days before what would have been the normal expiration of our contracts, U.S. investment bank Lehman Brothers collapsed and the global financial crisis hit like a ton of bricks. It would have been a terrible time to be bargaining a new contract in the middle of that crisis, and there's no hope in hell that we could have won the "stand-pat" agreement that we inked months earlier.

Among other differences I had with unions over my years with the CAW was the question of contract length. In an effort to avoid the possibility of strikes during the 1990s, companies began insisting on long-term contracts from unions. Instead of three-year agreements, the norm for the CAW, firms like Alcan began demanding contracts as long as 18 years, which I considered ridiculous. I understand how employers value the production stability that comes with a locked-in labour agreement running for eight or 10 years or more. I suspect that a bigger incentive to them is the way that long-term contracts tend to disconnect workers from their union, creating apathy and non-participation in union activities among the rank and file.

I'm especially amused when long-term contracts are demanded by companies that lecture workers on the need for flexibility in hiring, firing, work scheduling and other management decisions. Show me that kind of flexibility in a 10-year contract. Companies tried selling these long-term deals as a means of providing job security, but in essence they were a method of eliminating the power of workers to strike. These contracts inevitably were accompanied by threats to close the operation or cancel expansion plans. After a thorough debate at CAW council, our union's parliament, the delegates voted unanimously to reject agreements longer than three years.

Some of the first super-long collective agreements in Canada were negotiated by the United Steelworkers of America (USW) in the mid-1990s, including a 14-year deal with Hudson Bay Mining and Smelting in Manitoba, and an 18-year agreement with Alcan at a smelter in Quebec. These deals promised no strikes or lockouts during the term of the contract, with any disputes to be settled by arbitration. I stated publicly that the Steelworkers made a serious mistake in accepting these contracts, which did not endear me to their leadership. When Alcan sought an 18-year CAW agreement for their plant in Kitimat in 1998, we told them to get lost.

The CAW has found that the three-year agreement works best for members in all sectors of the economy. It addresses the desire of our members to have financial stability, enabling them to purchase homes, vehicles and furnishings, and plan vacations and other activities. Longer agreements tend to disengage the members from their union, and the union loses members' support for its struggles.

This is why I spoke out publicly against the 18-year no-strike deal for USW members, who loudly disagreed with me. "We still have the right to strike!" they said. I told them it was nonsense, and I was amazed when the same union agreed to a 15-year-deal with Hudson Bay Mining in Flin Flon, Manitoba, a multinational outfit that has made hundreds of millions of dollars in profit off the backs of its workers and the natural resources of this country. "Do the deal or we close the mine," Hudson Bay threatened, "and Flin Flon will become a ghost town!" The USW gave in.

Some people who are not attuned to trade unions continue to criticize the stand I took against these long-term deals. In reply, I come back to the point that union-management negotiations are by nature adversarial. This doesn't mean that I call every company executive an SOB. The fact is, I count some top management people as my friends, and I have great admiration for their abilities and for the human qualities that many have demonstrated. Labour negotiators are no different from lawyers on opposing sides. Outside the courtroom they may play golf, have drinks and trade jokes with one another, but put them in the middle of a legal argument in court and you can forget all that buddy-buddy bullshit.

I also took a stand, where necessary, to enforce discipline within my own union. I made it clear to CAW staff who participated in negotiations between local bargaining committees and employer representatives that they must ensure that key CAW policies such as our rejection of long-term agreements were never broken during these sessions. I knew employers would dangle a special deal in front of bargainers in return for wage concessions or contracts extending beyond our three-year maximum, and similar goodies. It would be tempting for a bargaining unit to agree to the proposal and to go say to their members, "Look what we got," ignoring the fact they had broken a firm CAW rule.

My instructions were clear: Anybody present at a bargaining session where the employer began offering five-year or seven-year contracts or similar deals opposed by the CAW was to advise the employer to call me before the discussion went any further. My answer was always "Not a chance!"

I wasn't just throwing my weight around as CAW president. Discipline was absolutely essential to protect the integrity of other contracts and other bargaining sessions. When a precedent was set with one local and one employer, I knew the word would spread far beyond that industry and that particular situation. Soon we would be inundated by employers demanding similar concessions or contract periods, or that other factors be written in their next contract. And who could blame them? We were one union, chosen to apply our universal principles on behalf of a quarter-million members in dozens of industry sectors. We worked like hell to accommodate each sector's special needs. But we also fought like hell to ensure that the union's fundamental principles, which were a source of strength to us since our split from the UAW in 1985, were never threatened. That built the unity that is the union's lifeblood today.

The importance of drawing a line in the sand, and making the most of the solidarity we've built between workers in different sectors and different regions of Canada, has never been clearer than in the case of the auto industry's current crisis. The Big Three auto companies harped for years about so-called high union wages and benefits. Unless we rolled back the wage levels we had won in collective bargaining over several years, the companies warned, they would not be able to compete. Most North Americans bought that argument and naturally blamed the unions for the failure of Ford, GM and Chrysler to compete successfully against imports. In their minds, the unions were the Bad Guys, wearing masks and black hats, robbing the companies at gunpoint; the car companies were the Good Guys, wearing white hats and protecting widows and orphans. That may be a good plot for an old cowboy movie, but it has damn little to do with reality and even less to do with the crises the North American car companies find themselves in today.

First, let's remember something I mentioned earlier: auto workers don't design, engineer or market the vehicles. They assemble them and—one more time—CAW workers have done at least as good a job in building those vehicles as any workers anywhere in the world. Next, assembly labour accounts for about 7 percent of the cost of building and selling a new car. This ratio actually has declined over time, even as our wages have increased because every increase in our wages has been justified by an *even faster* increase in the productivity of our work, reflecting the use of advanced technology and the increased efficiencies of our workplaces. With productivity growing faster than wages, the overall importance of labour costs in the auto industry's overall costs is declining. So why blame labour costs?

Third, people have amazing misconceptions about how much auto workers actually earn. This is not an accident; anti-union analysts and columnists never tire of berating CAW members, claiming we're paid as much as $75 or more per hour, which is nonsense. CAW production workers in the assembly plants start at $24 per hour. With top seniority, they work their way up to $34 per hour. Skilled trades members make a little more. But no one in any auto assembly plant in Canada makes anything remotely close to $75 per hour. Even our pensions and benefits add less than $10 per hour to our compensation. Yet, whenever the Big Three ran into financial trouble (and as I write this, they're up to their neck in it), many people see the union as the villain. And that's baloney.

The Big Three car companies were managed about as well as any manufacturing company you can name, which means they were good but they sure as hell weren't perfect. Earlier, I mentioned the $100 million paint facility that Chrysler built in Windsor that was never used. They tore the place down without one new vehicle rolling down the line. That's one example of mismanagement that puts "excessive union demands" into perspective when looking at the problems of the Big Three auto-makers. Here's another: Beginning in the late 1990s, the car companies did a hell of a job marketing vehicles through leasing deals. In 2005 you could pick up a new vehicle on a three-year lease at a 0.3 percent annual rate. If the new car, truck, minivan or SUV was a demo or a model that was not selling especially well, it would be heavily discounted, making the deal even better. Canadians jumped at the offer. Ford, GM and Chrysler moved a lot of vehicles out the door with these deals, with GM and Chrysler sometimes running three shifts to meet the demand. The car companies were happy, CAW members earning overtime were happy, and Canadians like Doug Steiner were *really* happy.

Steiner, who works in the investment industry, detailed his car-leasing experience in an article entitled "Canada 1, Detroit 0," in the October 2008 issue of *Report on Business Magazine,* which shone a light on one of the unacknowledged reasons behind the Big Three's problems. When Steiner's lease was about to expire in 2008, the dealer called and asked if he wanted to buy the car at the agreed-upon resid-ual value, which was 55 percent of the original price. Steiner, check-ing the used car listings, discovered that the vehicle was worth only 38 percent of its sticker price, and naturally declined the offer. The car went back to the dealer, and when Steiner added up the discounts, incentives, financing interest and miscalculation of residual value absorbed by the company, he calculated they cost the manufacturer— whom Steiner did not name—about $30,000 in total. All car makers add a healthy mark-up on their new vehicles, but I can assure you that none of them makes $30,000 profit on one car. Which means the car maker lost many thousands of dollars on Steiner's lease. Multiply this by thousands of similar leases the car companies signed over the years, launched by marketing geniuses trying to score new and bigger sales figures at any price, then tell me that the CAW's wages are responsible for all the problems faced by automakers.

This didn't stop the car companies from demanding over and over again that unions roll back wage increases earned over the past couple of decades. The CAW refused, on the basis that you can't buy jobs with wage concessions. "We negotiated them, we earned them and we're keeping them," was our stance whenever the subject came up in negotiations. In the U.S., the UAW was not nearly as firm, and when the car companies put two-tier wages on the bargaining table, the UAW bought it.

The theory of two-tier wages was this: the union negotiated good deals for current workers who don't want to take a cut in income on contracts they had fought for, but new employees hired after the deal was signed did not vote on the offer. So the companies had an idea. Let's talk about those new workers coming in to replace current employees when they retire or when the company expands its workforce, they suggested. Why not start these new employees at a lower hourly wage than the guys already on the line? The current guys lose nothing, the new people get jobs, and the companies save a bundle. Isn't that a good idea?

No, it's not. It's a lousy idea. All the two-tier contracts I saw were designed so that new workers never caught up to the wages of the current workers. Even worse, they pitted the newer group of workers against both the older workers and the union, and undermined labour standards that generations of workers had fought to establish.

Imagine you're hired for a job paying $15 an hour, working next to somebody earning $25 an hour. Both of you have the same job responsibilities, work the same hours and perform the same function, yet at the end of a 40-hour week the other worker takes home $400 more than you. And you will never catch up with the other worker's income level.

This kind of artificial pay division creates tension and animosity on the line. It also produces resentment between the younger workers and the union, which under these terms is in no position to help those with lower wages. Sounds to me like a good way for management to dramatically weaken the influence of unions, and ultimately to destroy them.

It's a variation on a tactic employed several years ago by a company with two factories, one in Kingston, Ontario, and the other in the province of Quebec. Unionized workers in both plants were told that the employer was looking for wage cuts. "I'm going to close one of the factories," he announced. He didn't care which one. "Whichever one cuts its wages lowest, that's the one I'll keep open." He expected both groups of workers to start lowering their incomes, competing against each other to see who would do the most work for the least money, racing each other to the bottom. Survival of the fittest may be acceptable in the jungle, but what the hell is it doing in a society where the workers have dependants, where the cost of food and housing and heating your home is constantly rising?

Instead of the dog-eat-dog world of the factory owner, isn't it better to have equals bargaining across a table, even if they see each other as adversaries? That's the position I took when talking to the new owner of the Nackawic pulp plant I referred to earlier.

"You guys will have to cut your wages," the new owner said.

I told him to forget about it. The bargaining committee had voted unanimously not to cut wages.

"You can't be serious," he replied.

I told him we were totally serious.

He didn't believe we would refuse, because the employees were in a difficult bargaining position. They weren't working, so they could hardly threaten a strike. Most of them had lost their pensions, so they had little or nothing to fall back on. But they had worked hard for fair wages, they were damned if they were going to take money out of their pockets for anybody, and the union supported them 100 percent.

I suggested to the new mill owner that our members had put in a lot of years and a lot of sweat to reach the standard of living they enjoyed. They wanted their jobs but they wouldn't cut their incomes. So you tell us how much you think your total labour costs should be. We'll search for ways to meet those costs, then you can run the mill and our members can keep their jobs and income.

And that's what we did. By giving up some vacation time and a couple of extra holidays, and redesigning the bonus system, we found a way to meet the new owner's target. But we refused to give back hard-bargained wages.

This scenario happened time and again over my years with the CAW. We were not inflexible or insensitive to the plight of employers. They had to understand that our first obligation was to union members and their families. But any corporation that wanted to sit down and discuss both sides—theirs and ours—would be listened to.

Chrysler took this approach in 2007 when the company informed us about a new product they planned to produce at their Brampton plant. It would mean a $700 million investment in the plant and help secure 900 jobs on the plant's third shift. But they needed some cost cuts. Could we find them?

We did. Thanks to an earlier contract, workers at the Brampton plant were enjoying a bonus tied to the three-shift operating system developed by the CAW back in 1993. With the original three-shift system, it was impossible to run each shift for a full eight hours. Management needed a half-hour down-time between each shift to refill supplies and fix operational problems on the line. Our members didn't want to lose a half-hour's pay each day so the practice began of paying workers in a three-shift assembly plant eight hours pay for 7.5 hours of work. Eventually, management learned to operate the assembly line continuously for 24 hours per day with no down-time between shifts. Initially we retained the extra pay but with Chrysler in trouble and threatening to eliminate the third shift altogether, we gave it up in return for keeping 900 jobs that might have been lost otherwise.

That's what bargaining is all about: get what you can when you can, and be prepared to give a little when necessary. *But never cut your wages.*

On a very small number of occasions during my time in the CAW I saw union locals reject our "no concessions" policy and agree to wage cuts at their respective plants. I could count these exceptions on one hand. But within a couple of years, these plants always shut down. Wage cuts never solve the deeper challenges facing a troubled company. So where's the benefit?

You can't buy jobs. You can't walk out in the street, wave a lot of cash around and create secure jobs where there were none before. Nor can you buy your own job by handing money back to the employer. In the end, this won't help workers, and it will destroy their unions.

ELEVEN

It's All About Building Things— Including Our Future

Does manufacturing matter?

Back in the 1960s and 1970s, no one would have dared to ask this question. Of course manufacturing mattered. It mattered to millions of Canadians who earned a living manufacturing cars, trucks, appliances, toys, clothing and hundreds of items bearing a "Made in Canada" label. Those jobs have vanished, and with them went a lot of our national income and a good deal of our pride and identity. When was the last time you saw a "Made in Canada" stamp on a television set? A refrigerator? A piece of farm equipment? A home furnace? A pair of shoes?

During those years when other manufacturing activity was leaving the country, the success of Canada's automotive industry shone like a beacon of hope and prosperity. Assembling cars and trucks sure as hell mattered right through the beginning of the 21st century. In

1999, Canada produced over 3 million assembled vehicles—the highest number in its history, ranking our small, northern country as the fourth-largest automotive producer in the world and, on a per capita basis, the most successful auto producer in the world. Cars, trucks and automotive parts accounted for almost one-third of our total exports, and we enjoyed a $15 billion auto trade surplus.

Over 60,000 Canadians were employed in auto assembly and almost 100,000 in auto parts production. And every assembly line job supported more than seven other jobs in the national economy via spinoff employment effects in the parts sector, supply industries and downstream consumer industries.

What a difference a decade makes. The year 1999 was also the year when the World Trade Organization ruled that the Canada–U.S. Auto Pact violated the so-called rules of free trade. Two years later the deal was dead, and Canada's auto industry started heading downhill. By 2009, a decade after the industry's peak year, we had lost more than 40,000 automotive jobs, our $15 billion auto trade surplus had melted away into a $14 billion auto trade deficit, and we barely ranked among the top 10 global auto producers, having been passed by France, Korea, Spain, Mexico, Brazil and China. By trusting free trade and global corporations with our industrial future, instead of taking the measures necessary to protect our share of this vital industry, we handed other countries a gift of billions of dollars in earnings, tens of thousands of jobs and future prosperity.

The decline of our auto industry is a parable for the broader economic and industrial decline Canada has experienced. While our natural resource industries grew like crazy (we Canadians were always adept at digging stuff out of the ground and selling it to foreigners), our manufacturing sector was rapidly eroding. We lost 600,000 manufacturing jobs in total between 2002 and 2009, many the result of the pointless, destructive rise in the value of our currency during the years of the global commodities boom. Even when our loonie came back to earth by late 2008, the damage was done: hundreds of plants and hundreds of thousands of jobs were gone, and they weren't coming back.

Many economists shrug at this decline in Canadian manufacturing jobs, noting that other countries in North America and Europe are undergoing the same change. We are joining them, the economists say, in a transformation toward service economies. Manufacturing jobs are shifting to emerging nations like China, India and Malaysia. Governments shouldn't try to interfere in this evolution, driven by free-market business decisions. The CAW represents employees in the service industries, in both private and public sectors. These members value the union's strength and representation, and the union is as committed to working on their behalf as it is to every other member. Whether in food/ hospitality, transportation or health care industries, service employees play vital roles. I understand and support that notion. But it's unrealistic to expect that our trade deficit in manufactured goods can be balanced through a spurt of growth in service industry exports. It simply isn't going to happen.

To just shrug at the plunge in Canada's manufacturing base, as though it's an inevitable development like a change in the weather, is not acceptable. Not to me, not to the hundreds of thousands of Canadian families who depend on jobs related to manufacturing and not, I hope, to politicians and business leaders. Manufacturing jobs are not "yesterday's industry"; they are different from those in the service industry in the impact they make on all of our lives, and they need to—they *must*— be encouraged and protected by government, for several reasons.

First, manufactured goods are essential to global trade. I'm obviously no fan of "globalization" if it means shipping jobs back and forth between countries in pursuit of ever-fatter profits. If we're going to be a player in international managed trade—not free trade—we need a manufacturing base to ensure success. Service-based jobs alone won't get the job done. If they did, India and other countries would be relying on call centres exclusively instead of trying to build their own manufacturing industries.

Second, manufacturing leads to higher productivity and higher rates of productivity growth. Countries with a small manufacturing base can generate only limited productivity growth. If you want high manufacturing productivity—and despite what conservatives and anti-unionists might think, unions are not fundamentally opposed to the idea—you need a broad manufacturing base.

Third, higher productivity yields higher worker incomes. Jobs in high-productivity manufacturing operations create worker incomes that are about 25 percent higher than those in the rest of the economy. The ripple effect is enormous. Communities grow and thrive on higher incomes. Homes are built, vehicles are purchased, furniture is bought, and all of this activity produces taxes to support quality health care, build better schools, open more parks and create a generally improved standard of living.

Finally, manufacturing companies invest far more in innovation and R & D than service industries. New "homegrown" ideas add to a country's competitive advantage, feeding its economy and generating new jobs and greater job security. There's lots of R & D in manufacturing and damn little in the service industries.

That's why manufacturing matters. And that's why I'm angry at the way successive federal governments have sold out our manufacturing industries on the basis of globalization, the "free market" and a refusal to stand up for Canada's rights.

No other industrialized country in the world, to my knowledge, takes such a hands-off attitude to its manufacturing industry as

Canada. Most federal government decision-makers, especially the neo-con Harperites occupying Parliament since 2006, lean on the "open market" model of the United States. In contrast with Canada, the erosion of that country's manufacturing base is not being treated like some minor adjustment, nor are its problems being dumped on the doorstep of unions and employee expectations. Here's what the Economic Policy Institute, a highly respected American think tank, proposed in response to the sharp decline in manufacturing jobs in the U.S. between 2000 and 2007:

> It seems appropriate for policy makers to lend support to the manufacturing industry. One way to do this is for the federal government to relieve the burden of the fixed costs of U.S. manufacturing firms by picking up some legacy costs that firms have incurred for retiree health and pension benefits. Manufacturing firms are far more likely to have offered sufficient retiree health and income benefits and are now suffering financially as a result. *Firms with large legacy costs should not be punished for being good employers, and workers and retirees should not be punished for economic events outside their purview.*[*] (italics added)

I've had it with people who point to the United States as a model for Canada to follow. Not because I disagree with them, but because the "model" doesn't exist—not the way some people on the right describe it.

Whenever I or anyone else in the CAW or other unions promoted the idea of supporting Canadian industries, we were told that we were practising protectionism, and we should accept the fact that

---

* Josh Bivens, "Shifting Blame for Manufacturing Job Loss," Economic Policy Institute Briefing Paper: April 2006, page 7.

we were living in the new era of globalism. To which I replied, We're not "practising" a damn thing. We're proposing that the federal government care about workers, especially in the manufacturing sector, at least as much as the Americans do. Sometimes the government appeared to bend over backward to avoid the idea.

In 2006, Ottawa announced plans to build three navy supply ships as part of its military expansion. The contract would be worth $2.1 billion. I supported the move, assuming the ships would be built in Canada. The contract would employ hundreds of Canadians, generate millions of dollars in tax revenue, create thousands of spinoff jobs, and enable several communities that counted on shipbuilding to survive.

Initially, Ottawa went through the motions, asking for bids from Canadian shipbuilders. But in 2008, the government announced no Canadian bidder had satisfied their criteria, which totally surprised the shipbuilding industry. The contract was put on hold, and word spread that the government might break its build-in-Canada policy and purchase the ships from offshore.

I couldn't believe it. Why this reluctance to spend our own money in our own country? How unfair would it be to have those ships built in Japan, a country that buys one buck's worth of Canadian manufactured goods for every three bucks of Japanese-made products we buy? Or in South Korea, where the ratio is just as bad? Or Norway? Or Chile? Should we hand them another 2 billion loonies for these ships?

Or maybe we should have the Americans build the ships, I suggested. They're our biggest trading partners. They're free trade advocates. Would they think we were being unfair if we favoured Buy Canadian? They'd better not. Not with the Jones Act in place.

The Jones Act dates back to 1920, and was one of the U.S. provisions exempted from the rules when NAFTA was negotiated. It had to be. The Jones Act rules that any cargo carried between U.S. ports must be aboard ships that are U.S. built, U.S. registered, U.S. owned, U.S. crewed, and serviced and repaired only by U.S. firms. Meanwhile, Canadians cannot build ships that might be used in the U.S., but U.S. shipbuilders can and do sell vessels and barges to Canada duty-free. Yet Ottawa thought it might risk "unfairly supporting Canadian industry" if it favoured Canadian shipbuilders. What kind of Alice in Wonderland world are they living in?

Shipbuilders in countries from Korea to Norway benefit from substantial government subsidies to support their own industries, which help them set a lower price than Canadian manufacturers can match. Yet we're supposed to send billions of dollars of our money overseas to add to the billions of dollars in aid those industries receive from their *own* governments. Meanwhile, Canada ignores the fiscal and economic dividends we would enjoy by doing the work at home. The income taxes paid by shipyard workers alone would return as much as one-third of the costs of the project back into the coffers of government. Why can't our own officials connect the dots?

Ottawa's approach to shipbuilding is just one example of the shameful way this country has failed both manufacturing companies and the workers they employ. People who dislike unions look at the decline in manufacturing jobs and start blaming "greedy workers and their union bosses." Well, that's unadulterated horseshit. There's no other description for it.

* * *

During my years as CAW president, I constantly told the leadership and members that unions must change. This didn't mean we were to start giving back the rights we had bargained and fought for over the years, including fair wages and job security. It meant we must constantly reassess labour's role in a changing world. I am as opposed to total inflexibility from unions as I am to featherbedding by workers and scab employment by management. I'm in favour of unions adjusting to change, as we did with CAMI Automotive Inc. and others over the past 20 years.

When General Motors and Suzuki announced plans in 1986 for a joint venture to be named CAMI with an assembly plant in Ingersoll, Ontario, the CAW naturally insisted on the right to represent the 2,300 wage-earning workers. We negotiated a "voluntary recognition" agreement, under which CAMI would accept the union in advance, before most of the workers even started working there. CAMI managers, however, insisted on running the plant according to a Japanese philosophy of teamwork and labour-management collaboration. This created an immediate conflict with the union's traditional approach to dealing with workplace grievances.

Bob White and I proposed finding a way to make things work; the opportunity to participate in a new greenfield auto plant doesn't come along every day. Many CAW members opposed the idea, claiming it would be a betrayal of union principles to cooperate with management. They rejected any talk of a team concept, noted that the grievance procedure was weak, and disliked the wage and benefits package, which was not up to the standards of the older Big Three plants. We countered with the concept of an independent union presence in the plant, working through an elected body of union representatives that was beholden to workers, not to management.

The debates were long and passionate. Voices and a few fists were raised. We were selling out, according to some members. Bob and I stuck to our guns, and finally won approval. Since opening in 1989 the CAMI plant has employed as many as 3,000 unionized workers operating three production shifts, and the union continues to play a role in resolving disputes and ensuring fairness to every one of them. What's wrong with that?

CAMI is unique in some ways, but it's not the only example of the CAW's policy of working with corporations and governments to benefit workers, their families and their communities. In early 2002 New Flyer Industries Inc., a bus manufacturer in Winnipeg, announced it was in deep financial trouble. If it couldn't find a buyer the company would close down, throwing hundreds of CAW members out of work.

Instead of throwing up our hands and walking away, we joined forces with Manitoba's NDP government to save New Flyer and its jobs. The provincial government offered $20 million in assistance, and the CAW agreed to open its contract for renegotiations. It worked. A buyer was located, a labour adjustment committee was formed to support laid-off employees, and hundreds of good-paying jobs were saved. In mid-2008 New Flyer employed over 1,000 workers in Winnipeg. What might have happened if the CAW had not chosen to get involved and join the government in saving the operation?

TWELVE

A Changing World
Demands a Changing Union

I could name dozens of examples where I pushed our union to be more innovative and open in its efforts to keep plants operating and union members working, especially in light of economic realities that seemed to get more depressing every year. None of these sparked more fire-and-brimstone debate than our deal with Magna International.

While building his chain of auto parts companies that make up Magna, Frank Stronach wasn't just non-union, he was anti-union. He spent millions of dollars fighting unions (especially the CAW) that wanted certification in his companies. Interestingly, his daughter, Belinda, has not been hostile to unions; as a Liberal MP she supported federal anti-scab legislation in 2007 and actively lobbied other Liberal MPs to her position.

In late 2005 Frank called me at CAW headquarters. "I need to talk to you about something," he said. "How soon can we get together?"

I told him I was pretty busy.

"You gotta stop for lunch some time," he responded. "How about tomorrow, in the dining room at my golf club?"

Too intrigued to say no, I called Ken Lewenza and asked him to join me.

Frank started off by reviewing all the things that we knew were happening in the auto industry. He talked about the growing number of imports, about the transfer of production offshore, about all the concerns the industry was facing and how they were affecting his Magna-owned companies. "We're a Canadian company, always will be," Frank said. "We're committed to Canada and want to grow here in Canada, contributing to this country's economy." Then he added: "Wherever the assembly plants go, we have to follow. We can't keep making parts in Aurora for shipment to Tennessee. It just doesn't make sense anymore."

We agreed that the North American auto industry was in trouble, and Frank suggested that we could do something to assist it. It would be better for everyone, he proposed, if the union and Magna stopped fighting each other and started finding ways to work together.

"If we accept the rights of the workers to join the union," he said, "and you accept our right to make a profit, we can eliminate all the wasted energy and resources. Then we can concentrate on convincing the government to do something to help the industry."

We began discussing details of a concept that Frank called the Framework of Fairness Agreement, or simply FFA. Basically, the terms would permit the CAW to recruit employees of Magna plants as union members. If the majority voted in favour of the union, the plant became CAW-certified and workers would be covered by a negotiated contract whose terms would include a means of resolving concerns.

The contract would include most of the features of other collective bargaining agreements, with a few exceptions. The most important of these was an understanding that the union would agree to a no-strike clause and management would agree to a no lockout clause. Any issue that could not be resolved through bargaining would be referred to an arbitrator for a final and binding decision. The bargaining committee would be elected by members of the CAW.

One unique feature of the offer was the guarantee of a wage increase in each year of the agreement. Historically, labour-management disputes are settled in one of three ways; the union can decide to strike to pursue their goals, the employer can decide to lock out the union members to pursue their goals, or both parties can agree to final and binding arbitration. The CAW used the right to strike only when it was clear the employer would not settle on reasonable terms, and it has used and will continue to use final binding arbitration when the elected leadership and the membership decide it is in their best interest to do so. The Magna agreement was one occasion when both sides could abandon their dislike of the arbitration process.

I never made a substantial decision without consulting with CAW executive and local leaders, and I sure as hell wasn't going to change my policy with this one. Back at CAW headquarters I discussed the proposal in detail with several people, including secretary-treasurer Jim O'Neil and my assistants Bob Chernecki, Hemi Mitic, Tom Collins, Carol Phillips and Peter Kennedy. When they appeared comfortable with the idea we brought in the chairs of the CAW master bargaining committees at the Big Three—Ken Lewenza for Chrysler, Chris Buckley for GM and Mike Vince for Ford—along with Tim Carrie, chair of our Independent Parts Supplier council.

I explained how the arrangement would work, and Jim Stanford, our economist, reviewed the historical decline of union presence in auto parts manufacturing. At that time, we were falling toward 25 per-cent density where auto parts manufacturing was concerned, about half where we had been 10 years earlier. The more our density dropped, I reminded everybody, the more that non-union plants would set the wage and benefits standard, not us.

These were hard-nosed, dedicated unionists, and if any of them had expressed deep reservations about the idea, I would have scrapped it. "We can't sit by and watch all the progress we've made over the years vanish," I suggested, "and that's going to happen unless we improve our presence in these plants. We have the potential of representing 18,000 workers at 45 different Magna plants, which would raise our density back to about 50 percent. There's no other way to achieve this." The proposal was endorsed unanimously by the CAW's auto leadership and senior staff. So we contacted Stronach, wrapped up some details, and broke the news.

"With this agreement," I commented in the press, "Magna and the CAW will develop a new way of working together. It will strengthen the CAW's ability to support auto parts workers at an incredibly challeng-ing time, in a way that also strengthens Canada's auto industry. This isn't about driving up costs. It's about a long-term relationship com-mitted to helping build this industry and provide jobs for Canadians."

Frank Stronach, who had a long record of criticizing unions, surprised everyone with some of his comments. "We're not afraid of labour organizations," he told the press. "We never, ever said we should not be unionized," adding that the company and the union shared the same mandate: "To be efficient and to be competitive, and that takes a lot of goodwill. Society needs checks and balances, and unions do fulfil that important role." Then he added a real kicker. "Union workers," Stronach declared, "are better motivated than non-union workers."

He meant that employees backed by a strong union feel more independent and less intimidated than non-union workers, and thus are more motivated to perform their duties well. I had been preaching that idea to Stronach and others for years. To hear him repeat this fact publicly was music to my ears.

Since the signing of the Magna agreement, three bargaining units have voted overwhelmingly in favour of joining the CAW and accepting the new contract rules, and their decision has been criticized by other unions. But what's the problem? The issue is clear to me and should be clear to anyone else concerned about workers' rights and job security. These Magna workers did not have a union, did not have the protection of a contract, enjoyed no seniority rights, job postings or grievance procedure, and missed a lot of other benefits provided by a strong union. Now they have all these rights, guaranteed by a union agreement in exchange for a no-strike clause. Are they better off? They sure as hell are in my view, and in the view of most of the workers as well. Yet other union leaders blasted them for their decision and the CAW for making it possible.

As far as I'm concerned the anti-CAW sentiment in the labour movement was pure envy coming from people who simply could not accept our continuing success. Sid Ryan, president of the Canadian Union of Public Employees (CUPE), was especially critical, despite the fact that a large number of his own members settle their deals with employers through voluntary binding arbitration. Deborah Bourque, who was president of CUPW at the time, was also critical even though she had just signed an eight-year no-strike clause on behalf a newly organized group of postal workers. Others in unions that had signed long-term agreements, and had used or were using arbitration to settle their contracts, were equally critical of the CAW for allegedly giving up the right to strike. Leaders of CUPE, the Steelworkers and the SEIU had all accepted no-strike provisions in their own local contracts, yet they piled on me and the CAW for trying something innovative at Magna.

This was more than a little hypocritical. In my opinion it was pure envy that we were able to achieve success and prove once again that the CAW remained on the leading edge of change. As a result of this agreement and others, the CAW was being recognized as the leading union in bargaining strategies dealing with social, economic and political issues not only in Canada but also around the world.

Instead of viewing CAW's success as a challenge and perhaps an inspiration to improve the status of their own unions, many labour leaders chose to undermine the CAW. It didn't work then and it won't work in the future, thanks to the culture of the CAW that has developed over many years.

It's a culture of hard work by elected local and national leaders and their staff on behalf of CAW members and their families. My attitude as CAW president was that we could not claim we represented hardworking union members if the top level of the union itself wasn't working just as hard or even harder. When I was elected national president in 1992, I promised to maintain open dialogue and communication with all staff members and all local union leadership, and to consult with my assistants and the CAW national executive board. Part of this commitment was a guarantee to return every phone call made to my office, my cellphone or my home phone by the end of the day. Later I made a similar commitment to answer all e-mails within 48 hours of receiving them, and required the staff to do the same. Any CAW member who contacted the union's head office knew he or she would receive a prompt response. The policy convinced members that the union took their concerns seriously, and it emphasized to the CAW executive and staff that we were there to serve the members, not vice-versa. All in all, it made the CAW a better organization.

Was the Magna agreement a perfect deal? Of course not. We would have preferred open access to all Magna facilities and overwhelming support from every plant authorizing the CAW to engage in traditional collective bargaining. But that wasn't going to happen. And the workers under the Framework of Fairness Agreement (FFA) were clearly better off than having no union at all.

* * *

You don't make omelettes without breaking eggs, and you don't make changes in any organization—especially the change that the FFA represented—without drawing criticism, and our deal with Stronach was no exception.

Leaders of other unions were the first to jump all over me for proposing and implementing the program. One attack on both the program and me came from a column that appeared in the *Financial Post* on November 23, 2007. The article was signed by six Ontario union leaders: Wayne Fraser of the United Steelworkers; Sid Ryan of the Canadian Union of Public Employees (CUPE); Cec Makowski of the Communications, Energy and Paperworkers Union of Canada (CEP); Sharleen Stewart of the Service Employees International Union (SEIU); Dave Ritchie of the International Association of Machinists and Aerospace Workers (IAMAW); and Warren (Smokey) Thomas of the Ontario Public Sector Employees Union (OPSEU). The article called the deal a major blow against independent unionism.

"It seems pretty clear," they wrote, "that this deal will help production and employment to flow out of the Big Three auto assemblers and other auto parts makers and into Magna, where workers will lack time-tested union rights and capacities, and where labour costs are significantly lower." This statement revealed a total lack of understanding about the auto industry. Unionized auto workers already faced brutal competition from non-union plants (including Magna) where strikes could not legally occur. How the hell could unionizing Magna, even in a non-traditional way, make the situation any worse? By strengthening the wages and benefits of Magna workers, the FFA would reduce the downward pressure on our existing CAW members in the auto parts sector. That's precisely why we did what we did. We knew that if unionization in auto parts continued to slip, our ability to defend standards in our existing unionized shops would crumble. With this agreement Magna employees would see an increase in their incomes, not a decrease, and the CAW would exert influence in plants where it had no influence before the agreement.

I expected to hear criticism from other unions, but I didn't see Chris Buckley's accusations coming from inside the CAW itself. President of CAW Local 222 in Oshawa and head of the CAW-GM Master Bargaining Committee, Chris had supported the FFA during our internal discussions. But when he returned to Local 222 in Oshawa, he apparently got an earful about it from his members. They didn't like it, and their opposition carried more weight with Chris than his commitment to the union's decision. This may have been especially the case with the local union about to head into its own elections. Instead of responding to his members' complaints with the same arguments we had used in our discussions, Chris simply fired their dissatisfaction back at me in a scathing letter. "Our principles state 'In our society, private corporations control the workplace and set the framework for all employees,'" Chris wrote. "Does this no longer apply? Are we now bowing to corporations like Magna?"

Chris's position was soon supported by a small number of CAW locals, including Local 112, representing workers at the Bombardier plant in Toronto. A storm of back-and-forth discussion began. I never expected things to go smoothly, but I spent a lot of time and effort trying to defend the concept against the criticism coming from Chris and the others. There was a real irony to Chris's complaints. If he had not voted in favour of the FFA, I would not have proceeded with it. Nor would I have pushed the idea if key CAW leaders like Ken Lewenza, Mike Vince or Tim Carrie had objected. I needed unanimous agreement on the idea from our auto sector leadership; without it, the idea would have been dropped on the spot. Chris had provided the unanimity we needed, and when he had second thoughts he tried to take it back.

If Chris Buckley had a serious problem with the proposal during our discussion he could have killed it easily, and he knew it. Only when it proved unpopular with some members of his local did he change his mind and do a 180 on me. I understand his discomfort over their reaction, but good leadership doesn't involve making only easy decisions; it demands that you make the hard decisions as well. (And it's a measure of tolerance for free speech within the CAW that Chris's right to speak out against the idea, even after he approved it initially, was never questioned, nor was he ever chastised. In fact, two weeks later I offered him a promotion. Do you think this kind of tolerance for free speech exists in corporations or political parties? Not bloody likely.)

At this point former CAW head Bob White stepped into the battle, taking some of the pressure off me. The words of no labour leader in the country carry more weight than Bob's, and an op-ed article published on October 30, 2007 in the *Toronto Star* he helped calm the waters. "A strong union leader must challenge employers to respect workers' rights and treat their employees fairly," Bob wrote. "But equally important, a strong leader must also challenge our own movement." Bob noted that the voluntary recognition deal with CAMI had also been controversial when first proposed, but was now working to everyone's satisfaction. Then he attacked the critics of the Magna agreement. And he did it with the usual Bob White right-between-the-eyes style.

"I am surprised and disappointed by the arrogant tone of many of the critics," he wrote. "They show no respect for Magna workers. It is they, not armchair critics or academics, who will make the final decision whether or not to approve this arrangement." He went on to note some important terms of the deal. Magna workers would have a quality contract, negotiated every three years and ratified by secret ballot; the contract would be enforced by a dispute-settlement system that included, as a last resort, binding arbitration; workers would get annual wage increases and quality benefits; they would be served by full-time local union representatives; and they would benefit from the resources and programs of the national union. None of these was available to the Magna workers without agreeing to CAW certification.

No-strike agreements are unusual in the auto industry, but are common in other sectors in the CAW and most other unions. Having the right to strike is preferable but not always possible. More than 30,000 CAW members in the public sector, from nursing home attendants to air traffic controllers, do not have that right either, yet important gains have been made by them and their unions. Bob made this point, adding, "I think it is important to keep finding new strategies and innovations to make a positive difference in workers' lives, as long as workers have the ultimate say in determining whether they accept the union and the collective agreement, as they do in the CAW–Magna deal."

Despite Bob White's defence of our arrangement with Frank Stronach, the complaints kept pouring in. One situation was especially difficult for me to deal with and led to the only time during my presidency of the CAW when I actually applied the full power of that office to a CAW staff member.

Vic Tomiczek, a regional director of the union from Nova Scotia, opposed the deal with Magna and spoke his mind about it, which was fine with me and everyone else. He joined the CAW's elected board and their assistants, regional directors and department heads to discuss and vote on the proposal. More than 60 people in all exchanged their views, which were representative of the union membership right across the country. Everyone respected Vic's position, but when the vote was taken he was on the losing side and we agreed to move on.

Once back in Nova Scotia, Vic continued voicing his opposition, which didn't disturb me. I knew the Magna agreement would be a controversial move and I never expected everybody to agree with it, nor did I expect those who opposed it to suddenly become silent. But a few weeks later, while I was out of the country attending an international conference, I received a call from Bob Chernecki informing me that Vic had started taking his complaints beyond his own staff assignment and union local into the offices of other union locals in his region. He was calling the deal "a sellout" and creating hostility against it and CAW union executives in places where he didn't belong.

I told Bob Chernecki to inform Vic that he had no right to visit other union locals and stir up resentment against a decision that had been made by the union executive. If he still disagreed, fine—but interfering in the business of local unions, trying to persuade them to oppose a legitimate union decision, was unacceptable.

Bob passed my message to Vic, who basically ignored it. When I received word that Vic was still working actively to overturn the deal I suspended him with pay and scheduled a hearing with his union upon my return to Canada. Based on the hearing, I announced that I would fire Vic, the first time I had taken such a step. However, following discussions with the staff union; I agreed that Vic's departure would be an early retirement. This was fine with me; he couldn't adapt to a changing environment, which can be a challenge for some people. This went beyond his problem about dealing with change, and affected a much bigger situation. Just because you have problems adapting doesn't give you the right to actively undermine your organization with others, especially those outside your staff assignment.

In December 2007, the CAW council endorsed the FFA with opposition from only a handful of delegates. The internal wounds soon healed. Chris Buckley and the others who opposed the deal put aside the debate and got back to work building the union and protecting its members, and CAW organizing and servicing staff began implementing the FFA. Like the original debate, this has proven more difficult than we expected.

By early 2008, of course, the North American auto industry was sliding into crisis and Magna, despite its strengths, was not immune. When its sales of parts to the assemblers fell with the drop-off in vehicle production, Magna indicated it would close several Canadian plants. Sensibly, Magna's management indicated it would serve no purpose to unionize a plant and then close it for demand-related reasons, a move that would reflect badly on both the company and the union.

As I write this, three new bargaining units at Magna have been certified under the FFA, with strong membership support in each case. Along with two units previously organized in Windsor and Mississauga, this makes a total of five CAW-represented plants in the company. Magna's CEO Don Walker is the chairperson of the auto industry's main policy group, the Canadian Automotive Partnership Council, and a fair and thoughtful guy. It won't be easy to carry on building a new model for labour-management relations, but I believe the FFA approach is worthwhile and I wish Walker and my successor Ken Lewenza all the best as they try to make it a reality.

* * *

The world keeps changing, whether we like it or not, and not everything moves in the direction we want it to go. But you deal with the things that are real, not the things you wish were in front of you.

Employers don't act the same way they did when I entered the union movement more than 40 years ago. This doesn't mean they necessarily act better, just differently. It seemed to me that one of the surest ways for the union movement to seal its own doom would be refusing to adapt to change. Union goals of protecting and improving the status of workers can and should remain the same, but the tactics and strategy to attain them have to be flexible.

In an article entitled "Reports of Labour's Demise Overlook Encouraging Trends," David Gouter, a professor in the labour studies program at McMaster University, noted that many union people believed the arrival of mass production industries spelled the end of unions "because assembly lines reduced the role of skilled-trades workers who were the core of unions. Then the organizing drives of the 1930s and 1940s changed the character of the labour movement and industrial work itself." Gouter added that, until the 1960s, few people believed the public sector would be unionized, and for many years before that, women and immigrants were never considered prospects for union membership, yet today these groups represent pillars of strength for the union movement in Canada. Gouter concluded, "There are good reasons to doubt smug dismissals of organized labour as a spent force" (*Toronto Star*, September 1, 2008).

The world has changed but unions still count, are still relevant, and are still necessary to ensure fairness for workers. Union membership has been sliding over the past two decades or so, helped along by the recent economic disaster caused, I have to say, not by "greedy labour" but by outrageously greedy financial wizards driven by their own gluttony and regulated by no one.

We could hang our heads and cry over the fact that unions represent fewer than 30 percent of all workers in Canada and much less in the private sector. Or we could gnash our teeth and vent our rage with speeches, marches and unnecessary strikes. But does anyone think this would change the situation? My view is that we must adapt where we can, without losing sight of our goals, and take pride and comfort where things have swung our way.

At the turn of the twenty-first century, globalization appeared to be inevitable, sweeping away jobs and progressive changes in labour-management relations. Things have begun to change, fuelled by the current economic crisis. People are beginning to appreciate the importance of homegrown industries, where decisions that influence their society are made within their own borders and not by some officious bean counter using long-distance communication to fire workers, close plants and devastate communities. Canadian jobs and investments may still be heading overseas, but the swing no longer appears inevitable.

The energy wasted on trying to protect and maintain old ways of doing things, even when it's clear they aren't working, should instead be spent challenging ourselves, listening to both our members and non-unionized workers, and thoughtfully but fearlessly experimenting with new approaches. In March 2006, I was honoured to receive an annual visiting lectureship at Queen's University in Kingston. The award was named after Don Wood, the long-time director of industrial relations at Queen's. I titled my keynote lecture "The State of the Union Movement in Canada: The Challenges We Face, and the Innovations We Must Undertake." Here's what I said at the conclusion of my lecture:

> I sincerely believe that we are fighting for the life of our movement, and we have to act as if that was true. That means ruthlessly reviewing what is working, and what is not working, in our current organizing,

bargaining, education, and political activism. It means being willing to fearlessly innovate: to try new approaches, where old ones aren't working.

This will inherently be a painful, controversial process. As anyone who knows me understands well, I have never been one to shy away from controversy. And I believe our movement should be more willing to debate, to take on those tough issues, to call it like it is—rather than thinking we can iron out our differences under some blanket of phony consensus, as the power of the labour movement continues to erode under our feet.

I know I sparked more than my share of controversy during my time as a CAW leader, including plenty of it within our own ranks. But I don't mind the bumps and bruises, the scrapes and hard feelings built up as a result of those debates. We need more debate, not less. Because if our movement doesn't face its challenges and come up with innovative ways to confront and solve them, it will die.

And hiding behind a façade of fake solidarity won't change that fact for a minute.

THIRTEEN

How—and Why—to Save the North American Auto Industry

"In free fall."

As I write this, that's the description of the global economy. Stock markets, house prices, employment levels and almost everything else is dropping in value. Governments around the world are pouring hundreds of billions of dollars into banks and investment firms to keep them afloat. Untold billions more are going toward tax cuts and stimulus efforts. No one knows for sure where the bottom is, or when the economy will turn around. Everyone is concerned about the future, as they should be. Meanwhile, new car buyers can't get loans at attractive rates, auto leasing has almost completely dried up, car dealers can't get credit to place wholesale orders with the manufacturers, and the automakers themselves need capital to retool their plants for new environmentally friendly cars and trucks. What a mess.

The economic situation shouldn't surprise anyone familiar with the North American auto industry. We've been watching similar developments in Canada's most important manufacturing sector for years. In fact, the most frightening thing about the potential collapse of our auto industry and the possible disappearance of GM, Ford and Chrysler is the fact that the top executives of those firms didn't recognize what was happening. Or if they knew, they refused to take effective action. How else can you explain GM executives, for example, signing a contract and committing to keep the Oshawa truck plant open in May and then changing their minds in June?

Nevertheless the depth and impact of the crisis are shocking. Nothing prepared people for the extent of the damage this recession has caused, including enormous losses in pension funds that threaten the security of workers on a pension or close to retirement. Billions of people around the world have been badly affected by this crisis, losing their jobs, their homes, their pensions. Auto workers in North America have been one of the hardest-hit groups.

For years before the automotive companies dropped the bomb about their possible demise in late 2008, I had been making speeches in and out of the industry warning about the risk. The three companies, I repeated to whomever would listen, could not survive operating as they were. No business model existed that showed corporations losing both market share and billions of dollars every quarter and still managing to stay alive, and no country's industry can survive a continual one-way flow of imports into the domestic market, with virtually nothing go back the other way. Capitalism doesn't work like that. How could a trade unionist recognize and acknowledge this fact while whole regiments of MBAs in the executive offices of the car companies, and governments in both Canada and the U.S., pretended it wasn't happening?

So all the frantic discussion about the possible failure of the Big Three auto companies in late 2008 wasn't news to me. The only surprise was how quickly it came about. And it's interesting, isn't it, that through 20 or 30 years of right-wing complaints about unions and the power of the left, the biggest economic mess to hit the world since the Great Depression began on Wall Street, among all those smart-asses who believed in total deregulation and letting "market forces" set the standards.

The only apparent reaction by the auto companies to the impending crisis was to show a smiling face to the public and a different one to the unions. From 2003 to 2008 each company came to the CAW with proposals that required unionized workers to give up benefits, take early retirement or accept layoffs. It was part of the firm's restructuring, we were told over and over again, and necessary to save the company. Well, none of those steps "saved" the companies, and none could as long as imports kept flowing unrestricted into North America. We kept repeating this to both the automobile companies and the federal government. Nobody paid attention.

Meanwhile GM, Ford and Chrysler kept losing market share and money, and the auto workers kept losing their jobs. From May 2001 to December 2008, the number of jobs in Canada's auto assembly plants dropped by 13,000 with another 23,000 jobs lost in parts manufacturing. About 36,000 fewer workers and more than $2 billion in workers' income vanished from Canada's economy in that period.* Not surprisingly perhaps, the lost jobs were more distressing to the CAW than to the automotive company executives, who seemed to expect either a miracle to occur or their brilliant decision making to turn things around. It appears to me that they failed to realize the implications of these job

---

* Based on data from Statistics Canada, CANSIM Matrix 281–0024; assumes $70,000 annual income in assembly and $50,000 annual income in parts.

losses. They were like someone who stands around watching his next-door neighbour's house on fire, ignoring the likelihood that the flames will spread to his own home.

Sometimes it seemed that government and the public believed the people running GM, Ford and Chrysler could never be wrong because they were so clever and their companies were so big. Their positions gave them status compared to union leaders, and too many people confuse status with trust when it comes to deciding which conflicting opinion they choose to believe. The auto company executives may have had the status with their titles, their office suites and their private jets, but the CAW had the truth. Too bad it took so long for the rest of the world to acknowledge it.

It wasn't just the automotive companies who seemed to ignore the impending crisis. In 2002 I grew alarmed about two events that promised to spell nothing but trouble for our industry and for Canada. One was that year's drop-off in this country's auto trade surplus. Just three years earlier Canada had been the fourth-largest auto producer in the world and the largest in per capita terms, producing more motor vehicles for our size than any other nation and creating an annual trade surplus in vehicles of almost $15 billion. By 2002 the surplus had slipped to barely $5 billion and it kept falling. Meanwhile, several states in the U.S. were offering tens of millions of dollars in public funds to attract new plants to their region, and the auto companies were responding to the deals.

If we were to regain our automotive trade surplus, or even keep it from sliding into a trade deficit, we needed to take action on two fronts: control the one-way wave of imports, and provide the industry with economic incentives similar to those being extended in the southern U.S.

On September 25, 2002, I wrote Prime Minister Jean Chrétien imploring him to take action, noting at the beginning of my letter all the success the CAW had achieved recently: "Since I became President of the CAW in 1992, we have achieved contracts without a work stoppage in nine of the last 10 Big Three contracts that have been negotiated."

Then, after listing a number of announcements to expand facilities in Canada by GM totalling $1.3 billion, I pointed out:

> Both the company and the CAW are proud of the fact that such a significant investment commitment could be mobilized without direct government assistance. This demonstrates, contrary to the arguments of some commentators, that neither the CAW nor the auto industry are somehow "addicted" to government "handouts." Canada's auto industry has a lot going for it: productivity, quality, location, and competitive operating costs. In many cases (such as with the recent GM announcements), these advantages will be sufficient to win commitments for new investments to protect existing jobs. In these cases, obviously, no investment subsidies are required, and neither we nor the company asked for them.

All well and good, but we were not out of the woods. I continued:

> It would be a major mistake to conclude, as some commentators obviously have, that since some investments in Canada's auto industry (like GM's recent $1.3 billion commitments) can be won without government involvement, there is therefore no need for government involvement of any kind. Clearly, some new investment will continue to flow to Canada even in the absence of an active government strategy, based on the momentum of previous investment decisions and the continuing quality and competitiveness of our output. No one has suggested that investment will fall to zero in the absence of a government policy. The real question, rather, is do we want more investment or less investment? Do we want to build on our past successes or watch the industry decline, threatening Canada's position as a world automotive leader?

If we rely solely on private cost-benefit decisions to determine how much investment we attract in Canada, we will receive an amount of new investment that is not consistent with preserving Canada's current status as a top-10 global automaker. We will not receive greenfield plants, we will lose at least two major assembly plants in the next 18 months, and our overall auto manufacturing base will gradually decay. Yes, we will win some investments and some new product commitments; not all of our auto assembly plants will suddenly close. But we will follow Britain, Italy and other former automaking powerhouses down in the global rankings. With all the new North American plants going to Mexico or the U.S. South, and our existing plants losing momentum, our industry will be unable to play the role we have come to rely on—as a leading engine of Canadian growth, exports and productivity.

What we needed was a comprehensive national policy on the automotive industry. We needed a strategy to protect and enhance our most important export industry, using every tool in the government's toolbox: investment supports, trade policy, support for skills and technology, and modern infrastructure. Every other successful auto-exporting nation has a policy like this. But Canada doesn't.

Canada's $15 billion trade surplus in automotive products in 1999 dissolved into a $14 billion trade deficit by 2008. In less than a decade, Canada's trade balance in motor vehicles slid almost $30 billion, and nobody but me, along with other CAW leaders and union members, seemed to give a damn.

Linked to the plunge from surplus to deficit was the declining North American market share of the Big Three companies, now well below 50 percent. The response of management to this decline was curious on the one hand and maddeningly logical on the other.

Their most apparent action was to downsize their operations by closing plants, laying off workers and cutting back production. I'm familiar enough with business practices to know that this is not the response in any other industry. When Coca-Cola begins losing market share to Pepsi, it doesn't respond by shutting down its bottling plants. It works like hell to get back the lost sales at Pepsi's expense. Obviously, there's a lot less involved in choosing a soft drink than in deciding which new car to buy, but the fact remains that GM, Ford and Chrysler basically abdicated a large part of the market to offshore competition.

The logic of their decision was this: The car companies do not care where their products are manufactured as long as they can make a profit. So while they were closing plants and generally downsizing in the U.S. and Canada, they were opening new plants in Latin America, Eastern Europe and Asia, and some of the cars produced there find their way back into our market.

I understand that business decision. I don't agree with it, but I understand it. And it's wrong.

First of all, downsizing didn't work. Over and over again the companies would announce with great fanfare that they had restructured, closing plants and laying off workers to deal with the problem, promising things would be hunky-dory from that day on. But they never were. A year later, another downsizing announcement would be made with another promise that this one, like the last, would be the breakthrough needed to ensure the firm's future success.

Yet each time one of these restructure/reorganize/reposition events occurred the company would write off billions of dollars in plants, facilities and severance payments to workers. That was the short-term loss. They also remained committed to covering retiree benefits. In the U.S. this meant making regular health benefit and other payments to almost a million retirees, payments they had to fund with lower auto production and a smaller market share. Downsizing only added to the car makers' problem, weighing them down in ways that assembly line wages didn't and never could.

While the North American companies were downsizing, foreign automakers were expanding, and their biggest expansion market was North America. The year 2008 marked the first time in history that more vehicles were sold on this continent by foreign manufacturers than were built here by GM, Ford and Chrysler. Of those foreign-branded cars, half arrive from countries whose markets are effectively closed to the vehicles we build here.

The top management at the Big Three knew the situation as well or better than me. They saw their losses mounting, their market share slipping, and their foreign competition unloading more and more vehicles here every year. So why didn't they see the crisis coming? Why were they less aware than me about the inevitable outcome of the situation?

Maybe because they were so busy reassuring everybody, especially their shareholders and dealers, that they were in control. For the past few years, it seemed that each month one or more of the companies would announce a new business model for their operations, sprinkling the press releases with news of workplace closings, shift reductions and layoffs. Every announcement came with an assurance that the company was now on track for recovery and the future never looked brighter.

The naiveté of the corporate leadership was shocking. Were they reading the same sales reports as me? Did they honestly believe that the best way to counter competition was to make fewer vehicles? From time to time I'd raise the question with Rick Wagoner or Gary Cowger at GM, or Tom LaSorda at Chrysler, or Joe Hinrichs at Ford. "I don't think you can solve this problem the way you're going," I'd say to them. "You can't shrink your way out of this mess. You have to start dealing with the imports, especially from Japan and Korea, or you'll never get anywhere."

This didn't cut much ice, especially with GM, for a good reason. GM had a substantial interest in Daewoo, a Korean manufacturer whose small cars were rebadged and shipped to North America and Europe as GM models. The most popular Daewoo/GM car in Canada is the subcompact Chevrolet Aveo, also marketed as the Pontiac Wave. This made it awkward, of course, for GM to go to Washington and Ottawa to demand a restriction on unfair importation when they were making a profit from the practice. To its credit, GM did actively oppose the free trade agreement that Canada's federal government has attempted to negotiate with Korea.

The North American automakers could have applied their political and media influence to point out that every other country with a domestic automotive industry restricts imports, either openly with tariffs or underhandedly with "gentlemen's agreements"—except for Canada and the U.S. The import restrictions used by other countries to give their own industries a protected home base aren't even on the radar of the WTO. This is an open secret that all the players understand, acknowledge and accept. Apart from a few largely token efforts, the North American automakers failed miserably to confront this free trade charade.

Year after year, automotive imports to countries in the European Community total around 10 percent of the total market; all other vehicles sold there are made in the EU. Meanwhile, the Europeans export enough of their manufactured vehicles to other markets, including North America, that they essentially break even on the deal. You will not find any law limiting import levels on the books, and no EU politician or bureaucrat will discuss it openly, but the global automobile manufacturers have all heard the same warning, delivered with a smile and a handshake: Keep your share of the market around 10 percent or we'll find ways to do it for you. That's the EU version of managed trade, and look how well it works for them.

In Japan and Korea the rules are even stricter. Imports there account for a tiny fraction of domestic sales (well below 5 percent), thanks to a wide range of policies, from non-tariff barriers to manipulating exchange rates, to keep it that way. It's only North America that allows so much of its market (almost 30 percent now) to be conquered by imports.

* * *

One of the knocks against the North American car makers concerns the quality of the vehicles they turn out, and back in the 1970s and 1980s this may have been a valid complaint. The demand for new cars and trucks in those years was tremendous. People were buying whatever they could get their hands on, and the manufacturers worked like hell to produce as many vehicles as possible in the shortest amount of time.

The car companies deserve a kick in the ass for putting production and quick profits ahead of quality. They paid for it with a bad reputation for quality and they're still paying for it in the minds of some people today. But that's all in the past. There have been huge changes in the quality levels reached in North American plants, and many of the steps to make better vehicles originated not with management but with the union. Surprised? You shouldn't be.

Nobody enjoys hearing they do shoddy work. If you have special skills and are paid well for them, you take pride in what you do, and CAW workers are no different from anyone else. When the workers on the line saw a problem they tried to fix it, or alerted management about it. The workers or shop stewards would point out that a particular part didn't fit correctly, or that it might be better if one assembly procedure took place before another, stuff like that. Eventually, when they realized their sales were hurting because of quality issues, the companies started listening to the workers and implementing techniques to build better vehicles. Today they are built as well as and in many cases better than anyone else builds them anywhere in the world.

But that old reputation still hangs on with people who believe you have to look to Asia or Europe to get a well-built car. Here's the real story.

GM, Ford and Chrysler have all been selling vehicles in Canada for 100 years or more. Imports like Honda, Toyota and Nissan really got their start here in the late 1970s after the oil crisis. That's when people started looking for smaller cars, and the Japanese had been building small cars for years. They knew how to do it efficiently and they grabbed a large share of the market. They're good, but they're not perfect.

The imports have had just as many quality problems and recalls as the North American companies, if not more. In January 2009, Toyota, the company everybody holds up as an example of exceptional quality, announced a major recall of 1.3 million cars because, as Toyota's own release explained, "These cars, in certain crashes, will use a small pyro-technic explosion to tighten the seatbelts to hold passengers in place. The hot gas given off in the act of pre-tensioning could damage the faulty insulator pad and trigger a fire." Sounds like a pretty major flaw to me, proving only that Toyota can make as serious an error in engineering or assembly as any other company.

Independent firms like J.D. Power confirm that North American-made vehicles have higher quality levels than those manufactured in Europe, and that the quality gap between North America and Asia has been effectively eliminated.

* * *

The global economic crisis of 2008–2009 wasn't triggered by problems in the automobile and truck industry, but it's difficult to imagine any group suffering the effects more severely than those who make automobiles and parts for a living. Not long ago people worried about the likelihood of Chrysler surviving. Now they worry about the chances of General Motors and even Ford being around over the next five years.

At least the United States now has a president who is prepared to step in and take action instead of simply telling Americans to "go shopping." While I applaud President Barack Obama's style, I'm concerned about the wisdom of some of his decisions, especially those relating to the automotive industry. The task force Obama set up to deal with the auto companies included nobody with experience in the auto industry. There were, however, lots of number crunchers straight from Wall Street to oversee the auto-restructuring exercise, the same people who got us into the whole mess with their derivatives and credit default swaps and ultra-short-term views.

Telling Chrysler in March 2009 that the company had 30 days to negotiate a merger with Fiat or face liquidation was a gift to the Italians because it took all the bargaining power away from Chrysler. I understand the importance of a deadline but if the task force insisted on imposing one they should have played an active role in the discussions instead of sending Chrysler into a room with Fiat and telling the company to come back in a month with a deal. It's a form of crisis management that leads to future disasters, usually performed not to find a long-term solution to a problem but to make a short-term positive impact on voters.

The abrupt firing of Rick Wagoner by the White House is another example of making a decision based more on creating an impression of being decisive than on solving the problem at hand. Sure, I've had my differences with Wagoner and I was damned angry about GM's reneging on our May 2008 contract and closing the Oshawa truck plant. But Wagoner was one of the brightest top executives I encountered in the industry over 40 years. He knew the industry as well as anybody and the task force could have used his experience. Instead, he became something of a sacrificial lamb.

I don't know all the circumstances of Wagoner's firing, although I suspect he was axed because he wouldn't cut the company as quickly and deeply as Washington wanted. But Wagoner had already cut GM effectively in half since 2000. He had agreed to get rid of Hummer, Saturn and Saab, and Pontiac was the next to go, but the guys calling the shots in Washington wanted him to downsize the company even more ruthlessly and violently. Why? The company had been trying to dig its way out of a hole for the last decade by downsizing and it hadn't worked. The more GM shrank the larger its per-unit costs for product development, marketing and retiree benefits grew.

Firing a guy like Wagoner after telling him how to run the company, and dictating a 30-day schedule to Chrysler for its merger talks, suggests a level of arrogance on the part of Obama's team that I dislike. I know the demands were made in exchange for loans provided to the companies, but I don't believe this gesture qualified the politicians and their staff as automotive executives overnight. And by the way, whatever Wagoner's and GM's failings might have been, they didn't trigger the global economic turndown. That started on Wall Street. So why wasn't Washington as quick on the trigger with banking, finance and investment CEOs as it was with the head of General Motors? Some people have claimed it demonstrates an anti-blue collar (read: anti-manufacturing) bias on the part of government. Some people just might be correct.

When I first heard Wagoner's replacement would be Fritz Henderson I was appalled. Basically a numbers guy, Henderson collected a fair amount of foreign experience, running GM's operations in South America for a while before being sent to oversee things in Europe and

Asia and being appointed GM's chief financial officer in 2006, moving up to chief operating officer in March 2008. He was the new guy on the block. GM took the Oshawa truck plant away from us in June 2008 and I suspected he influenced the decision. I met him at the meeting after GM announced it was closing the truck plant and at the time I found him cold and uncommunicative, not the kind of person I'd want to deal with on a regular basis. I also worried that he focused too much on the company's U.S. interests and to hell with the Canadian operations.

Well, I may have been wrong. Or maybe Henderson had some kind of epiphany where he found the Truth and the Light. Anyway, within a couple of days of moving into Rick Wagoner's job he began complimenting Ken Lewenza and the CAW, saying the union had met the challenge GM set, making GM's Canadian plants more than competitive with the U.S. plants. He also publicly noted that 80 percent of the vehicles manufactured in Canada were shipped to the U.S., and that's where they had to be competitive. A GM CEO defending the CAW and admitting the importance of Canadian plants to the U.S. market? Hey, I've got no problem with that kind of guy.

While GM and Chrysler had their hands out to accept government money, Ford stepped back and said the company didn't need it. This led a number of people to assume that Ford had some kind of magic solution to the problems facing the other guys. What was it doing that GM and Chrysler weren't? The answer wasn't what it was doing at the time; it's what it *had* done in 2006 when the company hired Alan Mulally as its CEO. Mulally, who left a top position at Boeing, came to Ford only after he had an agreement from the Ford family that they would support him in restructuring the company. In 2007, before the economic crisis hit, Mulally arranged financing for $23.5 billion in available cash.

He did it by mortgaging almost everything the company owned—

the factories and the land they sat on, the technology used to design and build the cars, and even the company's famous blue Ford logo. He also sold Ford's investment in Jaguar, Land Rover and Aston Martin, and announced that Volvo was for sale as well. He took a lot of flak for risking everything including the company's own brand to get his hands on the cash, but he did it while the credit was still available. It was a gutsy move, I'll admit. Was it a smart move? We'll see. Ford has suffered market-share losses similar to their competition's and faces similar dangers. I must admit that their new product line appears to be broader and more fuel efficient than the others,' which should give them an edge. In April 2009, Ford announced it had cut $10 billion from its loan obligations, making its future look even more solid, but there are a lot of potholes in the road ahead.

Mulally handled himself better in many ways than Tommy LaSorda of Chrysler when he visited Ottawa in March 2009 looking for financial support. If he didn't get what he wanted from the union and tax relief from the government, LaSorda lectured a parliamentary committee, Chrysler would move its operations out of Canada. It was an empty threat, made by a guy on his knees looking for a handout. How smart is that?

Consider the facts. In 2009 Chrysler built all of its minivans in Windsor, having closed a plant in St. Louis, Missouri, to consolidate production. They chose Windsor because it took 5.5 hours less labour to assemble a minivan in Windsor than in St. Louis, which meant a productivity advantage of almost 25 percent. In fact the Windsor plant was the most productive minivan plant in North America, of any manufacturer, thanks to a range of innovative sourcing and work practices introduced there. We weren't happy to see another U.S. plant close, but the CAW members at Windsor had done what was required to enhance their own job security.

To close the Windsor plant and shift production to St. Louis, as Tommy LaSorda threatened, was just about the dumbest suggestion I've ever heard from an automotive company executive. It would cost the company between $300 million and $400 million just to reconfigure the plant to build both models. Not only that, but Chrysler began assembling Volkswagen Routan model vans in the same plant back in mid-2008. Closing Windsor would require shifting that production to Missouri as well, costing the company another couple of hundred million and creating some bad blood with Volkswagen, which raved about the quality and productivity of CAW workers in Windsor.

On top of that, Chrysler would be obligated to make large severance payments to the Windsor workers, adding at least another $500 million to the cost, plus hire and train hundreds of Missouri workers after making huge severance payments to workers let go when Chrysler closed the plant just a year earlier. Does that make any sense? Off the top of my head I figure it would cost Chrysler well over $1 billion to pull out of Windsor. For what? For a plant and workforce that weren't nearly as efficient as the Windsor operation? And for a dramatic drop in market share when Canadians turned against the company for pulling out?

Brampton, the other Chrysler plant in Canada, is the only facility building the larger vehicles the company produces—the Dodge Charger, Chrysler 300 and so on—in a modern, high-productivity plant. Closing it and moving production to the U.S. would cost it even more in expenses and lost profits.

The threat had no credibility with CAW members at Chrysler, or with people who know the auto industry. All it did was generate a bunch of nervous headlines in the press, and reduce the credibility of everything Tommy LaSorda said after that.

* * *

Can the Big Three auto companies survive? They'd better. But they need to follow a new direction plus get help from government, and not all of the help involves cash.

I'm the first to agree that the challenges of the automotive industry, especially in Canada and the U.S., will not be met solely by governments throwing money into the pot. Too many factors will change people's expectations for the cars they drive. I include concern for the environment and a shift toward alternative fuels as two of the biggest changes. Nothing less than a revolution in the way people choose and use their cars is on its way. The first shift, toward electric power as either a primary or secondary energy source, has already begun, and I expect it to reshape the industry over the next five to 15 years. Beyond that it may be hydrogen or some other motive power—who knows?

Change of this magnitude always seems to inspire and produce a breakthrough of some kind that few people see coming and that almost always comes from some source out in left field. It wasn't IBM who developed the personal computer that has changed our lives since 1980; they were content to make million-dollar computers for companies, and to hell with homes and families. It was two kids in a garage in California who called their product Apple. IBM jumped on board, and nothing has been the same since.

The same kind of game-changer may come along in automobiles. When it happens, it's unlikely to originate with the Big Three, not only because they've been slow to react in the past but because they'll be focused over the next few years on handling their finances to stay alive. How will they be able to afford billions on the research and development major innovation requires?

Frank Stronach's deal with Ford to develop an all-electric car may pave the way. The structure and flexibility of Magna and similar companies let them switch direction and remain open to new ideas in radical ways that GM, Ford and Chrysler can't match, regardless of their good intentions and dedication. I see new alliances and partnerships springing up outside the industry, not necessarily among current manufacturers like Chrysler and Fiat. Sure, Fiat may show Chrysler how to build small cars more effectively but much bigger technological shifts are coming.

The industry needs both new ideas and new players. Where will they come from? And how will they deal with new problems created by solving old problems? Electric cars, for example, are promoted as a remedy for high carbon levels in the environment, and they probably are. But the batteries that store energy are made using some of the most polluting materials in manufacturing. Imagine if 10 million battery-powered electric cars were produced in North America each year, and each of them needed new batteries after three or four years. What happens to the old batteries? How much can be safely recycled, how much will become trash, and what becomes of it?

* * *

As soon as word spread about the financial problems of GM, Ford and Chrysler, people began blaming unionized workers. They're entitled to their opinion, but the facts say otherwise.

When I started in the industry back in the mid-1960s, assembly line labour accounted for about 25 percent of the cost of a new car or truck. Through improved productivity, better utilization of manufacturing facilities and other advances—many of them originating with the unions—the labour cost of new vehicles has been reduced to about 7 percent today. Think of it this way: *Even if the CAW built cars for free, it would cut the sticker price by only 7 percent.*

On a dollar-for-dollar basis, with the loonie at below 90 cents

U.S., Canadian auto labour is unquestionably cheaper than American, Japanese and German labour. Here's something else to ponder: the dealer profit in each GM, Ford and Chrysler car, including the commission to the salesperson who sells it, is bigger than the labour cost to build it.

If those two facts don't open your eyes to the reality of Canadian auto worker efficiency, let's start by comparing some 2007 productivity stats from the Big Three's assembly plants in Canada and the U.S.:[*]

Productivity Measure	Canada	U.S.	Canada's Edge
Hours per vehicle	21.0	22.9	9.2%
Vehicles assembled per worker annually	54.4	48.2	12.8%

How do CAW workers compare with workers in Asian or European "transplants" operating in North America when it comes to the number of hours needed to assemble a vehicle? Here are the 2007 figures from the same sources:

CAW Plants	Canadian Transplants	U.S. Transplants
21.0 hrs./vehicle	21.66 hrs./vehicle	25.24 hrs./vehicle

This data demolishes the stereotype about union members being unproductive. CAW-represented factories in Canada are 6 percent more productive than non-union assembly plants here and 24 percent more productive than non-union factories in the U.S. Everyone looks at how much we make per hour, compared with non-union facilities, but nobody compares how much we produce in that hour of work compared with non-union plants.

---

[*] Data from *The Harbour Report*, Statistics Canada, Ward's Automotive and U.S. Bureau of Labor Statistics.

If anything, these numbers underestimate the true value of the Canadian productivity advantage. Measuring productivity in terms of hours per vehicle does not take into account the quality or the complexity of the vehicles produced (let alone all the parts and other value-added products that go into those vehicles). Government data indicates that the average auto worker in Canada (including both the assembly and the parts sectors) produces 40 percent more value-added per year than in the U.S.*

It's true that CAW wages are higher than average Canadian weekly earnings, but not nearly as much as our critics claim. At the top of the seniority scale CAW assemblers make $34 per hour compared with average wages in Canada of about $22 per hour. But you have to factor in productivity. The average auto assembly worker in Canada produces about $300,000 of value-added each year, which is four times the national average. If you produce more output with each hour of work, shouldn't you be paid more in wages?

Internationally, too, auto wages in Canada are fully competitive with those paid in other leading automotive nations. When the exchange rate is at its long-run average level (below 90 cents U.S.), Canadian auto wages are lower than those paid in the U.S., Germany and Japan. Analysts and commentators are quick to blame labour costs for all the problems in the North American auto industry. If that was true, then why are Germany and Japan the most successful auto exporting nations in the world? Their labour costs are even higher. In Japan, on top of healthy wages, auto workers also receive enormous lump-sum bonuses that can amount to $20,000 or more per worker per year, and that boost compensation costs considerably. There is no credible case that the wages of auto workers, whether in Canada or

---

* Data reported by CAW, *Auto Industry on the Brink* (2009).

anywhere else in the world, are the source of the dramatic problems faced by this crucial sector.

When GM, Ford and Chrysler sat down with the CAW in the spring of 2008, the union recognized—perhaps with more clarity then the automakers did—that the looming global financial crisis and the resulting credit freeze (which cut deeply into vehicle sales and dealer wholesale orders) would hit the auto industry badly. Even though none of the industry's problems could be attributed to union wages, more fingers were pointed at us than at anybody else. We accounted for 7 percent of the cost of producing a selling a new vehicle but we were assigned 99 percent of the blame.

We pushed back against the scapegoating of workers for a problem we didn't create, but we knew we had to be part of the solution and protect ourselves against the coming catastrophe. We opened early bargaining with the Big Three in spring 2008, before the worst of the financial crisis hit home, becoming the first major player in the industry to respond to the crisis. A deal was hammered out in near-record time. Contracts extending through 2011 included no wage increases, an 18-month suspension of COLA (cost of living allowance), loss of one week's paid vacation pay, modifications to our health plans and various other cost savings in local agreements.

When fully implemented, the new contracts provided annual bottom-line cost savings for the whole industry of $300 million. Here's the real kicker: Even with the loonie at par (far above its normal long-run value) and the U.S. plants phasing in a two-tier wage system, Canadian workers would remain fully competitive on a unit-cost basis with U.S. workers thanks to their greater productivity and Canada's universal health care.

Remember that it's not the workers who design, engineer and market the cars and trucks they make. For all of their abilities, the executives running Ford, GM and Chrysler have made their share of mistakes in choosing and designing the vehicles to manufacture and sell. From the Ford Edsel to the Pontiac Aztec, design disasters have cost the car companies billions over the years, no matter how well they were built by union workers. Surely one of the fundamental goals of any car company is to produce vehicles that people want to buy. GM's own research indicated that consumers would reject the Aztec, but they went ahead and built it anyway. No car manufacturer has a perfect record in this area, but during the golden years of the Big Three they really believed they could sell whatever the hell they marketed. They were wrong over and over again, even when they consciously attempted to break the mould with Saturn and other ventures.

Between 2005 and 2008 General Motors lost an estimated $72 billion, and tens of thousands of their employees, especially production line and assembly workers, lost their jobs, yet you can count on the fingers of one hand the number of executives whose bad decisions put them on the street.

One of the many challenges faced by GM, Ford and Chrysler in the last decade has been meeting the demand in Canada and the U.S. for smaller, more fuel-efficient vehicles that could outperform those from Japanese and Korean manufacturers. I'm sure the ability to do it was there, but the commitment was lacking. In 2000, Ford launched a project called "Blue" to design small fuel-efficient cars to counter imports from Honda and Toyota. After a big investment of money and time, the whole idea was abandoned because gas was cheap. Who needed inexpensive small cars?

There wasn't much motivation to make small, efficient cars because it was easier—and more profitable—to make and sell SUVs and pickup trucks. A compact car sells for maybe $18,000 and earns the company maybe $1,000 in profit; an SUV or full-size pickup sells for $38,000 and earns the company more than $5,000 in profit. If you were calling the shots at Ford, GM and Chrysler, where would you put your money?

Let's remember that the Asian companies whose imports have proven so successful—Toyota, Honda, Nissan, Subaru, Hyundai, Kia and the rest—got started by building cars for their own markets where gasoline is expensive, roads are narrower, and communities are much closer together than in North America. The companies learned how to build good small cars for their home markets, which were protected against offshore imports. Then they parlayed their experience into global market success by taking advantage of the willingness of North American governments to tolerate massive, one-way imbalances in trade.

Meanwhile, North American car companies responded to their own market demands with larger, more powerful vehicles designed carry more people at faster speeds for longer distances and in greater comfort. In Canada and the U.S., gasoline has been relatively cheap, roads are wider, and travelling 800 kilometres a day is not unusual. The market called for large, powerful vehicles, and the industry built them. When the market changed, and features like fuel economy and smaller size became more important, the North American manufacturers were at a disadvantage. Anyone who believes it's easy to shrink a full-size Ford or Chevrolet down to 30 or 40 percent of its original size and come up with a successful product at a competitive price knows very little about building cars. It takes an entirely different expertise and approach to build compact and subcompact vehicles.

Full-size pickups are another example. Toyota and Honda came into the market late, and for all of their vaunted capability they couldn't build pickup trucks to match the Ford F-150, the Chevrolet Silverado or the Dodge Ram at anything near a competitive price. Why? Because they lack the expertise acquired by the Big Three over 75 or 80 years of building pickups. Toyota launched an aggressive strategy to conquer the Big Three's large pickup trucks with its massive Tundra, produced at a new plant in Texas. The Tundra proved as much of a macho gas-guzzler as anything made by the Big Three, and their timing was terrible: they spent billions on this and other large vehicles, only to see the bottom drop out of the market when gasoline hit US$4 per gallon, followed by the devastating effects of the credit freeze.

Being able to build small cars better than the Big Three gave Toyota and Honda more than sales success. It gave them a mystique that's not totally deserved, especially when comparing family cars. You think a Toyota Camry is a good car? Sure it is. But compare it with a Buick Allure, built in Oshawa, Ontario, by union labour in a plant that was declared among the best in the world for initial quality four out of six times between 2002 and 2008. The only cars that matched Buicks coming out of Oshawa Plant #2 in initial quality, according to J. D. Power, were Lexus sedans costing nearly twice as much. Don't tell me that CAW members can't build quality cars at a fair labour cost, because they've done it for years.

I compared a 2009 middle-of-the-line Camry with a 2009 middle-of-the-line Buick Allure, using data from the Toyota and GM websites. They both have similar-sized V6 engines, airbags, stereo systems, automatic transmissions, a power driver's seat, and all the other bells and whistles consumers expect. The Buick is roomier inside, with a bigger trunk. The Toyota has a six-speed automatic; the Buick's is four-speed. Any opinion about their exterior design is subjective. Personally, I prefer the look of the Buick. Let's focus on fuel economy, warranty and price. You can do the same thing I did, but I'll save you the trouble:

	Buick Allure CXL	Toyota Camry SE V6
Hwy Fuel Economy	7.2 L/100 km	7.0 L/100 km
Warranty	Bumper to Bumper	Bumper to Bumper
	48 mo./80,000 km	36 mo./60,000 km
Powertrain	60 mo./160,000 km	60 mo./100,000 km
Corrosion Perforation	72 mo./160,000 km	60 mo./unlimited km
Roadside Assistance	60 mo./160,000 km	36 mo./60,000 km
Courtesy Transport	60 mo./160,000 km	None
Accessories	48 mo./80,000 km	12 mo./unlimited km
List Price	$29,695	$31,350

It looks like I'm trying to sell Buicks here. Well, I am and I'm not. I'd rather you bought a car built by CAW members using North American parts, of course. But my point is to counter people who still believe we can't build a good car at a good price here in Canada, because we sure as hell can. We build them as well as or better than the Japanese or the Koreans, and the country benefits substantially more from the Big Three's investments, production and parts purchases. Every job in an auto assembly or powertrain plant supports 7.5 jobs somewhere in the national economy, counting both "upstream" jobs in the parts and supply industries and "downstream" jobs in consumer goods and services. So every time I see an imported vehicle on the highway, I start counting the jobs lost for Canadians.

The Canadian auto industry is worth saving because it produces good cars at good prices, and because to lose it—to have every motorized vehicle on Canadian roads built outside of the country—would prove a bloody disaster. Canada would go from a recession to a depression in the blink of an eye. A study released in late 2008 by the Centre for Spatial Economics measured the cost of the Big Three disappearing: Canada would lose 600,000 jobs, our GDP would decline by 5 percent, our trade balance would drop by $28 billion per year, and governments would see a massive increase in their own deficits thanks to the disappearance of the industry that has paid the bills for so long. According to the study, the federal deficit would rise by $13 billion per year, and the Ontario deficit by $4 billion per year. No wonder both levels of government decided they could not afford to sit back and let the industry wither away.

The Big Three have taken some important steps to respond to a changing world while struggling to stay afloat. At times, I really wondered how hard they were trying to cut their internal costs. For years Chrysler had two co-presidents. How can you justify two presidents running one company? Why pay two salaries for one job? One of them, Tommy LaSorda, was the son of a Chrysler assembly line worker I knew back in the 1960s. Yet he was as aggressive as any other corporate executive in threatening to leave Canada if we didn't cut our labour costs.

LaSorda said exactly that in the middle of our spring 2008 contract negotiations. In an interview with Bloomberg News, a reporter quoted from the statement and asked what I had to say in response to LaSorda. I said Chrysler should fire one of its two presidents and I left it up to the Bloomberg News audience to guess which one should go. "How the hell do you ask workers to give up everything," I said, "when you've got two presidents of a company, each drawing fat salaries?" It wasn't about the few million dollars a year each was drawing. It was about leadership and fairness and setting a model of behaviour.

Tommy LaSorda aside, the problems of the North American auto industry are so numerous and deep that blaming the unions is ludicrous. Much more damaging than the attitude of the unions has been the attitude of the U.S. and Canadian governments toward the industry, creating problems that a bunch of interest-free loans offered a week before calling an election won't solve. Are some decisions made in Ottawa and Washington regarding the auto industry the result of blindness, stupidity or some kind of obligation to Japan and Korea? Sometimes, it's hard to tell. In the U.S. at least, no one seems interested in consulting the unions, whose members' jobs are on the line.

Back in late 2006 the CEOs of the Big Three, after practically begging for more than a year, were given a chance to meet with President George W. Bush. The CEOs got almost an hour with him, for photo ops and drinks, I guess. They tried to explain the seriousness of the situation to the president, especially the impact of unfair trade from Japan and Korea (while the American government was negotiating a free trade agreement with Korea that would have made things worse). Bush, who always called himself a free trader, didn't respond with anything of value, and I wasn't surprised. I was amazed, however, to note that Ron Gettelfinger, the president of the UAW who represented almost a half-million auto workers, wasn't invited. The workers just didn't count, I suppose.

No CAW union leader would be absent from such a critical event in Canada, because the federal government knows we would scream bloody murder. That's another difference between the U.S. industry and the Canadian industry that's worth noting. Too bad, because sometimes it takes a union point of view to make an impression on government.

Some time after the White House get-together, I was invited to a discussion dealing with the introduction of a Clean Air Act in Canada. Thinking it would be just a handout of government policy papers I planned to skip the session. Jim Flaherty called to say it would be a major event, with several federal cabinet ministers in attendance, and they wanted my input. So I went.

At the meeting Flaherty and others indicated that Ottawa's Clean Air Act might duplicate the California greenhouse gases standards, and that the Conservatives planned to introduce them in 2009. The California standards were praised as a model for Canada and the world.

I'm all for clean air and environmental protection. In fact, the CAW promoted the idea of reducing Canada's greenhouse emissions when Stephen Harper was still sneering at global warming. But the impact on the auto industry of Flaherty's proposal would have been massive.

Sure, the auto industry must evolve to produce cleaner vehicles, but it needs support to get there, including measures to ensure that Canada gets a fair share of jobs in the "green" car industry of the future. You can't suddenly dictate a whole new regulatory structure without notice and support for industrial adjustment. The California approach, based on corporate-average standards, would have given a huge head start to off-shore producers by virtue of the fact that the vehicles they produce are smaller, on average, than those in North America. So they could meet the new standards with a fraction of the investment needed by the Big Three. It makes no sense to shoot your own industry in the foot, while simultaneously aiding the imports, all in the name of protecting the environment.

It was no surprise that California came up with the process. California doesn't have an auto industry, of any significance. Their share of the industry could vanish and nobody would notice. California had nothing to lose.

No industry is more important in Canada than the auto industry, especially in Ontario. The California model would have cost us tens of thousands of jobs. I'm in favour of progress, but not when it creates collateral damage, meaning tens of thousands of workers and their families becoming destitute. There had to be better ways of dealing with the problem.

The planned introduction of the California standards also suggested that nobody in Ottawa knew what the hell was going on in the rest of the country. When the meeting ended, I approached Flaherty and told him I couldn't believe what I had just heard about adopting the standards of the California Clean Air Act, applying it as though Vancouver were San Francisco and Toronto were Los Angeles. "You and I were in Oshawa just a few weeks ago when GM announced it would build the new Camaro there," I reminded him. "It's a muscle car with a V8 engine, and if you bring that California Act in as it stands, you're going to be telling GM that they can build the car in Canada but they can't sell it here. Do you know what GM will say? They'll say, 'If we can't sell it here, we won't build it here.' And who can blame them?"

The hypocrisy of the Conservatives is amazing. Flaherty and the Tories have refused to back the Kyoto Accord, which the CAW supported, but they appeared ready to impose California-designed standards, without changes, that would have thrown thousands of Canadian workers out on the street. I sensed from Flaherty's response that this may not have occurred to him, even though his constituency of Whitby-Oshawa is home to the GM auto plants. Could he really be so oblivious to the impact his announcement would make right in his own backyard?

I made my point. Flaherty and his people backed away from applying the California standards and chose to follow the more flexible Environmental Protection Agency standards instead.

You may question GM's decision to introduce a V8-powered muscle car if you like, especially with oil prices moving higher and the economy sinking. But I repeat: the union doesn't choose the vehicles to be built, and many people would be upset if we tried. That's a decision to be made by management, and when they chose to build the Camaro in Oshawa, it promised work for our members. Should we have told GM, "We don't like the idea of building that car," and written off the chance of saving an entire plant? As it turned out, the Camaro was a hit with consumers, becoming GM's hottest product (measured by low inventories in 2009).

Meanwhile, many people keep shrugging their shoulders at the possible collapse of the auto industry and raging at union workers, claiming they're wholly responsible for this mess. In January 2009, my replacement as CAW president, Ken Lewenza, told me he was getting hundreds of e-mails each week ripping a strip off his hide and the hides of every CAW member, blaming them as the sole source of the auto companies' situation. The letter writers acted as though the workers had no right to explain their position or to reject charges that the problem was based on their greed.

The easiest thing for Ken Lewenza to have done in those situations would have been to go to the CAW executive and the rank and file and say, as they do in Newfoundland, "The arse is out of 'er, boys!" and to agree they had to accept the wage cuts being demanded of them. He didn't say that. Instead he argued effectively that since CAW wages were not the problem, cutting those wages could not be the solution. That's his job, to get the facts straight and protect the advances that his members have earned over so many years of struggle, and it upset a lot of people who didn't want their stereotypes and preconceptions disturbed. It had been my job for almost 20 years, and I knew exactly what he was going through.

The CAW wants to be part of the solution. Lewenza and I and every union leader before us and all the people who will come after us are guided by a commitment that workers have a right to make progress, even during the most difficult times. The progress may be limited by the economic, social and political environment they find themselves in, but they can't limit their goals by deciding to go along with the rest of the crowd and accept any decision handed down to them. That's not how unionism works. That's not what strong union leaders do.

* * *

When Washington began talking about providing funds to GM, Ford and Chrysler, Ottawa's response was to wait around to see what the

Americans would do. I said at the time, and I repeat now, that the federal government should not have waited for the U.S. to take the lead. We have a major industry here, and we should have taken the initiative in offering assistance to the auto companies.

Harper should have called the CEOs to a meeting and proposed granting them sufficient funds to restore and maintain their operations in Canada. Attached to the agreement would be two conditions: The companies would have to maintain the Canadian production footprint they enjoyed through 2008, meaning that Canadian operations would continue to supply 20 percent of the North American markets; and they would agree to produce replacement vehicles for current products, such as the Chevrolet Impala, here in Canada.

I have no doubt that the companies would have agreed to the deal. Why not? All of them know they can get greater productivity and profit margins from the Canadian plants. They were getting beat up in Washington. They were looking for a friend, and if Canada had made this offer, I'm convinced the Big Three would have snapped it up. Then they could have gone to Congress with the agreement and used it as leverage in their request for American funding. Meanwhile, Canada would have been assured of the same export advantage we've had for some time.

By waiting for the Americans to make the first move, the federal government put Canada at a severe disadvantage. We became a target for any U.S. politicians who wanted to claim they were protecting American jobs. Rumblings from many in Washington insisted that money from American taxpayers should be used to protect American jobs. I didn't blame them for that attitude. I want Canada to take the same aggressive position where Canadian workers are concerned, but we never seem to. We stood around waiting for the Americans to make the first move then, like a puppy walking in the tracks of a bigger dog, we trotted along behind. All Harper asked for was "a fair share" of North American production in exchange for billions of federal dollars. "This will maintain Canada's fair share of production," Stephen Harper said when he announced the funding, meaning a proportional 10 percent. But we didn't have 10 percent of their production, we had 20 percent. Using the same proportional measurement, Washington could insist that the industry dedicate only 10 percent of its production to Canadian plants. By permitting the U.S. deal to be completed first, we stood to lose half of our potential production. In my opinion, this was incompetence at the highest level of our federal government.

There were occasional glimmers of encouraging news in early 2009. Car sales showed signs of a rebound in the spring and government "scrappage" incentives and other programs in Europe and Asia were making a difference. Vehicle sales in some markets were actually up on a year-over-year basis.

Discussions between Ford and Magna to build an electric car based on the Ford Fusion were another promising development. Magna knows the automotive industry as well as anyone, and they are well advanced in developing a battery and drive system for electric cars. They have the technology, they have the commitment, and they have the affiliation with the Ford name to make this a serious proposition. They also have experience in sub-assembly of parts and, in my opinion, could easily make the move to operating a full auto assembly plant. In fact, Magna has run an assembly plant in Austria for several years, an economical alternative to large automotive assemblers.

The profit-making point for large integrated assembly plants like most of those in Canada is about 200,000 vehicles a year. When volume drops below this figure it's virtually impossible for big plants to make money. Frank Stronach's plant in Austria is structured differently. It's efficient to run and flexible in its configuration. The big plants may not be able to make a buck producing just 75,000 or 100,000 vehicles a year, but Magna's can, and he made deals to assume production on behalf of various companies if they dropped below the 200,000 figure. When I visited Magna's Austrian operation a few years ago I was amazed to see five different kinds of vehicles coming out of the plant, including BMWs, Chrysler minivans, Land Rovers and others, following the same kind of complex scheduling that Canadian companies used in the 1950s before the Auto Pact was signed. Thanks to the organizing genius of Frank and his staff, assisted by computerized scheduling and flow control, the Magna plants are highly efficient.

I met with Frank Stronach a few days before Christmas 2008 to discuss his plans to develop and produce an electric car in conjunction with Ford. Frank explained that Magna wanted recognition for its work and technology. He needed to be careful in constructing this deal because he didn't want Magna going head to head with GM and Chrysler, who remain major buyers of Magna-made parts. But one way or another, Frank was determined to become a leader in electric car development and manufacturing, and I for one love the idea. Magna is a Canadian company that has long committed 6 percent of its earnings to research and development. He also has a policy of assigning responsibility for plant success to the individual plant manager. As long as the plant follows what Frank cleverly calls the Magna Charter, a guide to the company's operating principles, and reaches its profit target, managers run their own shows. Because the guy who walks the plant floor every day has a better idea what's happening there, and also has a closer relationship with the workers, a good working environment is more likely to result. Frank's strategy is paying off.

* * *

For all of Frank Stronach's genius and success, the problem of restoring the North American automotive industry is far bigger than any one person can handle. I have no doubt that CAW President Ken Lewenza, incoming secretary-treasurer Peter Kennedy and their staff will do whatever they can to help the industry survive, but first the American and Canadian governments have to deal with the import problem. There is no sense in the union on either side of the border saying they're going to do something to help the industry when we know the imports are going to kill it anyway. Any action taken by the unions has to be conditional on the government dealing with the real challenge of imports.

With the Auto Pact no longer in effect, Canada is free to follow its own path. I think it should take the lead in managing the trade in vehicles, especially with Barack Obama and the Democrats in power. I'm a great admirer of Obama and his party, but Democrats have a record of managing trade when it hurts their workforce and economy. Once again, I admire that approach. Free trade is great in theory but managed trade is better in practice. If Canada takes the lead in saying to Korea, Japan and others, "If you want free access to our markets, you have to give us similar access to your markets," and enforces the idea, it will pay off. When it does, the U.S. will sit up and take notice, and I expect they would create and enforce similar rules. Why not? UAW President Ron Gettelfinger began making noises along this line in early 2009. He wasn't as loud and strong as I think he should be, but it was a beginning.

Here's what we should do. We should say to the countries and their car manufacturers, whose imports into Canada account for about 25 percent of new car sales, "Either you voluntarily reduce your imports to 15 percent of our market or we'll take steps to limit them ourselves." That 15 percent figure, it seems to me, is reasonable and approximates the unspoken limit that the European Community imposes. We already apply similar limits to food items like imported cheese to protect the country's dairy industry. If we can say, "This much cheese and no more," why the hell can't we say, "This many cars and no more"? Are dairy farmers more important than auto workers and dealers? Or consider the American precedent of restrictions on Canadian softwood lumber and their attempts to control steel imports.

A lot of free market true believers will tut-tut about restricting trade or charge that I am not in touch with reality. First, I suggest they review some guidelines from the World Trade Organization, especially the one that permits a country to restrict imports if the imports are causing "undue harm" to an industry at the national level. No one who studies the figures can deny the undue harm being caused in North America by unrestricted vehicle imports. I'm not proposing some kind of trade revolution. I'm proposing just the opposite of a revolution: let's start doing what other countries do when their own trade is being harmed by the unfair policies and practices of other countries.

It would be a bold move for Canada to lay down the trade law that way. Traditionally we've been nice guys on this subject, and you know where nice guys finish. If we took the step of blocking imports from countries that refuse to open their markets to us, it would make a massive impact around the world, and help revive our automotive industry. It would also take a lot of courage on the part of our federal politicians, something they haven't demonstrated in the past.

* * *

The industry will need input from both labour and management if it has any hope of surviving the global economic crisis that began in 2008.

Summing up, here's my 10-point plan for the critical moves that government and industry must take:

1. Demand that foreign auto companies agree to managed trade with Canada. Not "free trade"—managed trade. That was the basis for the Canada–U.S. Auto Pact, the most successful trade agreement in history. For every dollar of vehicles or parts that Japan, Korea and soon India and China sell in Canada, they have to buy a dollar's worth back from us. I see nothing unfair about this idea.

2. Convince federal and provincial governments to stop blaming workers for problems and to start dealing with unfair competition. Governments in Canada keep talking about how much money they can take away from workers and retirees, how to force the companies to downsize, and how to get the companies to build vehicles that no one is sure Canadians want to buy. Governments are good at setting policy, companies are good at making decisions, and our workers are first-rate at building vehicles. People and organizations should be left alone to do what they do best.

3. Manage the loonie to keep it around 80 cents American. We may take pride in a Canadian dollar that's worth more than a Yankee greenback, but pride doesn't create and ensure jobs. A cheaper Canadian dollar will.

4. Obtain government assistance to create and produce fuel-efficient vehicles in Canada. No matter how much the price of gasoline may fluctuate—often the result of greedy speculation—everyone knows that we are taking more petroleum out of the ground than we are finding. Sooner or later it will dry up completely, and we're all better off if we are prepared in advance.

5. Provide similar assistance, via grants or tax breaks, for R & D on vehicles propelled by something other than fossil fuels. Assurance will have to be made that successful R & D conducted in Canada will lead to Canadian manufacturing of the products resulting from it. I think that's doable. More than that, it's essential.

6. Start development of an alternative fuel infrastructure. The most likely solution will be plug-in electric-powered cars similar to the Chevrolet Volt that GM plans to introduce. The Volt's range initially will be about 100 kilometres, which makes it okay for commuting but impractical for longer trips. Even when its range is extended to 160 kilometres between plug-in charges, this won't be adequate for vacations and business trips, and no one will want to stand around for three hours while the battery recharges. Perhaps the answer is battery exchange centres where, just as you fill up with gasoline at service stations now, you switch your current battery for a fully charged one and are on your way in minutes. We also need a fueling infrastructure to support ethanol, flex-fuel and clean diesel, as well as less polluting vehicles.

7. Start from scratch to create, design, engineer and build reliable small vehicles expressly for the North American market. People got very excited about the Nano car built in India and sold there for $2,500, but that's not the future of cars in this part of the world. It lacks all kinds of safety, reliability and comfort features demanded by North Americans. Instead of panicking over a threat that will never develop, we should be looking at a vehicle that will meet North American needs.

8. Make sure governments demonstrate to domestic auto manufacturers that they are taking the lead in protecting and encouraging

the car companies to deal with the multiple crises they're facing. The auto industry is the most dynamic, influential and technologically innovative business in the world. If it vanishes from Canada and the U.S., displaced by vehicles created in Asia, Europe and India, it will leave an enormous gap in our economic and social structure.

9. Support the production and purchase of made-in-Canada mass transit equipment. Part of the solution to global warming involves expanding public transit. Luckily, Canada has a strong transit manufacturing industry, supporting tens of thousands of jobs that are every bit as important to our economy as auto assembly jobs. We should leverage our upcoming purchases of buses, subway equipment and trains into Canadian manufacturing jobs, through strong Buy Canadian policies. This will help to offset the loss of auto jobs.

10. Spread this attitude across the entire manufacturing sphere. We cannot have a strong economy in this country and deliver a decent standard of living for most people without a substantial and successful manufacturing base. Service industries, as innovative and technologically based as they may be, do not provide a well-balanced economy on their own.

* * *

In spring 2009, with all the scary news of the credit crisis still occupying the front pages of newspapers around the world, Toyota announced that for the first time in its history it suffered a loss in the fiscal year ending in March 2009, totalling US$4.4 billion.

I found the news item interesting for a number of reasons.

First, because the Japanese found it shocking that Toyota could actually lose money. This kind of thing just didn't happen to Toyota. For 70 years the company had consistently shown a profit. Toyota lose money? Things must be serious.

Next, the size of the loss seemed impossible to many people. US$4.4 billion is a lot of money, to be sure. But let's put it in perspective. General Motors lost that much money every two months in 2008, and had been recording losses well before the market tanked in the U.S. That's how seriously the economic downturn was hitting the biggest automaker in North America. Here's another perspective to consider: In its previous fiscal year, Toyota recorded an operating profit of 2.27 trillion yen or, at the December 2008 exchange rate of 90 yen to the dollar, about US$25 billion. The 2009 loss was small compared to Toyota's previous profits.

Another announcement from Toyota was equally interesting. Due to its losses, management announced, the company would be forced to lay off workers. No surprise there; that's the textbook response of North American auto companies whenever the market turns cold and red ink appears on their books. But there was a difference: Toyota planned to lay off about 1,000 workers worldwide, and not one of the jobs would be in the company's Japanese facilities.*

I'm not being critical of Toyota's policies in the least, but what in hell is going on here? How can North American car makers dump 100,000 employees without blinking, and Toyota spreads their layoffs around the world without one full-time worker at Toyota in Japan losing his or her job? In fact, Toyota had not laid off a single full-time employee in Japan since 1950.

Japanese culture plays a role here, perhaps. So does Toyota's management ability, and hats off to them. But surely the fact that Toyota and

---

* "Toyota Mulls Cutting 1,000 Full-time Jobs," Associated Press, January 23, 2009.

other Japanese and Korean manufacturers have easy, open access to the largest auto buying markets in the world, without fear of competition in their protected home market, enables them to stay paternalistic at home and run a lean machine elsewhere in the world.

Wouldn't it be wonderful if North American companies could operate in the same manner? And do not tell me it's impossible.

* * *

After months of brinkmanship involving financiers, politicians, suppliers and union leaders, the North American auto crisis finally came to a culmination in the spring of 2009. U.S. President Barack Obama held two historic live news conferences (one at the end of May for Chrysler, and then another at the end of June for GM) to announce details of his final rescue plan to a skeptical public.

Who would have ever predicted that the U.S. government, supposedly the greatest defender of free enterprise in the world, would take a majority ownership stake in these two enormous companies? Even more surprising was that Stephen Harper, Canada's most right-wing prime minister of all time, would join the nationalization bandwagon. He approved many billions of dollars in assistance to the two industrial icons, including an equity share in both firms. There was one final twist of fate: the UAW's health care trust fund now also has a substantial ownership share in both companies.

Imagine that: U.S. autoworkers partly own their employers, through the middleman of their own health care trust. A few idealistic commentators actually think this is somehow a positive step forward, a sign of "worker empowerment" or some such nonsense. That's totally wrong. GM and Chrysler will operate no differently than they ever did, governed just as ruthlessly by the hunger for profit and the drive to survive. The UAW has even pledged not to actively use the voting power of its shares to influence corporate direction. And it will sell off its shares as soon as market conditions recover, thus raising needed cash for its health fund. After all, you can't pay a doctor's bill with GM shares. You need real money for that.

The U.S. and Canadian governments plan to do the same thing with their shares, selling them off as soon as the stock market is ready. They have no intention or desire to hang on to to their new investments. So don't worry; socialism hasn't suddenly arrived in the North American auto industry.

The fact that the U.S. and Canadian governments and the UAW health trust are now part-owners (more by default than design) of two of the largest industrial corporations in the world is proof of the profound failure of the right-wing agenda we've been following for decades. And I'm not thinking only about the dramatic financial collapse that began with the American sub-prime mortgage meltdown. That was obviously the precipitating factor, the straw that broke the camel's back. But the stage was set for the auto industry's catastrophe by years of neglect and rose-coloured wishful thinking on the part of both politicians and auto executives.

Will the joint U.S.–Canada rescue package "save" the auto industy in the long run? There's no doubt the emergency aid was essential to keeping GM and Chrysler alive. Without it, both companies would now be liquidated. We'd have suffered the permanent loss of tens of thousands of direct jobs and hundreds of thousands more among suppliers, dealers and local businesses in auto-dependent communities.

But I am deeply worried that our governments have not learned the lessons from the decade-long decline in North America's auto sector. I've argued here that this long erosion of a once-mighty industry was caused by the irrationalities and injustices of near-religious faith in free markets and free trade. Allowing Japan, Korea and soon China to sell as much as they want here, without buying anything back. Pinning our economic hopes on the latest financial fad, rather than investing in building a real industrial base. Leaving the fate of crucial strategic sectors like auto to chance, rather than taking pro-active measures to ensure that we get a fair share of these valuable jobs.

In the midst of the current crisis, have North American governments fundamentally changed their views on any of these issues? Far from it; even as they rushed to put out the fires of the meltdown, they reinforced their commitment to the same policies (free trade at all costs) that lit the flames.

Consider, for example, the U.S. "clunker" bill implemented in the summer of 2009. The program came into effect about a year later than in other countries such as France, China or Germany. But better late than never. The program provided generous subsidies to consumers who traded in old gas-guzzlers for new, more fuel-efficient cars and trucks.

It's a sensible idea, for sure. Good for the economy (putting some life back into auto sales). And good for the environment. The only problem is that the Obama government didn't put any domestic content requirement on the bill. Imported Hyundais and Hondas are eligible for just as much support, courtesy of the U.S. taxpayer, as Chevrolets and Chryslers (made by the U.S. companies that were at death's door).

How strange that the government would actually subsidize the continued conquest of the North American market by offshore firms. Offshore nameplates received over half of the total funds provided. In Canada, meanwhile, no "clunker" subsidies were provided at all.

The flood of one-way imports to North America continues all the while. In fact, amidst the crisis, Korean auto sales to North America have surged to their highest share of the market ever, and in the second quarter of 2009, Korea's Hyundai declared its largest quarterly profit ever. Imagine that: in the middle of the worst global recession since the 1930s, Korea's automakers (backed as always by generous government subsidies and an undervalued exchange rate) are raking in more profits than at any time in history, thanks to the one-sided generosity of North America's governments, which not only tolerate lopsided trade imbalances but actually further subsidize imports with their own handouts). Unless and until we rein in this travesty of globalization, our domestic producers will continue to lose market share. As their sales fall, their unit costs will grow. Excess capacity will accumulate and the red ink will flow again. Sooner rather than later, we'll be right back in the same mess.

So while the U.S. and Canadian governments have been forced by economic necessity to ride to the rescue of GM and Chrysler, it seems they haven't changed their fundamental approach to managing the industry or the overall economy. Free markets and free trade will continue to rule the world. I fear that this means the North American auto industry will continue to decline in the years to come. A slow decline, rather than sudden death. But painful and unnecessary just the same.

With the industry on death's door and hundreds of thousands of jobs at stake, you'd think this would have been the time to finally address the true causes of the industry's crisis. But instead, the politicians and the media alike fell back on their tried-and-true scapegoat. When it doubt, blame the union.

George Bush started it all when he demanded, in one of his last acts as president, big concessions from the UAW as a condition of interim financial support to GM and Chrysler. Anyone who hoped that Barack Obama would take a different approach was quickly disappointed. He rubber-stamped Bush's demand for concessions and actually sent the union back to give more as the crisis dragged on. The

Canadian government followed suit, demanding big concessions from the CAW as a condition of their support for GM and Chrysler.

The government claimed this was simply good business sense. If governments were going to put their money on the line, they had to prove there was a good "business case." And what better way to construct a business case than by socking it to the workers?

However, there's not an economist on the continent who could convincingly argue that shaving a few bucks an hour from labour costs could save the North American auto industry. Sure, lots of analysts joined the dogpile on the union, supporting the government demand for concessions. But there's a difference between overheated rhetoric and economic reality.

It takes around 20 hours of labour to assemble a vehicle. Cutting all-in labour costs by $20 per hour (a massive concession) therefore reduces the cost of a new vehicle by $400, or just 1 or 2 percent of its total price. Toyota and Honda and the other importers have been raking in as much as ten times that in profits per vehicle. They can easily offset any labour cost savings extracted from the UAW and the CAW by slimming down their profit margins. The government-imposed concessions won't alter the playing field one iota. In reality, they'll simply distract everyone's attention—including that of the media and the public at large—from the real problems we should be addressing.

No, the government-imposed labour concessions were not motivated by economics. They were motivated by politics. The governments wanted to be "seen" to be cracking down on the big bad union, to help them manage the "optics" of the overall rescue effort, which was unpopular with many open-line radio hosts and other commentators. Now, in the wake of the concessions, what has changed? Labour costs have been clawed back a bit. But labour costs were only 7 percent of the total cost in the first place. How will cutting labour costs from 7 percent to 6 percent of the total vehicle cost suddenly turn things around for the North American automakers? Answer: it won't.

Ken Lewenza, my successor at the helm of the CAW, has had a real trial by fire in his first year in the post. Against the odds, with a gun pointed right at its head, the union under Lewenza managed to hold the line on the concessions and cost cutting. The most important victory for the union was defending the autoworkers' pensions. That was a historic achievement. The battle was especially fierce at GM, where the pension plan had been badly underfunded since 1992 (thanks to an Ontario government loophole that allowed GM to fund its plan at a weaker standard than that of other companies).

True to form, the CAW mounted major public pressure, including a massive rally of about 15,000 people at Queen's Park, followed by the occupation of the offices of several provincial MPPs. That campaign forced the Ontario government to acknowledge its own role in creating GM's pension mess, and it abandoned its previous demands for major cuts in pension benefits. In the end, pensions weren't cut by a single dollar, and the GM pension fund will be boosted back up to normal funding levels as part of the company's overall restructuring.

That's a true victory for the union and its retirees, present and future. In my experience, workers feel more passionate about their pension than about any other part of their compensation package. It's like the light at the end of the tunnel, keeping them going through the long, tough years of working on an assembly line. That's what motivated thousands of active and retired autoworkers to take a stand. And once again, fighting back made a difference. The union came through the crisis with its head held high.

In contrast to GM and Chrysler, Ford has been able to survive the crisis (so far, anyway) without seeking bankruptcy protection or government ownership. This is due as much to good luck as to good management. Ford mortgaged everything including the family silver in 2007, just before the onset of the global credit freeze, to finance its restructuring. Thus when the crisis hit, the company had enough reserve funds in the coffer to get through the downturn. Then adversity turned to opportunity. Ford's executives deliberately portrayed themselves as more "independent" than their government-supported North American rivals. This translated into improved market share and pricing. Ford took advantage of its rivals' tough times to build its own market share at their expense. I guess that's how capitalism works.

But even Ford's long-term outlook in North America is not encouraging. In a mature market, and under continual pressure from Asian and European imports, it's unlikely Ford's North American market share will bounce back nearly enough to absorb its abundant excess capacity. More plant closures and layoffs seem inevitable. For GM and Chrysler, whose market share declined notably in the wake of the government rescue, the situation is much worse. Despite closing dozens of plants and cutting their North American workforce in half, they are still carrying far more capacity than they need. Once again, our industry executives will be left trying to dig themselves out of a hole.

I don't know if you've ever tried that in your own garden. It doesn't work. It's a basic fact of physics that the more you dig, the deeper in the hole you get. Too bad this simple lesson is lost on our politicians and auto executives.

I have no doubt that, as corporations, the Detroit Three automakers will survive and eventually recover. They will expand their presence in fast-growing China. They will focus their sales effort on other offshore markets. They will continue to relocate production to low-cost jurisdictions such as Mexico, Korea and Eastern Europe. They will perpetually seek new global dance partners, as Chrysler has done with Fiat. It's all part of their effort to offset continuing market share losses in North America. They would happily abandon North America altogether if they could find their fortune more reliably elsewhere in the world.

So the companies will survive. But whether auto manufacturing in North America survives is another issue altogether. And for workers, what matters is keeping good auto jobs here, not whether particular corporations make a profit somewhere in the world.

Ironically, the one industry leader actually thinking about bringing new work to North America is my old nemesis, Frank Stronach. He made a bid to take over the Opel division of GM and mused publicly about building Opel-branded vehicles in Canada. He'd need the right package to make it happen, including government support (not nearly as much as was required to rescue GM and Chrysler), a first-class supply base and an effective, modern working relationship with the union. I think Stronach's idea is one of the more hopeful signs in the current industrial carnage that passes for our continental auto industry.

In the meantime, those hundreds of thousands of hard-working Canadians who depend on this industry for their livelihood will just have to keep on working, hoping and speaking out for a brighter future. Maybe one day, if governments realize that we need a full-fledged industrial strategy for this vital sector (something like the ten-point plan I outlined earlier), that brighter day will dawn.

FOURTEEN

So Much More to Do

What a turn my life has taken since I stepped down as CAW president. I've been named an Officer of the Order of Canada, one of my proudest achievements and a near-impossible dream for the kid growing up in poverty in New Brunswick. I've become a regular radio and TV commentator, including a regular appearance on a panel on Toronto's AM 640, with former Ontario premier Ernie Eves. And I'm back at work, in a different setting from the shop floor at Chrysler or the offices of the CAW—in a classroom at Ryerson University in Toronto, where I lecture as a Distinguished Visiting Professor on international trade, trade between provinces in Canada, labour relations, and various economic, social and political issues. I love interacting with young people, challenging them with new perspectives, and I love being challenged myself, something that happens frequently at Ryerson. Outside the classroom I participate in organizing conferences with keynote speakers on the auto manufacturing sector and others, and exploring ideas on how to strengthen Canada's economy.

I'm also working with the National Hockey League Players' Association (NHLPA). I initially served on their advisory board and now I'm the NHL players' ombudsman. It's fascinating, of course, to get to meet these high-profile sports personalities. But it's also sobering to see how they, just like ordinary factory workers, need a union to level the playing field with the owners of the hockey clubs they work for. Without their union, NHL players, despite their incredible ability, would never receive a fair share of the incomes and profits that they generate. Many of the player representatives I have met through the NHLPA are as dedicated and selfless as any trade unionists you'll ever meet, giving generously of their time and talent to build a strong and effective union.

Among all these new duties I have more time to spend with my family, something I've not done enough of over the years.

I'll certainly continue my urge to keep up with international events, especially those concerning the constant search for world peace and the continued problem of poverty around the world. As I mentioned earlier, trade unionists have traditionally addressed these challenges and done their best to influence them, participating in peace marches and providing assistance to poverty-stricken people in Canada and beyond.

Now and then, someone in the labour movement makes a wrong turn or fires a salvo at the wrong target, which casts a pall over the entire movement. One person with a tendency to shoot himself in the foot, or some other part of his anatomy, is Sid Ryan, president of the Ontario branch of the Canadian Union of Public Employees (CUPE), who has proposed banning Israeli academics from speaking at Canadian universities about the Palestinian conflict and compared the Jewish state's military actions in Gaza to Nazi tactics.

Sid has a right to speak his mind, of course, but even he later agreed that his Nazi reference was over the top. Mind you, in my opinion Sid is frequently off the wall. I suspect that, as a principled and passionate guy, Sid may come under pressure from a small number of more radical members. One thing you can't do as head of a union is to allow the most vocal, and usually most radical, minority to dominate your thinking on issues or the decision-making process.

National unions, I submit, have an obligation to comment when innocent lives are lost, no matter who the combatants are. Traditionally, unions have been advocates of peace, not war, and have spoken out on these issues. This has left them vulnerable to charges from the right wing, including some suggestions that we don't support Canadian troops serving in Afghanistan and elsewhere, a totally wrong assumption. The men and women in the armed forces are unquestionably superb in their training, ability and dedication to restoring peace, and they enjoy the total backing of the CAW and other Canadian unions. We can support the troops without supporting the unjust and ultimately failed war to which our government has committed them.

We want them home, as soon as possible, however, and they no doubt share that desire. This doesn't make Canadian unions any less patriotic than other groups. In fact, I would submit that union members, who constantly ask Canadians to favour Canadian-made products when they make a purchase, are more patriotic than most. It simply means we favour solving problems with negotiations rather than bombs and bullets.

The problems of the Middle East have stymied better minds than mine over the past 60 years. I don't have a magic formula, nor does anyone else. I just don't want to see more children with missing limbs, more mothers wailing over their dead husbands, sons and daughters, or more soldiers on either side firing bullets or artillery shells toward innocent people's homes.

My position is simply this: Israel is a fact, and it was carved out of land that had once been part of Palestine. I understand the anger that has simmered among Palestinians since the founding of Israel, but at some point anger must be replaced with reality. Look at a map of the United States. Texas, New Mexico and Arizona, and much of Colorado, Kansas and California were once part of Mexico before military action by the Americans led to their absorption into the U.S. I suspect some Mexicans still harbour resentment over their loss but the countries no longer shoot at one another, leaving thousands dead and wounded.

The map of the world is redrawn over and over. We don't have to like the changes that take place, but eventually we have to accept them and find a way to live with the new reality. Israel has a right to exist, and both Palestinians and Jews have a right to live in peace. The "two-state solution" to the conflict always made a lot of sense to me. That's the position I maintained while president of the CAW and the one I support today. I never gave a council report without referring to events in the Middle East, praising efforts for peace and condemning warfare and conflict, no matter where they began and who launched them.

So I'm all for Sid Ryan or any other union leader speaking out on international events. I would hope their efforts are directed toward promoting peace, and that they are fair about any criticism they make. Ryan's opposition to Israeli speakers was clearly discriminatory.

However important international problems might be, we have enough issues in our own backyard. At the top of this list is how we treat First Nations people. The challenges they face extend beyond poverty to abuse by our governments and corporations. For thousands of years before the arrival of European settlers in North America, First Nations people drank water and ate fish without fear of sickness or poisoning. Now, in some of the most remote areas of Canada, their descendants are told to boil their water before drinking it and to avoid eating fish from those same waters or risk mercury poisoning. The same government that permitted and encouraged industries to exploit and scar the land, polluting the water and dumping toxic waste into rivers and streams for 100 years, ignored the plight of our aboriginal people. It was and remains a disgrace, and some of my proudest moments in the union movement were those spent with other union members, helping to clean up a mess among First Nations communities, people who our governments often refuse to acknowledge.

* * *

Beyond the auto industry and beyond our own country, I expect the next decade will see us undergoing so many social, political and economic changes that we may have trouble recognizing the world. It's certain that a lot of us will have trouble adjusting to it.

Countries are building protectionist walls around their key market sectors. Some, like India and China, are doing it openly while the others are achieving the same thing quietly and secretly. This is an understandable if unfortunate reaction to the global economic crisis. The only two countries that are not acting this way—not to any extent at least—are the United States and Canada. Our auto markets are still wide open to the Japanese, South Koreans and others despite the damage that imports have inflicted on our domestic industry. The World Trade Organization agrees that a country can take action when its own industries are being harmed, and nobody can argue that the North American industry isn't being harmed.

I expect to see a growing trend toward protectionism, although I hope it will be limited to countries and industries that truly are suffering under unfair and inequitable trade policies. Along with protectionism we will see a move back to international regulation of certain industries and actions, such as finance and investment. We need oversight of these transactions on a worldwide basis to avoid financial shenanigans—such as the peddling of near-worthless securities across borders without anyone confirming their value—in the future.

We will also witness, I believe, a new opportunity for trade unionism to expand in coming years as a result of this recession, just as unions grew during the Great Depression. Any confidence that people had in business executives to handle the economy vanished when it became apparent just how badly many large corporations were managed. Governments in Canada, the U.S. and elsewhere haven't demonstrated a whole lot of skill in avoiding disaster either. Under those circumstances, it's natural for people to look a little closer when it comes to improving their economic situation. The more working people who have reasonable job security and financial stability, the stronger the entire economy will become. You don't need to be an economist to understand that fact.

Unions have been striving for job security for generations, so this is right up their alley, but they cannot and will not take full advantage of the situation if they limit their goals to expanding their membership in traditional ways. Simply trying to attract new members by threatening to strike if they don't achieve their collective bargaining goals won't do the unions much good. Our best hope is to redefine ourselves and develop unique ways of proving we can be part of the overall solution. Unions must find new ways to reach out to workers, for example, by providing short-term social benefits to members who lose their jobs.

The major challenge is to counter the fear of the whole idea of unions. Employees are afraid of upsetting their bosses and losing their jobs if they support the idea of a union, and of giving up weeks of income if they have to go on strike. These fears are real and deep-seated, and until unions can find a way to dissolve them in every instance they won't be able to extend their influence and power as widely as they should.

I wish I could say that a swing to the left in Canadian politics will drive the move toward wider unionism but I don't think this is necessarily the case. Governments have been forced to seemingly adopt "leftist" policies of late, such as nationalization of banks and certain industries, because there has been no other alternative except to pour money into them during the current crisis. No matter which end of the political spectrum you're on, you don't hand over enormous amounts of money to any organization without claiming some control over its direction and management, and that implies some degree of ownership.

No politician in North America, especially in the U.S., would dare call this socialism, but that depends on your definition of the term. Socialism cannot be defined the same way it was when I entered the workforce and became committed to the union movement and left-wing politics. Back then, socialism was based on public ownership of major industries and institutions as the key to all of our problems. That's no longer a valid argument. Socialism today, in my view, involves using the tools of government to support workers, their families and their communities, and isn't that exactly what has been happening since the summer of 2008? In a crisis far too large and complex for private industry to handle, government must and did step in. The potential for using government ownership as a tool to influence economic and social outcomes has never been so clear in my lifetime.

Look, on most days people don't need government and don't want government looking over their shoulder and telling them how to live their lives. But in the middle of a crisis that may cost them their jobs, their homes, their health care benefits and their children's future, they need to know government will intervene. Government can do this by taking the lead and challenging the private sector to do what's right not only for owners and shareholders but for workers and their families as well.

While few people are consciously thinking, "It's time to shift to the left and introduce some socialist principles," this change is taking place anyway. Maybe it's coming about because, after 30 years of watching the right wing screw things up so much, from the Reagan/Thatcher/Mulroney era to George W. Bush and Stephen Harper, voters are saying, "What the hell—might as well give the socialists a try. They can't make a bigger mess of things than those yahoos."

President Obama has told Americans that his policies are not socialism, but just a temporary bridge to help the country move from its crisis back to pure capitalism. But a lot of these policies look long term to me, and the longer they're in place and, I hope, start proving their worth, the easier it will be for people, Americans in particular, to say, "You know, this isn't such a bad idea after all." Once you have a left-wing economic agenda in place, will it be that difficult to shift to a left-wing political agenda?

This shift to the left may eventually generate support for what I consider essential moves in America, such as the introduction of a universal health care system. To introduce this idea, even though the United States remains the only industrialized nation without such coverage, represents a gigantic challenge, given all the political and economic clout of the insurance industry and the medical profession. My expectation is that government health care will be introduced in increments until everybody gets used to the idea. Obama's proposal that all children under the age of six be assured of medical care is a start. When it's in place, perhaps they'll extend it to children under 12 and eventually to everyone. He'll also face a battle to introduce new labour laws, including the Employee Free Choice Act that will permit union accreditation based on a simple majority of workers signing union cards, instead of going through a secret ballot process after 30 percent of cards have been signed. Business lobbyists are frantically mobilizing to oppose this move, which would finally give unions in the U.S. a fair shot at stopping and reversing the erosion of union membership that has so badly weakened their clout over the last three decades. It will take an all-out campaign by unions, anti-poverty activists and their allies to win this battle, but it's essential to the future of the labour movement south of the border, and it could have a very positive spill-over effect in Canada if it succeeds.

* * *

I can look back on my years in the union and the broader labour movement with pride and satisfaction. I didn't win all the battles I fought, but I didn't expect to. As I said during my days as CAW president: "If you take on a fight, you have no guarantee of winning. But if you don't take it on, you're guaranteed to lose." Besides, at this stage of my life it makes even less sense than ever to dwell on things I failed to accomplish.

I'll admit the way my thinking has evolved with time. During the first days on the job at the Chrysler plant back in the mid-1960s I was a hard-line traditionalist when it came to key elements of trade unionism—you fight and you claw for every penny you can squeeze from the employer, and you never consider closing the gap between you and the other side. Time, of course, changes everything eventually, and 35 years of trying to organize Magna without success changed me.

Over those years I watched the auto parts sector in the U.S. transform itself into a different industry from a generation ago. At one time unionized parts suppliers set the standards in the industry and it was up to the non-union shops to match them if they wanted to retain their best workers. In recent years, the roles became reversed. Now barely 7 percent of auto parts manufacturers in the U.S. are unionized, and the union shops are bargaining down to save their jobs.

I could see this happening in Canada, and I didn't like it. We need to increase, not decrease, union penetration in the industry, and strengthen, not weaken, the CAW and unions in general. If it takes building a bridge across that gap between us and the other side, it's worth pursuing, and it will require full commitment to innovative, determined efforts to organize new members in all sectors of the economy.

The economic crisis of 2008–2009 saw tens of thousands of union members out of work with no resources to cover the cost of prescription drugs, life insurance, eyeglasses, pension credits and other benefits. Why couldn't unions find ways to extend these benefits for unemployed members over a reasonable period of time before they obtain new employment with another unionized shop? Imagine how much appeal unions would hold for unorganized workers if membership brought them into a more family-oriented and socially focused organization.

* * *

My heart will always be with the CAW and its members. On shop floors, in bargaining committee rooms, at conferences and, when the need arises, on picket lines, some part of me will be there. Whatever becomes of workers in the automotive industry and all the other CAW members employed in jobs that range from running railroads and providing health care to hospitality services and mining, I believe I, and all the good union people around me, helped them achieve job satisfaction and job security. My driving force over these many years was a passionate belief in unionism.

Our members produce the valuable goods and services that drive our economy. Nothing would happen without their labour, yet they face an endless struggle to gain a reasonable degree of control and security in their work lives, and a fair share of the wealth they produce. By linking arms and wielding their collective strength through a union, whether in the workplace or in the broader social and political arenas, workers maintain their hope for a fair deal. The tactics will change over time; unionists must be open to imagining and debating new ideas, new responses to the challenges we face. But the fundamental concept that energizes the endless hours spent building and managing our movement must not change. Workers deserve a better deal, and independent, principled unions are the only vehicle that can win it for them. Over all my years as a unionist I fixed my sights on the problem at hand and stuck to doing what I believed was right and fair. That consistency and determination were my major strengths.

Of all people, perhaps John Diefenbaker put this part of my philosophy best. During Question Period in the House of Commons, a young opposition member named Richard Cashin, a fiery Newfoundlander who helped organize workers in the fishing industry, raised some side issue with Diefenbaker. The prime minister refused to acknowledge the question, so the young MP raised it again, demanding to know why he'd failed to respond. Finally Diefenbaker rose, harrumphed and said, "Mr. Speaker, I never get sidetracked by rabbits when I'm hunting big game."

Now, when was the last time you heard a union leader—sorry, a former union leader—say something admirable about a Conservative prime minister?

Anyway, I too always refused to be sidetracked by rabbits.

Still do.

ACKNOWLEDGEMENTS

After 40 plus years of union leadership, it has been a difficult task to narrow down the key issues to make this book into what I believe will be of interest to Canadians—especially union members and labour relations practitioners. As part of the top leadership team of the CAW/UAW, I was extremely fortunate to have been involved with every major issue facing our union for over 30 years. It was an interesting, exciting and challenging period of my life, and I will continue to appreciate the memories, both good and bad, as well as the people I have had the opportunity to meet, the travel to many parts of Canada and around the world, and the experiences in collective bargaining, CAW council meetings and conventions.

I especially enjoyed working with the union's National Executive Board, local union leadership, staff and support staff in the ongoing effort to build a strong, united and diversified union. I liked dealing with the media and took advantage of every opportunity to defend CAW members publicly. I have made every effort to bring a progressive trade union perspective to the broader social, economic and political issues facing our country.

I have had unforgettable experiences—the many tours of CAW workplaces, getting to meet thousands of union members and understand the work they do day-in and day-out, the respectful relationships I developed with the management of the many companies I dealt with and the many important relationships I had with labour leaders and trade union activists in Canada and around the world.

I would like to recognize and thank the leadership and membership of the CAW Local 444 in Windsor, Ontario. Without my home local's encouragement and support over many years, I would not have had the many experiences that allowed me to write this book.

I would like to thank my good friends and colleagues, the leadership team of CAW that worked so hard to build our union: Jim O'Neil, Bob Chernecki, Hemi Mitic, Peter Kennedy, Peggy Nash, Ken Lewenza and Carol Phillips, all of whom contributed immensely to the success of CAW. Without their support, this book would not have been possible.

A special thank you to Jim Gifford, senior editor, HarperCollins; my agent, Rick Broadhead; and John Lawrence Reynolds and his wife, Judy, for their assistance and support.

I would like to thank Ryerson University for sponsoring one of the book launches—it is very much appreciated.

Finally, a very special thank you to my good friend and colleague, CAW economist Jim Stanford. Thank you for your support, guidance and assistance in writing this book.

INDEX

Bush, George W., 132, 145, 147, 148,
158, 159, 281, 297, 310

CAMI Automotive Inc., 37fn, 236–37,
247
Canada Industrial Relations Board
(CIRB), 63
Canada–U.S. Auto Pact, 13–15, 105,
112, 133, 140, 149, 230, 287, 288, 290
Canadian Airline Employees Associa-
tion (CALEA), 69–70
Canadian Airlines International,
163–68, 171–74, 178–79, 185
Canadian Auto Workers union
(CAW):
changing membership, 73–74
charitable activities, 41–44, 46
Family Education Centre, 121–22
formation of, 149–52
Social Justice Fund, 45
support staff strike (2000), 60–61
wages of members, 5, 223, 274–75
Canadian Journal of Communication,
96
Canadian Labour Congress, 142, 158
Canadian Union of Postal Workers
(CUPW), 243
Canadian Union of Public Employees
(CUPE), 118, 243–44, 245
Carrie, Tim, 241

Casino Niagara, 201
CBC Television, 78–79
Centre for Spatial Economics, 279–80
Cerberus Capital Management, 182
Cheney, Dick, 159
Chernecki, Bob, 136, 197, 214, 241, 249
Chevrolet Volt, 291
Chrysler Canada Inc., 12, 13, 16, 17,
25–26, 81–86, 111, 150–51, 224,
227–28, 266, 269–70, 280, 298
Clark, Brad, 193–95
Clark, Cyril, 12
Clarke, Troy, 88–89, 91
Clean Air Act, 138, 281–82
Clement, Tony, 122, 130
CN Rail, 66–68, 199
collective bargaining, 49–51, 52–53,
80–81, 117, 205–18, 219–23
Collenette, David, 167–68
Collins, Tom, 241
Common Sense Revolution, 120
Communications, Energy and Paper-
workers Union (CEP), 73, 245
Companies' Creditors Arrangement
Act (CCAA), 180
Competition Act, 168
Corcoran, Terence, 96, 98
Côté, Paul, 203
Couillard, Julie, 138
Cowger, Gary, 88, 91, 92, 262

Ryan, Sid, 243, 245, 304–05, 306
Ryerson University, 303

Saillon, Claude, 169
Sairanen, Sari, 185
Salmers, David, 93–93, 95
same-sex benefits, 211–12
Schwartz, Gerry, 23–24, 98, 163, 164,
    168–74, 176, 177, 182
September 11, 2001 attacks, 147, 179
Service Employees International
    Union (SEIU), 73, 214, 243, 245
Short Brothers, 58
Smith, David, 117
Smith, Jack, 17
Social Contract, 118–19, 120, 126
social unionism, 41, 45
Sponsorship Scandal, 126, 129
Stanford, Jim, 133, 241
Ste. Anne Nackawic pulp mill, 103–05
Steiner, Doug, 224–25
Stewart, Sharleen, 245
strategic voting, 116, 123, 124,
    127–30, 131, 142
strikes, as bargaining tool, 214–16
Stronach, Belinda, 23, 239
Stronach, Frank, 19–22, 98, 108–09,
    239–43, 245, 248, 271, 286–87, 288,
    301
Suzuki Canada Inc., 156, 236

Telecommunications Workers Union
    (TWU), 61–66
Tellier, Paul, 199
Telus Communications Company,
    61–66
Tembec Inc., 105–06
Thomas, Warren (Smokey), 245
Tighe, Dick, 56
Tomiczek, Vic, 248–49
Toronto Star, 247, 251
Toyota Canada Inc., 37, 265, 278–79,
    292–93
trade unionism:
    benefits of, 18–19, 35–36
    decline in membership, 35, 251–52
    future of, 308–09, 311
    in service industries, 39
    women in, 34, 36, 251
two-tier wage system, 153–54,
    225–226, 275

United Auto Workers (UAW), 7, 15,
    20, 33, 54, 69, 70, 74, 75–76, 157,
    209, 225, 281, 294–95, 297
    CAW splits from, 149–54
United Steelworkers of America
    (USW), 220, 221, 243, 245
Ustian, Dan, 195, 196

Versatile Manufacturing, 143–44